OpenGL
Reference Manual

The Official Reference Document for OpenGL, Release 1

OpenGL Architecture Review Board

Addison-Wesley Publishing Company
Reading, Massachusetts   Menlo Park, California
New York   Don Mills, Ontario   Wokingham, England
Amsterdam   Bonn   Sydney   Singapore   Tokyo   Madrid
San Juan   Paris   Seoul   Milan   Mexico City   Taipei

Sponsoring Editor: David Rogelberg
Project Editor: Joanne Clapp Fullagar
Cover Image: Thad Beier
Cover Design: Jean Seal
Text Design: Electric Ink, Ltd., and Kay Maitz

Set in 10-point Stone Serif

ISBN 0-201-63276-4

First Printing, November 1992

123456789-AL-9695949392

Preface

OpenGL™ (GL for Graphics Library™) is a software interface to graphics hardware. This interface consists of several hundred functions that allow you, a graphics programmer, to specify the objects and operations needed to produce high-quality color images of three-dimensional objects. Many of these functions are actually simple variations of each other, so in reality there are only 120 substantially different functions.

As complements to the core set of OpenGL functions, the OpenGL Utility Library (GLU) and the OpenGL Extension to the X Window System™ (GLX) provide useful supporting features. This manual explains what all these functions do; it has the following chapters:

- **Chapter 1, Introduction to OpenGL**, provides a brief statement of the major underlying concepts embodied in OpenGL. It uses a high-level block diagram to discuss in conceptual terms all the major stages of processing performed by OpenGL.

- **Chapter 2, Overview of Commands and Routines**, describes in more detail how input data (in the form of vertices specifying a geometric object or pixels defining an image) is processed and how you can control this processing using the functions that comprise OpenGL. Functions belonging to GLU and GLX are also discussed.

Chapter 3, Summary of Commands and Routines, lists the OpenGL commands in groups according to what sort of tasks they perform. Full prototypes are given so that you can use this section as a quick reference once you understand what the commands accomplish.

Chapter 4, Defined Constants and Associated Commands, lists the constants defined in OpenGL and the commands that use them.

Chapter 5, OpenGL Reference Pages, which forms the bulk of this manual, contains descriptions of each set of related OpenGL commands. (Commands with parameters that differ only in data type are described together, for example.) Each reference page fully describes the relevant parameters, the effect of the commands, and what errors might be generated by using the commands.

Chapter 6, GLU Reference Pages, contains the reference pages for all the GLU routines.

Chapter 7, GLX Reference Pages, contains the reference pages for the GLX routines.

What You Should Know Before Reading This Manual

This manual is designed to be used as the companion reference volume to the *OpenGL Programming Guide* by Jackie Neider, Tom Davis, and Mason Woo (Reading, MA: Addison-Wesley Publishing Company). The focus of this *Reference Manual* is how OpenGL works, while the *Programming Guide*'s focus is how to use OpenGL. For a complete understanding of OpenGL, you need both types of information. Another difference between these two books is that most of the content of this *Reference Manual* is organized alphabetically, based on the assumption that you know what you don't know and therefore need only to look up a description of a particular command; the *Programming Guide* is organized like a tutorial—it explains the simpler OpenGL concepts first and builds up to the more complex ones. Although the command descriptions in this manual don't necessarily require you to have read the *Programming Guide*, your understanding of the intended usage of the commands will be much more complete if you have read it. Both books also assume that you know how to program in C.

If you don't have much of a computer graphics background, you should certainly start with the *Programming Guide* rather than this *Reference Manual*. Basic graphics concepts are not explained in this manual. You might also want to look at *Computer Graphics: Principles and Practice* by James D. Foley, Andries van Dam, Steven K. Feiner, and John F. Hughes (Reading, MA: Addison-Wesley Publishing Company). That book is an encyclopedic treatment of the field of computer graphics. Another, gentler introduction to the subject can be found in *3D Computer Graphics: A User's Guide for Artists and Designers* by Andrew S. Glassner (New York: Design Press).

Acknowledgments

This manual owes its existence to many people. Kurt Akeley of Silicon Graphics®, Sally Browning of SABL Productions, and Kevin P. Smith also of Silicon Graphics wrote most of the material, with contributions from Jackie Neider and Mark Segal (both from Silicon Graphics). *The OpenGL Graphics System: A Specification* (coauthored by Mark and Kurt), *The OpenGL Graphics System Utility Library* (written by Kevin), and *OpenGL Graphics with the X Window System* (written by Phil Karlton) served as source documents for the authors. Phil Karlton and Kipp Hickman assisted by helping to define and create OpenGL at Silicon Graphics, with help from Raymond Drewry of Gain Technology, Inc., Fred Fisher of Digital Equipment Corp., and Randi Rost of Kubota Pacific Computer, Inc. The members of the OpenGL Architecture Review Board—Murray Cantor and Linas Vepstas from International Business Machines, Paula Womack and Jeff Lane of Digital Equipment Corporation, Murali Sundaresan of Intel, and Chuck Whitmer of Microsoft—also contributed. Thad Beier together with Seth Katz and the Inventor team at Silicon Graphics created the cover image. Kay Maitz of Silicon Graphics, Arthur Evans of Evans Technical Communications, and Susan Blau provided production assistance; Tanya Kucak copyedited the manual. Finally, this book wouldn't exist unless OpenGL did, for which all the members of the OpenGL team at Silicon Graphics, Inc., need to be thanked for their efforts: Momi Akeley, Allen Akin, Chris Frazier, Bill Glazier, Paul Ho, Simon Hui, Lesley Kalmin, Pierre Tardif, Jim Winget, and especially Wei Yen, in addition to the previously mentioned Kurt, Phil, Mark, Kipp, and Kevin. Many other Silicon Graphics employees, who are too numerous to mention, helped refine the definition and functionality of OpenGL.

Contents

Preface iii

What You Should Know Before Reading This Manual v
Acknowledgments vi

1. **Introduction to OpenGL**... 1

OpenGL Fundamentals 2
Primitives and Commands 2
Procedural versus Descriptive 2
Execution Model 3
Basic OpenGL Operation.. 4

2. **Overview of Commands and Routines** 7

OpenGL Processing Pipeline 8
Vertices... 10
Primitives 11
Fragments 13
Pixels 15

Additional OpenGL Commands 16

    Using Evaluators 16

    Performing Selection and Feedback 16

    Using Display Lists 17

    Managing Modes and Execution 18

    Obtaining State Information 18

OpenGL Utility Library 19

    Manipulating Images for Use in Texturing 19

    Transforming Coordinates 19

    Polygon Tessellation 20

    Rendering Spheres, Cylinders, and Disks 20

    NURBS Curves and Surfaces 20

    Handling Errors 21

OpenGL Extensions to the X Window System 22

    Initialization 22

    Controlling Rendering 22

3. Summary of Commands and Routines 25

Notation 26

OpenGL Commands 27

    Primitives 27

    Coordinate Transformation 27

    Coloring and Lighting 28

    Clipping 28

    Rasterization 29

    Pixel Operations 29

    Texture Mapping 30

    Fog 31

    Frame Buffer Operations 31

    Evaluators 32

    Selection and Feedback 33

    Display Lists 33

    Modes and Execution 33

    State Queries 34

GLU Routines... 35
   Texture Images 35
   Coordinate Transformation 35
   Polygon Tessellation.. 36
   Quadric Objects... 36
   NURBS Curves and Surfaces 37
   Error Handling.. 38
GLX Routines... 39
   Initialization 39
   Controlling Rendering 39

4. **Defined Constants and Associated Commands**............................ 41

5. **OpenGL Reference Pages**... 55

6. **GLU Reference Pages** 305

7. **GLX Reference Pages** 357

Chapter 1

Introduction to OpenGL

As a software interface for graphics hardware, OpenGL's main purpose is to render two- and three-dimensional objects into a frame buffer. These objects are described as sequences of vertices (which define geometric objects) or pixels (which define images). OpenGL performs several processing steps on this data to convert it to pixels to form the final desired image in the frame buffer.

This chapter presents a global view of how OpenGL works; it contains the following major sections:

- **OpenGL Fundamentals** briefly explains basic OpenGL concepts, such as what a graphic primitive is and how OpenGL implements a client-server execution model.

- **Basic OpenGL Operation** gives a high-level description of how OpenGL processes data and produces a corresponding image in the frame buffer.

OpenGL Fundamentals

This section explains some of the concepts inherent in OpenGL.

Primitives and Commands

OpenGL draws *primitives*—points, line segments, or polygons—subject to several selectable modes. You can control modes independently of each other; that is, setting one mode doesn't affect whether other modes are set (although many modes may interact to determine what eventually ends up in the frame buffer). Primitives are specified, modes are set, and other OpenGL operations are described by issuing commands in the form of function calls.

Primitives are defined by a group of one or more *vertices*. A vertex defines a point, an endpoint of a line, or a corner of a polygon where two edges meet. Data (consisting of vertex coordinates, colors, normals, texture coordinates, and edge flags) is associated with a vertex, and each vertex and its associated data are processed independently, in order, and in the same way. The only exception to this rule is if the group of vertices must be *clipped* so that a particular primitive fits within a specified region; in this case, vertex data may be modified and new vertices created. The type of clipping depends on which primitive the group of vertices represents.

Commands are always processed in the order in which they are received, although there may be an indeterminate delay before a command takes effect. This means that each primitive is drawn completely before any subsequent command takes effect. It also means that state-querying commands return data that's consistent with complete execution of all previously issued OpenGL commands.

Procedural versus Descriptive

OpenGL provides you with fairly direct control over the fundamental operations of two- and three-dimensional graphics. This includes specification of such parameters as transformation matrices, lighting equation coefficients, antialiasing methods, and pixel update operators. However, it doesn't provide you with a means for describing or modeling complex geometric objects. Thus, the OpenGL commands you issue specify how a certain result should be produced (what procedure should be followed) rather than what exactly that result should look like. That is, OpenGL is fundamentally procedural rather than descriptive. Because of this procedural nature, it helps to know how OpenGL works—the order in which it carries out its operations, for example—in order to fully understand how to use it.

Execution Model

The model for interpretation of OpenGL commands is client-server. An application (the client) issues commands, which are interpreted and processed by OpenGL (the server). The server may or may not operate on the same computer as the client. In this sense, OpenGL is network-transparent. A server can maintain several GL *contexts*, each of which is an encapsulated GL state. A client can connect to any one of these contexts. The required network protocol can be implemented by augmenting an already existing protocol (such as that of the X Window System) or by using an independent protocol. No OpenGL commands are provided for obtaining user input.

The effects of OpenGL commands on the frame buffer are ultimately controlled by the window system that allocates frame buffer resources. The window system determines which portions of the frame buffer OpenGL may access at any given time and communicates to OpenGL how those portions are structured. Therefore, there are no OpenGL commands to configure the frame buffer or initialize OpenGL. Frame buffer configuration is done outside of OpenGL in conjunction with the window system; OpenGL initialization takes place when the window system allocates a window for OpenGL rendering. (GLX, the X extension of the OpenGL interface, provides these capabilities, as described in Chapter 2, under "OpenGL Extension to the X Window System.")

Basic OpenGL Operation

The figure shown below gives an abstract, high-level block diagram of how OpenGL processes data. In the diagram, commands enter from the left and proceed through what can be thought of as a processing pipeline. Some commands specify geometric objects to be drawn, and others control how the objects are handled during the various processing stages.

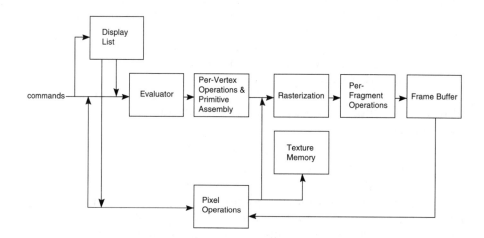

As shown by the first block in the diagram, rather than having all commands proceed immediately through the pipeline, you can choose to accumulate some of them in a *display list* for processing at a later time.

The *evaluator* stage of processing provides an efficient means for approximating curve and surface geometry by evaluating polynomial commands of input values. During the next stage, *per-vertex operations and primitive assembly*, OpenGL processes geometric primitives—points, line segments, and polygons, all of which are described by vertices. Vertices are transformed and lit, and primitives are clipped to the viewport in preparation for the next stage.

Rasterization produces a series of frame buffer addresses and associated values using a two-dimensional description of a point, line segment, or polygon. Each *fragment* so produced is fed into the last stage, *per-fragment operations*, which performs the final operations on the data before it's stored as pixels in the *frame buffer*. These operations include conditional updates to the frame buffer based on incoming and previously stored z-values (for z-buffering) and blending of incoming pixel colors with stored colors, as well as masking and other logical operations on pixel values.

Input data can be in the form of pixels rather than vertices. Such data, which might describe an image for use in texture mapping, skips the first stage of processing described above and instead is processed as pixels, in the *pixel operations* stage. The result of this stage is either stored as *texture memory*, for use in the rasterization stage, or rasterized and the resulting fragments merged into the frame buffer just as if they were generated from geometric data.

All elements of OpenGL state, including the contents of the texture memory and even of the frame buffer, can be obtained by an OpenGL application.

Chapter 2

Overview of Commands and Routines

Many OpenGL commands pertain specifically to drawing objects such as points, lines, polygons, and bitmaps. Other commands control the way that some of this drawing occurs (such as those that enable antialiasing or texturing). Still other commands are specifically concerned with frame buffer manipulation. This chapter briefly describes how all the OpenGL commands work together to create the OpenGL processing pipeline. Brief overviews are also given of the routines comprising the OpenGL Utility Library (GLU) and the OpenGL extensions to the X Window System (GLX).

This chapter has the following main sections:

- **OpenGL Processing Pipeline** expands on the discussion in Chapter 1 by explaining how specific OpenGL commands control the processing of data.

- **Additional OpenGL Commands** discusses several sets of OpenGL commands not covered in the previous section.

- **OpenGL Utility Library** describes the GLU routines that are available.

- **OpenGL Extension to the X Window System** describes the GLX routines.

OpenGL Processing Pipeline

Now that you have a general idea of how OpenGL works from Chapter 1, let's take a closer look at the stages in which data is actually processed and tie these stages to OpenGL commands. The figure shown on the next page is a more detailed block diagram of the OpenGL processing pipeline.

For most of the pipeline, you can see three vertical arrows between the major stages. These arrows represent vertices and the two primary types of data that can be associated with vertices: color values and texture coordinates. Also note that vertices are assembled into primitives, then to fragments, and finally to pixels in the frame buffer. This progression is discussed in more detail in the following sections.

As you continue reading, be aware that we've taken some liberties with command names. Many OpenGL commands are simple variations of each other, differing mostly in the data type of arguments; some commands differ in the number of related arguments and whether those arguments can be specified as a vector or whether they must be specified separately in a list. For example, if you use the **glVertex2f()** command, you need to supply x and y coordinates as 32-bit floating-point numbers; with **glVertex3sv()**, you must supply an array of three short (16-bit) integer values for x, y, and z. For simplicity, only the base name of the command is used in the discussion that follows, and an asterisk is included to indicate that there may be more to the actual command name than is being shown. For example, **glVertex*()** stands for all variations of the command you use to specify vertices.

Also keep in mind that the effect of an OpenGL command may vary depending on whether certain modes are enabled. For example, you need to enable lighting if the lighting-related commands are to have the desired effect of producing a properly lit object. To enable a particular mode, you use the **glEnable()** command and supply the appropriate constant to identify the mode (for example, GL_LIGHTING). The following sections don't discuss specific modes, but you can refer to the reference page for **glEnable()** for a complete list of the modes that can be enabled. Modes are disabled with **glDisable()**.

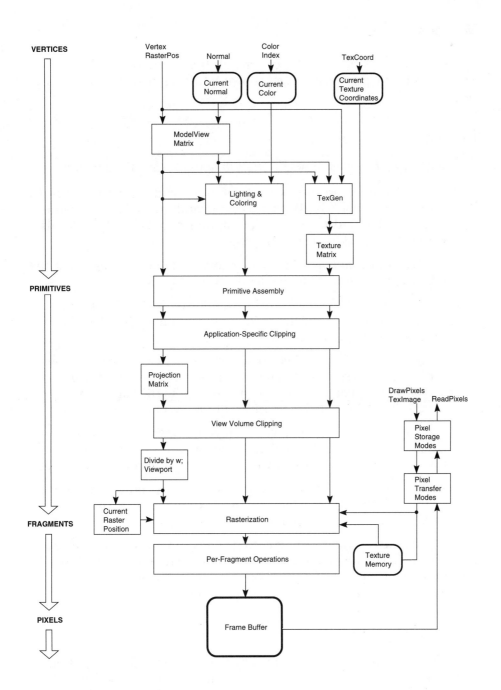

VERTICES

PRIMITIVES

FRAGMENTS

PIXELS

Vertex
RasterPos

Normal

Color
Index

TexCoord

Current
Normal

Current
Color

Current
Texture
Coordinates

ModelView
Matrix

Lighting &
Coloring

TexGen

Texture
Matrix

Primitive Assembly

Application-Specific Clipping

Projection
Matrix

View Volume Clipping

Divide by w;
Viewport

DrawPixels
TexImage

ReadPixels

Pixel
Storage
Modes

Pixel
Transfer
Modes

Current
Raster
Position

Rasterization

Per-Fragment Operations

Texture
Memory

Frame Buffer

Vertices

This section relates the OpenGL commands that perform per-vertex operations to the processing stages shown in the figure on the previous page.

Input Data

You must provide several types of input data to the OpenGL pipeline:

- Vertices—Vertices describe the shape of the desired geometric object. To specify vertices, you use **glVertex*()** commands in conjunction with **glBegin()** and **glEnd()** to create a point, line, or polygon. You can also use **glRect*()** to describe an entire rectangle at once.

- Edge flag—By default, all edges of polygons are boundary edges. Use the **glEdgeFlag*()** command to explicitly set the edge flag.

- Current raster position—Specified with **glRasterPos*()**, the current raster position is used to determine raster coordinates for pixel and bitmap drawing operations.

- Current normal—A normal vector associated with a particular vertex determines how a surface at that vertex is oriented in three-dimensional space; this in turn affects how much light that particular vertex receives. Use **glNormal*()** to specify a normal vector.

- Current color—The color of a vertex, together with the lighting conditions, determine the final, lit color. Color is specified with **glColor*()** if in RGBA mode or with **glIndex*()** if in color index mode.

- Current texture coordinates—Specified with **glTexCoord*()**, texture coordinates determine the location in a texture map that should be associated with a vertex of an object.

When **glVertex*()** is called, the resulting vertex inherits the current edge flag, normal, color, and texture coordinates. Therefore, **glEdgeFlag*()**, **glNormal*()**, **glColor*()**, and **glTexCoord*()** must be called before **glVertex*()** if they are to affect the resulting vertex.

Matrix Transformations

Vertices and normals are transformed by the modelview and projection matrices before they're used to produce an image in the frame buffer. You can use commands such as **glMatrixMode()**, **glMultMatrix()**, **glRotate()**, **glTranslate()**, and **glScale()** to compose the desired transformations, or you can directly specify matrices with **glLoadMatrix()** and **glLoadIdentity()**. Use **glPushMatrix()** and **glPopMatrix()** to save and restore modelview and projection matrices on their respective stacks.

Lighting and Coloring

In addition to specifying colors and normal vectors, you may define the desired lighting conditions with **glLight*()** and **glLightModel*()**, and the desired material properties with **glMaterial*()**. Related commands you might use to control how lighting calculations are performed include **glShadeModel()**, **glFrontFace()**, and **glColorMaterial()**.

Generating Texture Coordinates

Rather than explicitly supplying texture coordinates, you can have OpenGL generate them as a function of other vertex data. This is what the **glTexGen*()** command does. After the texture coordinates have been specified or generated, they are transformed by the texture matrix. This matrix is controlled with the same commands mentioned earlier for matrix transformations.

Primitive Assembly

Once all these calculations have been performed, vertices are assembled into primitives—points, line segments, or polygons—together with the relevant edge flag, color, and texture information for each vertex.

Primitives

During the next stage of processing, primitives are converted to pixel fragments in several steps: primitives are clipped appropriately, whatever corresponding adjustments are necessary are made to the color and texture data, and the relevant coordinates are transformed to window coordinates. Finally, rasterization converts the clipped primitives to pixel fragments.

Clipping

Points, line segments, and polygons are handled slightly differently during clipping. Points are either retained in their original state (if they're inside the clip volume) or discarded (if they're outside). If portions of line segments or polygons are outside the clip volume, new vertices are generated at the clip points. For polygons, an entire edge may need to be constructed between such new vertices. For both line segments and polygons that are clipped, the edge flag, color, and texture information is assigned to all new vertices.

Clipping actually happens in two steps:

1. Application-specific clipping—Immediately after primitives are assembled, they're clipped in *eye coordinates* as necessary for any arbitrary clipping planes you've defined for your application with **glClipPlane()**. (OpenGL requires support for at least six such application-specific clipping planes.)

2. View volume clipping—Next, primitives are transformed by the projection matrix (into *clip coordinates*) and clipped by the corresponding viewing volume. This matrix can be controlled by the previously mentioned matrix transformation commands but is most typically specified by **glFrustum()** or **glOrtho()**.

Transforming to Window Coordinates

Before clip coordinates can be converted to *window coordinates*, they are normalized by dividing by the value of *w* to yield *normalized device coordinates*. After that, the viewport transformation applied to these normalized coordinates produces window coordinates. You control the viewport, which determines the area of the on-screen window that displays an image, with **glDepthRange()** and **glViewport()**.

Rasterization

Rasterization is the process by which a primitive is converted to a two-dimensional image. Each point of this image contains such information as color, depth, and texture data. Together, a point and its associated information are called a *fragment*. The current raster position (as specified with **glRasterPos*()**) is used in various ways during this stage for pixel drawing and bitmaps. As discussed below, different issues arise when rasterizing the three different types of primitives; in addition, pixel rectangles and bitmaps need to be rasterized.

Primitives. You control how primitives are rasterized with commands that allow you to choose dimensions and stipple patterns: **glPointSize()**, **glLineWidth()**, **glLineStipple()**, and **glPolygonStipple()**. Additionally, you can control how the front and back faces of polygons are rasterized with **glCullFace()**, **glFrontFace()**, and **glPolygonMode()**.

Pixels. Several commands control pixel storage and transfer modes. The command **glPixelStore*()** controls the encoding of pixels in client memory, and **glPixelTransfer*()** and **glPixelMap*()** control how pixels are processed before being placed in the frame buffer. A pixel rectangle is specified with **glDrawPixels()**; its rasterization is controlled with **glPixelZoom()**.

Bitmaps. Bitmaps are rectangles of zeros and ones specifying a particular pattern of fragments to be produced. Each of these fragments has the same associated data. A bitmap is specified using **glBitmap()**.

Texture Memory. Texturing maps a portion of a specified texture image onto each primitive when texturing is enabled. This mapping is accomplished by using the color of the texture image at the location indicated by a fragment's texture coordinates to modify the fragment's RGBA color. A texture image is specified using **glTexImage2D()** or **glTexImage1D()**. The commands **glTexParameter*()** and **glTexEnv*()** control how texture values are interpreted and applied to a fragment.

Fog. You can have OpenGL blend a fog color with a rasterized fragment's post-texturing color using a blending factor that depends on the distance between the eyepoint and the fragment. Use **glFog*()** to specify the fog color and blending factor.

Fragments

OpenGL allows a fragment produced by rasterization to modify the corresponding pixel in the frame buffer only if it passes a series of tests. If it does pass, the fragment's data can be used directly to replace the existing frame buffer values, or it can be combined with existing data in the frame buffer, depending on the state of certain modes.

Pixel Ownership Test

The first test is to determine whether the pixel in the frame buffer corresponding to a particular fragment is owned by the current OpenGL context. If so, the fragment proceeds to the next test. If not, the window system determines whether the fragment is discarded or whether any further fragment operations will be performed with that fragment. This test allows the window system to control OpenGL's behavior when, for example, an OpenGL window is obscured.

Scissor Test

With the **glScissor()** command, you can specify an arbitrary screen-aligned rectangle outside of which fragments will be discarded.

Alpha Test

The alpha test (which is performed only in RGBA mode) discards a fragment depending on the outcome of a comparison between the fragment's alpha value and a constant reference value. The comparison command and reference value are specified with **glAlphaFunc()**.

Stencil Test

The stencil test conditionally discards a fragment based on the outcome of a comparison between the value in the stencil buffer and a reference value. The command **glStencilFunc()** specifies the comparison command and the reference value. Whether the fragment passes or fails the stencil test, the value in the stencil buffer is modified according to the instructions specified with **glStencilOp()**.

Depth Buffer Test

The depth buffer test discards a fragment if a depth comparison fails; **glDepthFunc()** specifies the comparison command. The result of the depth comparison also affects the stencil buffer update value if stenciling is enabled.

Blending

Blending combines a fragment's R, G, B, and A values with those stored in the frame buffer at the corresponding location. The blending, which is performed only in RGBA mode, depends on the alpha value of the fragment and that of the corresponding currently stored pixel; it might also depend on the RGB values. You control blending with **glBlendFunc()**, which allows you to indicate the source and destination blending factors.

Dithering

If dithering is enabled, a dithering algorithm is applied to the fragment's color or color index value. This algorithm depends only on the fragment's value and its x and y window coordinates.

Logical Operations

Finally, a logical operation can be applied between the fragment and the value stored at the corresponding location in the frame buffer; the result replaces the current frame buffer value. You choose the desired logical operation with **glLogicOp()**. Logical operations are performed only on color indices, never on RGBA values.

Pixels

During the previous stage of the OpenGL pipeline, fragments are converted to pixels in the frame buffer. The frame buffer is actually organized into a set of logical buffers—the *color, depth, stencil,* and *accumulation* buffers. The color buffer itself consists of a *front left, front right, back left, back right,* and some number of *auxiliary* buffers. You can issue commands to control these buffers, and you can directly read or copy pixels from them. (Note that the particular OpenGL context you're using may not provide all of these buffers.)

Frame Buffer Operations

You can select into which buffer color values are written with **glDrawBuffer()**. In addition, four different commands are used to mask the writing of bits to each of the logical frame buffers after all per-fragment operations have been performed: **glIndexMask()**, **glColorMask()**, **glDepthMask()**, and **glStencilMask()**. The operation of the accumulation buffer is controlled with **glAccum()**. Finally, **glClear()** sets every pixel in a specified subset of the buffers to the value specified with **glClearColor()**, **glClearIndex()**, **glClearDepth()**, **glClearStencil()**, or **glClearAccum()**.

Reading or Copying Pixels

You can read pixels from the frame buffer into memory, encode them in various ways, and store the encoded result in memory with **glReadPixels()**. In addition, you can copy a rectangle of pixel values from one region of the frame buffer to another with **glCopyPixels()**. The command **glReadBuffer()** controls from which color buffer the pixels are read or copied.

Additional OpenGL Commands

This section briefly describes special groups of commands that weren't explicitly shown as part of OpenGL's processing pipeline. These commands accomplish such diverse tasks as evaluating polynomials, using display lists, and obtaining the values of OpenGL state variables.

Using Evaluators

OpenGL's evaluator commands allow you to use a polynomial mapping to produce vertices, normals, texture coordinates, and colors. These calculated values are then passed on to the pipeline as if they had been directly specified. The evaluator facility is also the basis for the NURBS (Non-Uniform Rational B-Spline) commands, which allow you to define curves and surfaces, as described later in this chapter under "OpenGL Utility Library."

The first step involved in using evaluators is to define the appropriate one- or two-dimensional polynomial mapping using **glMap*()**. The domain values for this map can then be specified and evaluated in one of two ways:

- By defining a series of evenly spaced domain values to be mapped using **glMapGrid*()** and then evaluating a rectangular subset of that grid with **glEvalMesh*()**. A single point of the grid can be evaluated using **glEvalPoint*()**.

- By explicitly specifying a desired domain value as an argument to **glEvalCoord*()**, which evaluates the maps at that value.

Performing Selection and Feedback

Selection, feedback, and rendering are mutually exclusive modes of operation. Rendering is the normal, default mode during which fragments are produced by rasterization; in selection and feedback modes, no fragments are produced and therefore no frame buffer modification occurs. In selection mode, you can determine which primitives would be drawn into some region of a window; in feedback mode, information about primitives that would be rasterized is fed back to the application. You select among these three modes with **glRenderMode()**.

Selection

Selection works by returning the current contents of the name stack, which is an array of integer-valued names. You assign the names and build the name stack within the modeling code that specifies the geometry of objects you want to draw. Then, in selection mode, whenever a primitive intersects the clip volume, a selection hit occurs. The hit record, which is written into the selection array you've supplied with **glSelectBuffer()**, contains information about the contents of the name stack at the time of the hit. (Note that **glSelectBuffer()** needs to be called before OpenGL is put into selection mode with **glRenderMode()**. Also, the entire contents of the name stack isn't guaranteed to be returned until **glRenderMode()** is called to take OpenGL out of selection mode.) You manipulate the name stack with **glInitNames()**, **glLoadName()**, **glPushName()**, and **glPopName()**. In addition, you might want to use an OpenGL Utility Library routine for selection, **gluPickMatrix()**, which is described later in this chapter under "OpenGL Utility Library."

Feedback

In feedback mode, each primitive that would be rasterized generates a block of values that is copied into the feedback array. You supply this array with **glFeedbackBuffer()**, which must be called before OpenGL is put into feedback mode. Each block of values begins with a code indicating the primitive type, followed by values that describe the primitive's vertices and associated data. Entries are also written for bitmaps and pixel rectangles. Values are not guaranteed to be written into the feedback array until **glRenderMode()** is called to take OpenGL out of feedback mode. You can use **glPassThrough()** to supply a marker that's returned in feedback mode as if it were a primitive.

Using Display Lists

A display list is simply a group of OpenGL commands that has been stored for subsequent execution. The **glNewList()** command begins the creation of a display list, and **glEndList()** ends it. With few exceptions, OpenGL commands called between **glNewList()** and **glEndList()** are appended to the display list, and optionally executed as well. (The reference page for **glNewList()** lists the commands that can't be stored and executed from within a display list.) To trigger the execution of a list or set of lists, use **glCallList()** or **glCallLists()** and supply the identifying number of a particular list or lists. You can manage the indices used to identify display lists with **glGenLists()**, **glListBase()**, and **glIsList()**. Finally, you can delete a set of display lists with **glDeleteLists()**.

Managing Modes and Execution

The effect of many OpenGL commands depends on whether a particular mode is in effect. You use **glEnable()** and **glDisable()** to set such modes and **glIsEnabled()** to determine whether a particular mode is set.

You can control the execution of previously issued OpenGL commands with **glFinish()**, which forces all such commands to complete, or **glFlush()**, which ensures that all such commands will be completed in a finite time.

A particular implementation of OpenGL may allow certain behaviors to be controlled with hints, by using the **glHint()** command. Possible behaviors are the quality of color and texture coordinate interpolation, the accuracy of fog calculations, and the sampling quality of antialiased points, lines, or polygons.

Obtaining State Information

OpenGL maintains numerous state variables that affect the behavior of many commands. Some of these variables have specialized query commands:

glGetLight()	glGetTexEnv()	glGetTexParameter()
glGetMaterial()	glGetTexGen()	glGetMap()
glGetClipPlane()	glGetTexImage()	glGetPixelMap()
glGetPolygonStipple()	glGetTexLevelParameter()	

The value of other state variables can be obtained with **glGetBooleanv()**, **glGetDoublev()**, **glGetFloatv()**, or **glGetIntegerv()**, as appropriate. The reference page for **glGet*()** explains how to use these commands. Other query commands you might want to use are **glGetError()**, **glGetString()**, and **glIsEnabled()**. (See "Handling Errors" later in this chapter for more information about routines related to error handling.) Finally, you can save and restore sets of state variables with **glPushAttrib()** and **glPopAttrib()**.

OpenGL Utility Library

The OpenGL Utility Library (GLU) contains several groups of commands that complement the core OpenGL interface by providing support for auxiliary features. Since these utility routines make use of core OpenGL commands, any OpenGL implementation is guaranteed to support the utility routines. Note that the prefix for Utility Library routines is *glu* rather than *gl*.

Manipulating Images for Use in Texturing

GLU provides image scaling and automatic mipmapping routines to simplify the specification of texture images. The routine **gluScaleImage()** scales a specified image to an accepted texture size; the resulting image can then be passed to OpenGL as a texture. The automatic mipmapping routines **gluBuild1DMipmaps()** and **gluBuild2DMipmaps()** create mipmapped texture images from a specified image and pass them to **glTexImage1D()** and **glTexImage2D()**, respectively.

Transforming Coordinates

Several commonly used matrix transformation routines are provided. You can set up a two-dimensional orthographic viewing region with **gluOrtho2D()**, a perspective viewing volume using **gluPerspective()**, or a viewing volume that's centered on a specified eyepoint with **gluLookAt()**. Each of these routines creates the desired matrix and applies it to the current matrix using **glMultMatrix()**.

The **gluPickMatrix()** routine simplifies selection by creating a matrix that restricts drawing to a small region of the viewport. If you rerender the scene in selection mode after this matrix has been applied, all objects that would be drawn near the cursor will be selected and information about them stored in the selection buffer. See "Performing Selection and Feedback" earlier in this chapter for more information about selection mode.

If you need to determine where in the window an object is being drawn, use **gluProject()**, which converts specified coordinates from object coordinates to window coordinates; **gluUnProject()** performs the inverse conversion.

Polygon Tessellation

The polygon tessellation routines triangulate a concave polygon with one or more contours. To use this GLU feature, first create a tessellation object with **gluNewTess()**, and define callback routines that will be used to process the triangles generated by the tessellator (with **gluTessCallBack()**). Then use **gluBeginPolygon()**, **gluTessVertex()**, **gluNextContour()**, and **gluEndPolygon()** to specify the concave polygon to be tessellated. Unneeded tessellation objects can be destroyed with **gluDeleteTess()**.

Rendering Spheres, Cylinders, and Disks

You can render spheres, cylinders, and disks using the GLU quadric routines. To do this, create a quadric object with **gluNewQuadric()**. (To destroy this object when you're finished with it, use **gluDeleteQuadric()**.) Then specify the desired rendering style, as listed below, with the appropriate routine (unless you're satisfied with the default values):

- Whether surface normals should be generated, and if so, whether there should be one normal per vertex or one normal per face: **gluQuadricNormals()**
- Whether texture coodinates should be generated: **gluQuadricTexture()**
- Which side of the quadric should be considered the outside and which the inside: **gluQuadricOrientation()**
- Whether the quadric should be drawn as a set of polygons, lines, or points: **gluQuadricDrawStyle()**

After you've specified the rendering style, simply invoke the rendering routine for the desired type of quadric object: **gluSphere()**, **gluCylinder()**, **gluDisk()**, or **gluPartialDisk()**. If an error occurs during rendering, the error-handling routine you've specified with **gluQuadricCallBack()** is invoked.

NURBS Curves and Surfaces

NURBS (Non-Uniform Rational B-Spline) curves and surfaces are converted to OpenGL evaluators by the routines described in this section. You can create and delete a NURBS object with **gluNewNurbsRenderer()** and **gluDeleteNurbsRenderer()**, and establish an error-handling routine with **gluNurbsCallback()**.

You specify the desired curves and surfaces with different sets of routines—**gluBeginCurve()**, **gluNurbsCurve()**, and **gluEndCurve()** for curves or **gluBeginSurface()**, **gluNurbsSurface()**, and **gluEndSurface()** for surfaces. You can also specify a trimming region, which defines a subset of the NURBS surface domain to be evaluated, thereby allowing you to create surfaces that have smooth boundaries or that contain holes. The trimming routines are **gluBeginTrim()**, **gluPwlCurve()**, **gluNurbsCurve()**, and **gluEndTrim()**.

As with quadric objects, you can control how NURBS curves and surfaces are rendered:

 Whether a curve or surface should be discarded if its control polyhedron lies outside the current viewport

● What the maximum length should be (in pixels) of edges of polygons used to render curves and surfaces

● Whether the projection matrix, modelview matrix, and viewport should be taken from the OpenGL server or whether you'll supply them explicitly with **gluLoadSamplingMatrices()**

Use **gluNurbsProperty()** to set these properties, or use the default values. You can query a NURBS object about its rendering style with **gluGetNurbsProperty()**.

Handling Errors

The routine **gluErrorString()** is provided for retrieving an error string that corresponds to an OpenGL or GLU error code. The currently defined OpenGL error codes are described in the **glGetError()** reference page. The GLU error codes are listed in the **gluErrorString()**, **gluTessCallback()**, **gluQuadricCallback()**, and **gluNurbsCallback()** reference pages. Errors generated by GLX routines are listed in the relevant reference pages for those routines.

OpenGL Extension to the X Window System

In the X Window System, OpenGL rendering is made available as an extension to X in the formal X sense: connection and authentication are accomplished with the normal X mechanisms. As with other X extensions, there is a defined network protocol for OpenGL's rendering commands encapsulated within the X byte stream. Since performance is critical in three-dimensional rendering, the OpenGL extension to X allows OpenGL to bypass the X server's involvement in data encoding, copying, and interpretation and instead render directly to the graphics pipeline.

This section briefly discusses the routines defined as part of GLX; these routines have the prefix *glX*. You'll need to have some knowledge of X in order to fully understand the following and to use GLX successfully.

Initialization

Use **glXQueryExtension()** and **glXQueryVersion()** to determine whether the GLX extension is defined for an X server, and if so, which version is bound in the server. The **glXChooseVisual()** routine returns a pointer to an XVisualInfo structure describing the visual that best meets the client's specified attributes. You can query a visual about its support of a particular OpenGL attribute with **glXGetConfig()**.

Controlling Rendering

Several GLX routines are provided for creating and managing an OpenGL rendering context. You can use such a context to render off-screen if you want. Routines are also provided for such tasks as synchronizing execution between the X and OpenGL streams, swapping front and back buffers, and using an X font.

Managing an OpenGL Rendering Context

An OpenGL rendering context is created with **glXCreateContext()**. One of the arguments to this routine allows you to request a direct rendering context that bypasses the X server as described above. (Note that in order to do direct rendering, the X server connection must be local and the OpenGL implementation needs to support direct rendering.) You can determine whether a GLX context is direct with **glXIsDirect()**.

To make a rendering context current, use **glXMakeCurrent()**; **glXGetCurrentContext()** returns the current context. (You can also obtain the current drawable with **glXGetCurrentDrawable()**.) Remember that only one context can be current for any thread at any one time. If you have multiple contexts, you can copy selected groups of OpenGL state variables from one context to another with **glXCopyContext()**. When you're finished with a particular context, destroy it with **glXDestroyContext()**.

Off-Screen Rendering

To render off-screen, first create an X Pixmap and then pass this as an argument to **glXCreateGLXPixmap()**. Once rendering is completed, you can destroy the association between the X and GLX Pixmaps with **glXDestroyGLXPixmap()**. (Off-screen rendering isn't guaranteed to be supported for direct renderers.)

Synchronizing Execution

To prevent X requests from executing until any outstanding OpenGL rendering is completed, call **glXWaitGL()**. Then, any previously issued OpenGL commands are guaranteed to be executed before any X rendering calls made after **glXWaitGL()**. Although the same result can be achieved with **glFinish()**, **glXWaitGL()** doesn't require a round trip to the server and thus is more efficient in cases where the client and server are on separate machines.

To prevent an OpenGL command sequence from executing until any outstanding X requests are completed, use **glXWaitX()**. This routine guarantees that previously issued X rendering calls will be executed before any OpenGL calls made after **glXWaitX()**.

Swapping Buffers

For drawables that are double-buffered, the front and back buffers can be exchanged by calling **glXSwapBuffers()**. An implicit **glFlush()** is done as part of this routine.

Using an X Font

A shortcut for using X fonts in OpenGL is provided with the command **glXUseXFont()**.

Chapter 3

Summary of Commands and Routines

This chapter lists the prototypes for OpenGL, the OpenGL Utility Library, and the OpenGL extension to the X Window System. The prototypes are grouped functionally, as shown below:

- **OpenGL Commands**

  Primitives
  Coordinate Transformation
  Coloring and Lighting
  Clipping
  Rasterization
  Pixel Operations
  Texture Mapping

  Fog
  Frame Buffer Operations
  Evaluators
  Selection and Feedback
  Display Lists
  Modes and Execution
  State Queries

- **GLU Routines**

  Texture Images
  Coordinate Transformation
  Polygon Tessellation
  Quadric Objects
  NURBS Curves and Surfaces
  Error Handling

- **GLX Routines**

  Initialization
  Controlling Rendering

Notation

Since some of the OpenGL commands differ from each other only by the data type of the arguments they accept, certain conventions have been used to refer to these commands in a compact way:

void **glVertex2{sifd}{v}** (TYPE *x*, TYPE *y*);

In this example, the first set of braces encloses characters identifying the possible data types for the arguments listed as having data type TYPE. (The digit preceding the braces indicates how many arguments the command takes.) In this case, all the arguments have the placeholder TYPE, but in other situations some arguments may have an explicitly defined data type. The table shown below lists the set of possible data types, their corresponding characters, and the type definition OpenGL uses for referring to that data type.

character	data type	C-language type	OpenGL type definition
b	8-bit integer	signed char	GLbyte
s	16-bit integer	short	GLshort
i	32-bit integer	int	GLint, GLsizei
f	32-bit floating-point	float	GLfloat, GLclampf
d	64-bit floating-point	double	GLdouble, GLclampd
ub	8-bit unsigned integer	unsigned char	GLubyte, GLboolean
us	16-bit unsigned integer	unsigned short	GLushort
ui	32-bit unsigned integer	unsigned int	GLuint, GLenum, GLbitfield
		void	GLvoid

The second set of braces, if present, contains a **v** for the vector form of the command. If you choose to use the vector form, all the TYPE arguments are collapsed into a single array. For example, here are the nonvector and vector forms of a command, using a 32-bit floating-point data type:

void **glVertex2f**(GLfloat *x*, GLfloat *y*);

void **glVertex2fv**(GLfloat *v*[2]);

Where the use of the vector form is ambiguous, both the vector and nonvector forms are listed. Note that not all commands with multiple arguments have a vector form and that some commands have only a vector form, in which case the **v** isn't enclosed in braces.

OpenGL Commands

Primitives

Specify vertices or rectangles:

    void **glBegin** (GLenum *mode*);
    void **glEnd** (void);
    void **glVertex2{sifd}{v}** (TYPE *x*, TYPE *y*);
    void **glVertex3{sifd}{v}** (TYPE *x*, TYPE *y*, TYPE *z*);
    void **glVertex4{sifd}{v}** (TYPE *x*, TYPE *y*, TYPE *z*, TYPE *w*);
    void **glRect{sifd}** (TYPE x_1, TYPE y_1, TYPE x_2, TYPE y_2);
    void **glRect{sifd}v** (const TYPE *v_1, const TYPE *v_2);

Specify polygon edge treatment:

    void **glEdgeFlag** (GLboolean *flag*);
    void **glEdgeFlagv** (const GLboolean *flag*);

Coordinate Transformation

Transform the current matrix:

    void **glRotate{fd}** (TYPE *angle*, TYPE *x*, TYPE *y*, TYPE *z*);
    void **glTranslate{fd}** (TYPE *x*, TYPE *y*, TYPE *z*);
    void **glScale{fd}** (TYPE *x*, TYPE *y*, TYPE *z*);
    void **glMultMatrix{fd}** (const TYPE *m*);
    void **glFrustum** (GLdouble *left*, GLdouble *right*, GLdouble *bottom*,
                        GLdouble *top*, GLdouble *near*, GLdouble *far*);
    void **glOrtho** (GLdouble *left*, GLdouble *right*, GLdouble *bottom*,
                        GLdouble *top*, GLdouble *near*, GLdouble *far*);

Replace the current matrix:

    void **glLoadMatrix{fd}** (const TYPE *m*);
    void **glLoadIdentity** (void);

Manipulate the matrix stack:

    void **glMatrixMode** (GLenum *mode*);
    void **glPushMatrix** (void);
    void **glPopMatrix** (void);

Specify the viewport:

> void **glDepthRange** (GLclampd *near*, GLclampd *far*);
> void **glViewport** (GLint *x*, GLint *y*, GLsizei *width*, GLsizei *height*);

Coloring and Lighting

Set the current color, color index, or normal vector:

> void **glColor3{bsifd ubusui}{v}** (TYPE *red*, TYPE *green*, TYPE *blue*);
> void **glColor4{bsifd ubusui}{v}** (TYPE *red*, TYPE *green*, TYPE *blue*,
>   TYPE *alpha*);
> void **glIndex{sifd}{v}** (TYPE *index*);
> void **glNormal3{bsifd}{v}** (TYPE *nx*, TYPE *ny*, TYPE *nz*);

Specify light source, material, or lighting model parameter values:

> void **glLight{if}{v}** (GLenum *light*, GLenum *pname*, TYPE *param*);
> void **glMaterial{if}{v}** (GLenum *face*, GLenum *pname*, TYPE *param*);
> void **glLightModel{if}{v}** (GLenum *pname*, TYPE *param*);

Choose a shading model:

> void **glShadeModel** (GLenum *mode*);

Specify which polygon orientation is front-facing:

> void **glFrontFace** (GLenum *dir*);

Cause a material color to track the current color:

> void **glColorMaterial** (GLenum *face*, GLenum *mode*);

Obtain light source or material parameter values:

> void **glGetLight{if}v** (GLenum *light*, GLenum *pname*, TYPE **params*);
> void **glGetMaterial{if}v** (GLenum *face*, GLenum *pname*, TYPE **params*);

Clipping

Specify a clipping plane:

> void **glClipPlane** (GLenum *plane*, const GLdouble **equation*);

Return clipping plane coefficients:

> void **glGetClipPlane** (GLenum *plane*, GLdouble **equation*);

Rasterization

Set the current raster position:

    void **glRasterPos2{sifd}{v}**(TYPE *x*, TYPE *y*);
    void **glRasterPos3{sifd}{v}**(TYPE *x*, TYPE *y*, TYPE *z*);
    void **glRasterPos4{sifd}{v}**(TYPE *x*, TYPE *y*, TYPE *z*, TYPE *w*);

Specify a bitmap:

    void **glBitmap** (GLsizei *width*, GLsizei *height*, GLfloat *xorig*,
                GLfloat *yorig*, GLfloat *xmove*, GLfloat *ymove*,
                const GLubyte **bitmap*);

Specify the dimensions of points or lines:

    void **glPointSize** (GLfloat *size*);
    void **glLineWidth** (GLfloat *width*);

Specify or return a stipple pattern for lines or polygons:

    void **glLineStipple** (GLint *factor*, GLushort *pattern*);
    void **glPolygonStipple** (const GLubyte **mask*);
    void **glGetPolygonStipple** (GLubyte **mask*);

Choose how polygons are rasterized:

    void **glCullFace** (GLenum *mode*);
    void **glPolygonMode** (GLenum *face*, GLenum *mode*);

Pixel Operations

Select the source for pixel reads or copies:

    void **glReadBuffer** (GLenum *mode*);

Read, write, and copy pixels:

    void **glReadPixels** (GLint *x*, GLint *y*, GLsizei *width*, GLsizei *height*,
                GLenum *format*, GLenum *type*, GLvoid **pixels*);
    void **glDrawPixels** (GLsizei *width*, GLsizei *height*, GLenum *format*,
                GLenum *type*, const GLvoid **pixels*);
    void **glCopyPixels** (GLint *x*, GLint *y*, GLsizei *width*, GLsizei *height*,
                GLenum *type*);

Specify or query how pixels are encoded or processed:

> void **glPixelStore{if}** (GLenum *pname*, TYPE *param*);
> void **glPixelTransfer{if}** (GLenum *pname*, TYPE *param*);
> void **glPixelMap{f usui}v** (GLenum *map*, GLint *mapsize*,
>   const TYPE **values*);
> void **glGetPixelMap{f usui}v** (GLenum *map*, TYPE **values*);

Control pixel rasterization:

> void **glPixelZoom** (GLfloat *xfactor*, GLfloat *yfactor*);

Texture Mapping

Control how a texture is applied to a fragment:

> void **glTexParameter{if}{v}** (GLenum *target*, GLenum *pname*, TYPE
> *param*);
> void **glTexEnv{if}{v}** (GLenum *target*, GLenum *pname*, TYPE *param*);

Set the current texture coordinates:

> void **glTexCoord1{sifd}{v}** (TYPE *s*);
> void **glTexCoord2{sifd}{v}** (TYPE *s*, TYPE *t*);
> void **glTexCoord3{sifd}{v}** (TYPE *s*, TYPE *t*, TYPE *r*);
> void **glTexCoord4{sifd}{v}** (TYPE *s*, TYPE *t*, TYPE *r*, TYPE *q*);

Control the generation of texture coordinates:

> void **glTexGen{ifd}{v}** (GLenum *coord*, GLenum *pname*, TYPE *param*);

Specify a one- or two-dimensional texture image:

> void **glTexImage1D** (GLenum *target*, GLint *level*, GLint *components*,
>   GLsizei *width*, GLint *border*, GLenum *format*,
>   GLenum *type*, const GLvoid **pixels*);
> void **glTexImage2D** (GLenum *target*, GLint *level*, GLint *components*,
>   GLsizei *width*, GLsizei *height*, GLint *border*,
>   GLenum *format*, GLenum *type*, const GLvoid **pixels*);

Obtain texture-related parameter values:

> void **glGetTexEnv{if}v** (GLenum *target*, GLenum *pname*, TYPE **params*);
> void **glGetTexGen{ifd}v** (GLenum *coord*, GLenum *pname*,
> > TYPE **params*);
> void **glGetTexImage** (GLenum *target*, GLint *level*, GLenum *format*,
> > GLenum *type*, GLvoid **pixels*);
> void **glGetTexLevelParameter{if}v** (GLenum *target*, GLint *level*,
> > GLenum *pname*, TYPE **params*);
> void **glGetTexParameter{if}v** (GLenum *target*, GLenum *pname*,
> > TYPE **params*);

Fog

Set fog parameters:

> void **glFog{if}{v}** (GLenum *pname*, TYPE *param*);

Frame Buffer Operations

Control per-fragment testing:

> void **glScissor** (GLint *x*, GLint *y*, GLsizei *width*, GLsizei *height*);
> void **glAlphaFunc** (GLenum *func*, GLclampf *ref*);
> void **glStencilFunc** (GLenum *func*, GLint *ref*, GLuint *mask*);
> void **glStencilOp** (GLenum *fail*, GLenum *pass*, GLenum *zpass*);
> void **glDepthFunc** (GLenum *func*);

Combine fragment and frame buffer values:

> void **glBlendFunc** (GLenum *sfactor*, GLenum *dfactor*);
> void **glLogicOp** (GLenum *opcode*);

Clear some or all buffers:

> void **glClear** (GLbitfield *mask*);

Specify color, depth, and stencil values for clears:

> void **glClearAccum** (GLfloat *red*, GLfloat *green*, GLfloat *blue*, GLfloat
> *alpha*);
> void **glClearColor** (GLclampf *red*, GLclampf *green*, GLclampf *blue*,
> > GLclampf *alpha*);
> void **glClearDepth** (GLclampd *depth*);
> void **glClearIndex** (GLfloat *c*);
> void **glClearStencil** (GLint *s*);

Control buffers enabled for writing:

> void **glDrawBuffer** (GLenum *mode*);
> void **glIndexMask** (GLuint *mask*);
> void **glColorMask** (GLboolean *red*, GLboolean *green*, GLboolean *blue*,
>   GLboolean *alpha*);
> void **glDepthMask** (GLboolean *flag*);
> void **glStencilMask** (GLuint *mask*);

Operate on the accumulation buffer:

> void **glAccum** (GLenum *op*, GLfloat *value*);

Evaluators

Define a one- or two-dimensional evaluator:

> void **glMap1{fd}** (GLenum *target*, TYPE *u1*, TYPE *u2*, GLint *stride*,
>   GLint *order*, const TYPE *points*);
> void **glMap2{fd}** (GLenum *target*, TYPE *u1*, TYPE *u2*, GLint *ustride*,
>   GLint *uorder*, TYPE *v1*, TYPE *v2*, GLint *vstride*,
>   GLint *vorder*, const TYPE *points*);

Generate and evaluate a series of map domain values:

> void **glMapGrid1{fd}** (GLint *n*, TYPE *u1*, TYPE *u2*);
> void **glMapGrid2{fd}** (GLint *un*, TYPE *u1*, TYPE *u2*, GLint *vn*,
>   TYPE *v1*, TYPE *v2*);
> void **glEvalMesh1** (GLenum *mode*, GLint *i1*, GLint *i2*);
> void **glEvalMesh2** (GLenum *mode*, GLint *i1*, GLint *i2*, GLint *j1*, GLint *j2*);
> void **glEvalPoint1** (GLint *i*);
> void **glEvalPoint2** (GLint *i*, GLint *j*);

Evaluate one- and two-dimensional maps at a specified domain coordinate:

> void **glEvalCoord1{fd}{v}** (TYPE *u*);
> void **glEvalCoord2{fd}{v}** (TYPE *u*, TYPE *v*);

Obtain evaluator parameter values:

> void **glGetMap{idf}v** (GLenum *target*, GLenum *query*, TYPE *v*);

Selection and Feedback

Control the mode and corresponding buffer:

GLint **glRenderMode** (GLenum *mode*);
void **glSelectBuffer** (GLsizei *size*, GLuint **buffer*);
void **glFeedbackBuffer** (GLsizei *size*, GLenum *type*, GLfloat **buffer*);

Supply a token for feedback mode:

void **glPassThrough** (GLfloat *token*);

Control the name stack for selection:

void **glInitNames** (void);
void **glLoadName** (GLuint *name*);
void **glPushName** (GLuint *name*);
void **glPopName** (void);

Display Lists

Create or delete display lists:

void **glNewList** (GLuint *list*, GLenum *mode*);
void **glEndList** (void);
void **glDeleteLists** (GLuint *list*, GLsizei *range*);

Execute a display list or set of lists:

void **glCallList** (GLuint *list*);
void **glCallLists** (GLsizei *n*, GLenum *type*, const GLvoid **lists*);

Manage display-list indices:

GLuint **glGenLists** (GLsizei *range*);
GLboolean **glIsList** (GLuint *list*);
void **glListBase** (GLuint *base*);

Modes and Execution

Enable, disable, and query modes:

void **glEnable** (GLenum *cap*);
void **glDisable** (GLenum *cap*);
GLboolean **glIsEnabled** (GLenum *cap*);

Wait until all OpenGL commands have executed completely:

> void **glFinish** (void);

Force all issued OpenGL commands to be executed:

> void **glFlush** (void);

Specify hints for OpenGL operation:

> void **glHint** (GLenum *target*, GLenum *mode*);

State Queries

Obtain information about an error or the current OpenGL connection:

> GLenum **glGetError** (void);
> const GLubyte * **glGetString** (GLenum *name*);

Query state variables:

> void **glGetBooleanv** (GLenum *pname*, GLboolean *params*);
> void **glGetDoublev** (GLenum *pname*, GLdouble *params*);
> void **glGetFloatv** (GLenum *pname*, GLfloat *params*);
> void **glGetIntegerv** (GLenum *pname*, GLint *params*);

Save and restore sets of state variables:

> void **glPushAttrib** (GLbitfield *mask*);
> void **glPopAttrib** (void);

GLU Routines

Texture Images

Magnify or shrink an image:

int **gluScaleImage** (GLenum *format*, GLint *widthin*, GLint *heightin*,
　　　　　　　　GLenum *typein*, const void **datain*, GLint *widthout*,
　　　　　　　　GLint *heightout*, GLenum *typeout*, void **dataout*);

Generate mipmaps for an image:

int **gluBuild1DMipmaps** (GLenum *target*, GLint *components*, GLint *width*,
　　　　　　　　GLenum *format*, GLenum *type*, void **data*);
int **gluBuild2DMipmaps** (GLenum *target*, GLint *components*, GLint *width*,
　　　　　　　　GLint *height*, GLenum *format*, GLenum *type*,
　　　　　　　　void **data*);

Coordinate Transformation

Create projection or viewing matrices:

void **gluOrtho2D** (GLdouble *left*, GLdouble *right*, GLdouble *bottom*,
　　　　　　　　GLdouble *top*);
void **gluPerspective** (GLdouble *fovy*, GLdouble *aspect*, GLdouble *zNear*,
　　　　　　　　GLdouble *zFar*);
void **gluPickMatrix** (GLdouble *x*, GLdouble *y*, GLdouble *width*,
　　　　　　　　GLdouble *height*, GLint *viewport*[4]);
void **gluLookAt** (GLdouble *eyex*, GLdouble *eyey*, GLdouble *eyez*,
　　　　　　　　GLdouble *centerx*, GLdouble *centery*, GLdouble *centerz*,
　　　　　　　　GLdouble *upx*, GLdouble *upy*, GLdouble *upz*);

Convert object coordinates to screen coordinates:

int **gluProject** (GLdouble *objx*, GLdouble *objy*, GLdouble *objz*,
　　　　　　　　const GLdouble *modelMatrix*[16],
　　　　　　　　const GLdouble *projMatrix*[16],
　　　　　　　　const GLint *viewport*[4], GLdouble **winx*,
　　　　　　　　GLdouble **winy*, GLdouble **winz*);
int **gluUnProject** (GLdouble *winx*, GLdouble *winy*, GLdouble *winz*,
　　　　　　　　const GLdouble *modelMatrix*[16],
　　　　　　　　const GLdouble *projMatrix*[16],
　　　　　　　　const GLint *viewport*[4], GLdouble **objx*,
　　　　　　　　GLdouble **objy*, GLdouble **objz*);

Polygon Tessellation

Manage tessellation objects:

>GLUtriangulatorObj* **gluNewTess** (void);
>void **gluTessCallback** (GLUtriangulatorObj *tobj*, GLenum *which*,
>   void (**fn*)());
>void **gluDeleteTess** (GLUtriangulatorObj *tobj*);

Describe the input polygon:

>void **gluBeginPolygon** (GLUtriangulatorObj *tobj*);
>void **gluEndPolygon** (GLUtriangulatorObj *tobj*);
>void **gluNextContour** (GLUtriangulatorObj *tobj*, GLenum *type*);
>void **gluTessVertex** (GLUtriangulatorObj *tobj*, GLdouble *v*[3], void *data*);

Quadric Objects

Manage quadric objects:

>GLUquadricObj* **gluNewQuadric** (void);
>void **gluDeleteQuadric** (GLUquadricObj *state*);
>void **gluQuadricCallback** (GLUquadricObj *qobj*, GLenum *which*,
>   void (**fn*)());

Control the rendering:

>void **gluQuadricNormals** (GLUquadricObj *quadObject*, GLenum
>*normals*);
>void **gluQuadricTexture** (GLUquadricObj *quadObject*,
>   GLboolean *textureCoords*);
>void **gluQuadricOrientation** (GLUquadricObj *quadObject*,
>   GLenum *orientation*);
>void **gluQuadricDrawStyle** (GLUquadricObj *quadObject*,
>   GLenum *drawStyle*);

Specify a quadric primitive:

> void **gluCylinder** (GLUquadricObj *qobj*, GLdouble *baseRadius*,
> GLdouble *topRadius*, GLdouble *height*, GLint *slices*,
> GLint *stacks*);
> void **gluDisk** (GLUquadricObj *qobj*, GLdouble *innerRadius*,
> GLdouble *outerRadius*, GLint *slices*, GLint *loops*);
> void **gluPartialDisk** (GLUquadricObj *qobj*, GLdouble *innerRadius*,
> GLdouble *outerRadius*, GLint *slices*, GLint *loops*,
> GLdouble *startAngle*, GLdouble *sweepAngle*);
> void **gluSphere** (GLUquadricObj *qobj*, GLdouble *radius*, GLint *slices*,
> GLint *stacks*);

NURBS Curves and Surfaces

Manage a NURBS object:

> GLUnurbsObj* **gluNewNurbsRenderer** (void);
> void **gluDeleteNurbsRenderer** (GLUnurbsObj *nobj*);
> void **gluNurbsCallback** (GLUnurbsObj *nobj*, GLenum *which*, void
> (**fn*)());

Create a NURBS curve:

> void **gluBeginCurve** (GLUnurbsObj *nobj*);
> void **gluEndCurve** (GLUnurbsObj *nobj*);
> void **gluNurbsCurve** (GLUnurbsObj *nobj*, GLint *nknots*, GLfloat *knot*,
> GLint *stride*, GLfloat *ctlarray*,
> GLint *order*, GLenum *type*);

Create a NURBS surface:

> void **gluBeginSurface** (GLUnurbsObj *nobj*);
> void **gluEndSurface** (GLUnurbsObj *nobj*);
> void **gluNurbsSurface** (GLUnurbsObj *nobj*, GLint *uknot_count*,
> GLfloat *uknot*, GLint *vknot_count*, GLfloat *vknot*,
> GLint *u_stride*, GLint *v_stride*, GLfloat *ctlarray*,
> GLint *sorder*, GLint *torder*, GLenum *type*);

Define a trimming region:

> void **gluBeginTrim** (GLUnurbsObj *nobj*);
> void **gluEndTrim** (GLUnurbsObj *nobj*);
> void **gluPwlCurve** (GLUnurbsObj *nobj*, GLint *count*, GLfloat *array*,
> GLint *stride*, GLenum *type*);

Control NURBS rendering:

void **gluLoadSamplingMatrices** (GLUnurbsObj *nobj,
        const GLfloat modelMatrix[16],
        const GLfloat projMatrix[16],
        const GLint viewport[4]);
void **gluNurbsProperty** (GLUnurbsObj *nobj, GLenum property,
        GLfloat value);
void **gluGetNurbsProperty** (GLUnurbsObj *nobj, GLenum property,
        GLfloat *value);

Error Handling

Produce an error string from an OpenGL error code:

const GLubyte* **gluErrorString** (GLenum errorCode);

GLX Routines

Initialization

Determine whether the GLX extension is defined on the X server:

Bool **glXQueryExtension** (Display *dpy*, int *errorBase*, int *eventBase*);
Bool **glXQueryVersion** (Display *dpy*, int *major*, int *minor*);

Obtain the desired visual:

XVisualInfo* **glXChooseVisual** (Display *dpy*, int *screen*, int *attribList*);
int **glXGetConfig** (Display *dpy*, XVisualInfo *vis*, int *attrib*, int *value*);

Controlling Rendering

Manage or query an OpenGL rendering context:

GLXContext **glXCreateContext** (Display *dpy*, XVisualInfo *vis*,
    GLXContext *shareList*, Bool *direct*);
void **glXDestroyContext** (Display *dpy*, GLXContext *ctx*);
void **glXCopyContext** (Display *dpy*, GLXContext *src*,
    GLXContext *dst*, GLuint *mask*);
Bool **glXIsDirect** (Display *dpy*, GLXContext *ctx*);
Bool **glXMakeCurrent** (Display *dpy*, GLXDrawable *draw*,
    GLXContext *ctx*);
GLXContext **glXGetCurrentContext** (void);
GLXDrawable **glXGetCurrentDrawable** (void);

Perform off-screen rendering:

GLXPixmap **glXCreateGLXPixmap** (Display *dpy*, XVisualInfo *vis*,
    Pixmap *pixmap*);
void **glXDestroyGLXPixmap** (Display *dpy*, GLXPixmap *pix*);

Synchronize execution:

void **glXWaitGL** (void);
void **glXWaitX** (void);

Exchange front and back buffers:

void **glXSwapBuffers** (Display *dpy*, Window *window*);

Use an X font:

void **glXUseXFont** (Font *font*, int *first*, int *count*, int *listBase*);

Chapter 4

Defined Constants and Associated Commands

This chapter lists all the defined constants in OpenGL and their corresponding commands; these constants might indicate a parameter name, a value for a parameter, a mode, a query target, or a return value. The list is intended to be used as another index into the reference pages: if you remember the name of a constant, you can use this table to find out which functions use it, and then you can refer to the reference pages for those functions for more information. Note that all the constants listed can be used directly by the corresponding commands; the reference pages list additional, related commands that might be of interest.

Constant	Associated Commands
GL_2D, GL_3D, GL_3D_COLOR, GL_COLOR_TEXTURE, GL_4D_COLOR_TEXTURE	glFeedbackBuffer()
GL_2_BYTES, GL_3_BYTES, GL_4_BYTES	glCallLists()
GL_ACCUM	glAccum()
GL_ACCUM_ALPHA_BITS, GL_ACCUM_BLUE_BITS	glGet*()
GL_ACCUM_BUFFER_BIT	glClear(), glPushAttrib()
GL_ACCUM_CLEAR_VALUE, GL_ACCUM_GREEN_BITS, GL_ACCUM_RED_BITS	glGet*()
GL_ADD	glAccum()
GL_ALL_ATTRIB_BITS	glPushAttrib()
GL_ALPHA	glDrawPixels(), glReadPixels(), glTexImage1D(), glTexImage2D(), glGetTexImage()
GL_ALPHA_BIAS	glPixelTransfer*(), glGet*()
GL_ALPHA_BITS	glGet*()
GL_ALPHA_SCALE	glPixelTransfer*(), glGet*()
GL_ALPHA_TEST	glEnable(), glIsEnabled(), glGet*()
GL_ALPHA_TEST_FUNC, GL_ALPHA_TEST_REF	glGet*()
GL_ALWAYS	glAlphaFunc(), glDepthFunc(), glStencilFunc()
GL_AMBIENT	glLight*(), glGetLight*(), glMaterial*(), glGetMaterial*(), glColorMaterial()
GL_AMBIENT_AND_DIFFUSE	glMaterial*(), glGetMaterial*(), glColorMaterial()
GL_AND, GL_AND_INVERTED, GL_AND_REVERSE	glLogicOp()
GL_ATTRIB_STACK_DEPTH	glGet*()
GL_AUTO_NORMAL	glEnable(), glIsEnabled(), glGet*()
GL_AUX0 through GL_AUX3	glDrawBuffer(), glReadBuffer()
GL_AUX_BUFFERS	glGet*()

Constant	Associated Commands
GL_BACK	glColorMaterial(), glCullFace(), glDrawBuffer(), glReadBuffer(), glMaterial*(), glGetMaterial*(), glPolygonMode()
GL_BACK_LEFT, GL_BACK_RIGHT	glDrawBuffer(), glReadBuffer()
GL_BITMAP	glDrawPixels(), glReadPixels(), glTexImage1D(), glTexImage2D(), glGetTexImage()
GL_BITMAP_TOKEN	glPassThrough()
GL_BLEND	glTexEnv*(), glGetTexEnv*(), glEnable(), glIsEnabled(), glGet*()
GL_BLEND_DST, GL_BLEND_SRC	glGet*()
GL_BLUE	glDrawPixels(), glReadPixels(), glTexImage1D(), glTexImage2D(), glGetTexImage()
GL_BLUE_BIAS	glPixelTransfer*(), glGet*()
GL_BLUE_BITS	glGet*()
GL_BLUE_SCALE	glPixelTransfer*(), glGet*()
GL_BYTE	glCallLists(), glDrawPixels(), glReadPixels(), glTexImage1D(), glTexImage2D(), glGetTexImage()
GL_CCW	glFrontFace()
GL_CLAMP	glTexParameter*()
GL_CLEAR	glLogicOp()
GL_CLIP_PLANE	glEnable(), glIsEnabled()
GL_CLIP_PLANE0 through GL_CLIP_PLANE5	glClipPlane(), glGetClipPlane(), glEnable(), glIsEnabled()
GL_COEFF	glGetMap*()
GL_COLOR	glCopyPixels()
GL_COLOR_BUFFER_BIT	glClear(), glPushAttrib()
GL_COLOR_CLEAR_VALUE	glGet*()
GL_COLOR_INDEX	glDrawPixels(), glReadPixels(), glTexImage1D(), glTexImage2D(), glGetTexImage()
GL_COLOR_INDEXES	glMaterial*(), glGetMaterial*()
GL_COLOR_MATERIAL	glEnable(), glIsEnabled(), glGet*()

Constant	Associated Commands
GL_COLOR_MATERIAL_FACE, GL_COLOR_MATERIAL_PARAMETER	glGet*()
GL_COLOR_WRITEMASK	glGet*()
GL_COMPILE, GL_COMPILE_AND_EXECUTE	glNewList()
GL_CONSTANT_ATTENUATION	glLight*(), glGetLight*()
GL_COPY, GL_COPY_INVERTED	glLogicOp()
GL_COPY_PIXEL_TOKEN	glPassThrough()
GL_CULL_FACE	glEnable(), glIsEnabled(), glGet*()
GL_CULL_FACE_MODE	glGet*()
GL_CURRENT_BIT	glPushAttrib()
GL_CURRENT_COLOR, GL_CURRENT_INDEX, GL_CURRENT_NORMAL, GL_CURRENT_RASTER_COLOR, GL_CURRENT_RASTER_INDEX, GL_CURRENT_RASTER_POSITION, GL_CURRENT_RASTER_POSITION_VALID, GL_CURRENT_RASTER_TEXTURE_COORDS, GL_CURRENT_TEXTURE_COORDS	glGet*()
GL_CW	glFrontFace()
GL_DECAL	glTexEnv*(), glGetTexEnv*()
GL_DECR	glStencilOp()
GL_DEPTH	glCopyPixels()
GL_DEPTH_BIAS	glPixelTransfer*(), glGet*()
GL_DEPTH_BITS	glGet*()
GL_DEPTH_BUFFER_BIT	glClear(), glPushAttrib()
GL_DEPTH_CLEAR_VALUE	glGet*()
GL_DEPTH_COMPONENT	glDrawPixels(), glReadPixels(), glTexImage1D(), glTexImage2D(), glGetTexImage()
GL_DEPTH_FUNC	glGet*()
GL_DEPTH_RANGE	glGet*()
GL_DEPTH_SCALE	glPixelTransfer*(), glGet*()
GL_DEPTH_TEST	glEnable(), glIsEnabled(), glGet*()
GL_DEPTH_WRITEMASK	glGet*()

Constant	Associated Commands
GL_DIFFUSE	glLight*(), glGetLight*(), glMaterial*(), glGetMaterial*(), glColorMaterial()
GL_DITHER	glEnable(), glIsEnabled(), glGet*()
GL_DOMAIN	glGetMap*()
GL_DONT_CARE	glHint()
GL_DOUBLEBUFFER	glGet*()
GL_DRAW_BUFFER	glGet*()
GL_DRAW_PIXEL_TOKEN	glPassThrough()
GL_DST_ALPHA, GL_DST_COLOR	glBlendFunc()
GL_EDGE_FLAG	glGet*()
GL_EMISSION	glMaterial*(), glGetMaterial*(), glColorMaterial()
GL_ENABLE_BIT	glPushAttrib()
GL_EQUAL	glAlphaFunc(), glDepthFunc(), glStencilFunc()
GL_EQUIV	glLogicOp()
GL_EVAL_BIT	glPushAttrib()
GL_EXP, GL_EXP2	glFog*()
GL_EXTENSIONS	glGetString()
GL_EYE_LINEAR	glTexGen*(), glGetTexGen*()
GL_EYE_PLANE	glTexGen*()
GL_FALSE	glColorMask(), glGet*(), glIsEnabled(), glIsList()
GL_FASTEST	glHint()
GL_FEEDBACK	glRenderMode()
GL_FILL	glPolygonMode(), glEvalMesh2()
GL_FLAT	glShadeModel()
GL_FLOAT	glCallLists(), glDrawPixels(), glReadPixels(), glTexImage1D(), glTexImage2D(), glGetTexImage()
GL_FOG	glEnable(), glIsEnabled(), glGet*()
GL_FOG_BIT	glPushAttrib()
GL_FOG_COLOR, GL_FOG_DENSITY, GL_FOG_END	glFog*(), glGet*()
GL_FOG_HINT	glHint()

Constant	Associated Commands
GL_FOG_INDEX, GL_FOG_MODE, GL_FOG_START	glFog*(), glGet*()
GL_FRONT	glColorMaterial(), glCullFace(), glDrawBuffer(), glReadBuffer(), glMaterial*(), glGetMaterial*(), glPolygonMode()
GL_FRONT_AND_BACK	glColorMaterial(), glDrawBuffer(), glMaterial*(), glPolygonMode()
GL_FRONT_FACE	glGet*()
GL_FRONT_LEFT, GL_FRONT_RIGHT	glDrawBuffer(), glReadBuffer()
GL_GEQUAL, GL_GREATER	glDepthFunc(), glAlphaFunc(), glStencilFunc()
GL_GREEN	glDrawPixels(), glReadPixels(), glTexImage1D(), glTexImage2D(), glGetTexImage()
GL_GREEN_BIAS	glPixelTransfer*(), glGet*()
GL_GREEN_BITS	glGet*()
GL_GREEN_SCALE	glPixelTransfer*(), glGet*()
GL_HINT_BIT	glPushAttrib()
GL_INCR	glStencilOp()
GL_INDEX_BITS, GL_INDEX_CLEAR_VALUE, GL_INDEX_MODE	glGet*()
GL_INDEX_OFFSET, GL_INDEX_SHIFT	glPixelTransfer*(), glGet*()
GL_INDEX_WRITEMASK	glGet*()
GL_INT	glCallLists(), glDrawPixels(), glReadPixels(), glTexImage1D(), glTexImage2D(), glGetTexImage()
GL_INVALID_ENUM, GL_INVALID_OPERATION, GL_INVALID_VALUE	glGetError()
GL_INVERT	glLogicOp(), glStencilOp()
GL_KEEP	glStencilOp()
GL_LEFT	glDrawBuffer(), glReadBuffer()
GL_LEQUAL, GL_LESS	glDepthFunc(), glAlphaFunc(), glStencilFunc()
GL_LIGHT0 through GL_LIGHT7	glLight*(), glGetLight*(), glEnable(), glIsEnabled()
GL_LIGHTING	glEnable(), glIsEnabled(), glGet*()

Chapter 4: Defined Constants and Associated Commands

Constant	Associated Commands
GL_LIGHTING_BIT	glPushAttrib()
GL_LIGHT_MODEL_AMBIENT, GL_LIGHT_MODEL_LOCAL_VIEWER, GL_LIGHT_MODEL_TWO_SIDE	glLightModel*(), glGet*()
GL_LINE	glPolygonMode(), glEvalMesh*()
GL_LINEAR	glFog*(), glTexParameter*()
GL_LINEAR_ATTENUATION	glLight*(), glGetLight*()
GL_LINEAR_MIPMAP_LINEAR, GL_LINEAR_MIPMAP_NEAREST	glTexParameter*()
GL_LINES	glBegin()
GL_LINE_BIT	glPushAttrib()
GL_LINE_LOOP	glBegin()
GL_LINE_RESET_TOKEN	glPassThrough()
GL_LINE_SMOOTH	glEnable(), glIsEnabled(), glGet*()
GL_LINE_SMOOTH_HINT	glHint(), glGet*()
GL_LINE_STIPPLE	glEnable(), glIsEnabled(), glGet*()
GL_LINE_STIPPLE_PATTERN, GL_LINE_STIPPLE_REPEAT	glGet*()
GL_LINE_STRIP	glBegin()
GL_LINE_TOKEN	glPassThrough()
GL_LINE_WIDTH, GL_LINE_WIDTH_GRANULARITY, GL_LINE_WIDTH_RANGE	glGet*()
GL_LIST_BASE	glGet*()
GL_LIST_BIT	glPushAttrib()
GL_LIST_INDEX, GL_LIST_MODE	glGet*()
GL_LOAD	glAccum()
GL_LOGIC_OP	glEnable(), glIsEnabled(), glGet*()
GL_LOGIC_OP_MODE	glGet*()
GL_LUMINANCE, GL_LUMINANCE_ALPHA	glDrawPixels(), glReadPixels(), glTexImage1D(), glTexImage2D(), glGetTexImage()
GL_MAP1_COLOR_4	glMap1*(), glEnable(), glIsEnabled(), glGetMap*()
GL_MAP1_GRID_DOMAIN, GL_MAP1_GRID_SEGMENTS	glGet*()

Constant	Associated Commands
GL_MAP1_INDEX, GL_MAP1_NORMAL, GL_MAP1_TEXTURE_COORD_1 through GL_MAP1_TEXTURE_COORD_4, GL_MAP1_VERTEX_3, GL_MAP1_VERTEX_4	glMap1*(), glEnable(), glIsEnabled(), glGetMap*()
GL_MAP2_COLOR_4	glMap2*(), glEnable(), glIsEnabled(), glGet*()
GL_MAP2_GRID_DOMAIN	glGet*()
GL_MAP2_GRID_SEGMENTS	glGet*()
GL_MAP2_INDEX, GL_MAP2_NORMAL, GL_MAP2_TEXTURE_COORD_1 through GL_MAP2_TEXTURE_COORD_4, GL_MAP2_VERTEX_3, GL_MAP2_VERTEX_4	glMap2*(), glEnable(), glIsEnabled(), glGet*()
GL_MAP_COLOR, GL_MAP_STENCIL	glPixelTransfer*(), glGet*()
GL_MATRIX_MODE	glGet*()
GL_MAX_ATTRIB_STACK_DEPTH, GL_MAX_CLIP_PLANES, GL_MAX_EVAL_ORDER, GL_MAX_LIGHTS, GL_MAX_LIST_NESTING, GL_MAX_MODELVIEW_STACK_DEPTH, GL_MAX_NAME_STACK_DEPTH, GL_MAX_PIXEL_MAP_TABLE, GL_MAX_PROJECTION_STACK_DEPTH, GL_MAX_TEXTURE_SIZE, GL_MAX_TEXTURE_STACK_DEPTH, GL_MAX_VIEWPORT_DIMS	glGet*()
GL_MODELVIEW	glMatrixMode()
GL_MODELVIEW_MATRIX, GL_MODELVIEW_STACK_DEPTH	glGet*()
GL_MODULATE	glTexEnv*(), glGetTexEnv*()
GL_MULT	glAccum()
GL_NAME_STACK_DEPTH	glGet*()
GL_NAND	glLogicOp()
GL_NEAREST, GL_NEAREST_MIPMAP_LINEAR, GL_NEAREST_MIPMAP_NEAREST	glTexParameter*()
GL_NEVER	glDepthFunc(), glAlphaFunc(), glStencilFunc()
GL_NICEST	glHint()
GL_NONE	glDrawBuffer()

Constant	Associated Commands
GL_NOOP, GL_NOR	glLogicOp()
GL_NORMALIZE	glEnable(), glIsEnabled(), glGet*()
GL_NOTEQUAL	glDepthFunc(), glAlphaFunc(), glStencilFunc()
GL_NO_ERROR	glGetError()
GL_OBJECT_LINEAR	glTexGen*(), glGetTexGen*()
GL_OBJECT_PLANE	glTexGen*()
GL_ONE, GL_ONE_MINUS_DST_ALPHA, GL_ONE_MINUS_DST_COLOR, GL_ONE_MINUS_SRC_ALPHA, GL_ONE_MINUS_SRC_COLOR	glBlendFunc()
GL_OR, GL_OR_INVERTED, GL_OR_REVERSE	glLogicOp()
GL_ORDER	glGetMap*()
GL_OUT_OF_MEMORY	glGetError()
GL_PACK_ALIGNMENT, GL_PACK_LSB_FIRST, GL_PACK_ROW_LENGTH, GL_PACK_SKIP_PIXELS, GL_PACK_SKIP_ROWS, GL_PACK_SWAP_BYTES	glPixelStore*(), glGet*()
GL_PASS_THROUGH_TOKEN	glPassThrough()
GL_PERSPECTIVE_CORRECTION_HINT	glHint(), glGet*()
GL_PIXEL_MAP_*_TO_*	glPixelMap*(), glGetPixelMap*()
GL_PIXEL_MAP_*_TO_*_SIZE	glGet*()
GL_PIXEL_MODE_BIT	glPushAttrib()
GL_POINT	glPolygonMode(), glEvalMesh*()
GL_POINTS	glBegin()
GL_POINT_BIT	glPushAttrib()
GL_POINT_SIZE, GL_POINT_SIZE_GRANULARITY, GL_POINT_SIZE_RANGE	glGet*()
GL_POINT_SMOOTH	glEnable(), glIsEnabled(), glGet*()
GL_POINT_SMOOTH_HINT	glHint(), glGet*()
GL_POINT_TOKEN	glPassThrough()
GL_POLYGON	glBegin()
GL_POLYGON_BIT	glPushAttrib()
GL_POLYGON_MODE	glGet*()

Constant	Associated Commands
GL_POLYGON_SMOOTH	glEnable(), glIsEnabled(), glGet*()
GL_POLYGON_SMOOTH_HINT	glHint(), glGet*()
GL_POLYGON_STIPPLE	glEnable(), glIsEnabled(), glGet*()
GL_POLYGON_STIPPLE_BIT	glPushAttrib()
GL_POLYGON_TOKEN	glPassThrough()
GL_POSITION	glLight*(), glGetLight*()
GL_PROJECTION	glMatrixMode()
GL_PROJECTION_MATRIX, GL_PROJECTION_STACK_DEPTH	glGet*()
GL_Q	glTexGen*(), glGetTexGen*()
GL_QUADRATIC_ATTENUATION	glLight*(), glGetLight*()
GL_QUADS, GL_QUAD_STRIP	glBegin()
GL_R	glTexGen*(), glGetTexGen*()
GL_READ_BUFFER	glGet*()
GL_RED	glDrawPixels(), glReadPixels(), glTexImage1D, glTexImage2D(), glGetTexImage()
GL_RED_BIAS	glPixelTransfer*(), glGet*()
GL_RED_BITS	glGet*()
GL_RED_SCALE	glPixelTransfer*(), glGet*()
GL_RENDER	glRenderMode()
GL_RENDERER	glGetString()
GL_RENDER_MODE	glGet*()
GL_REPEAT	glTexParameter*()
GL_REPLACE	glStencilOp()
GL_RETURN	glAccum()
GL_RGB	glDrawPixels(), glReadPixels(), glTexImage1D(), glTexImage2D(), glGetTexImage()
GL_RGBA	glDrawPixels(), glReadPixels(), glTexImage1D(), glTexImage2D(), glGetTexImage()
GL_RGBA_MODE	glGet*()
GL_RIGHT	glDrawBuffer(), glReadBuffer()
GL_S	glTexGen*(), glGetTexGen*()

Constant	Associated Commands
GL_SCISSOR_BIT	glPushAttrib()
GL_SCISSOR_BOX	glGet*()
GL_SCISSOR_TEST	glEnable(), glIsEnabled(), glGet*()
GL_SELECT	glRenderMode()
GL_SET	glLogicOp()
GL_SHININESS	glMaterial*(), glGetMaterial*()
GL_SHADE_MODEL	glGet*()
GL_SHORT	glCallLists(), glDrawPixels(), glReadPixels(), glTexImage1D(), glTexImage2D(), glGetTexImage()
GL_SMOOTH	glShadeModel()
GL_SPECULAR	glLight*(), glGetLight*(), glMaterial*(), glGetMaterial*(), glColorMaterial()
GL_SPHERE_MAP	glTexGen*(), glGetTexGen*()
GL_SPOT_CUTOFF, GL_SPOT_DIRECTION, GL_SPOT_EXPONENT	glLight*(), glGetLight*()
GL_SRC_ALPHA, GL_SRC_ALPHA_SATURATE, GL_SRC_COLOR	glBlendFunc()
GL_STACK_OVERFLOW, GL_STACK_UNDERFLOW	glGetError()
GL_STENCIL	glCopyPixels()
GL_STENCIL_BITS	glGet*()
GL_STENCIL_BUFFER_BIT	glClear(), glPushAttrib()
GL_STENCIL_INDEX	glDrawPixels(), glReadPixels(), glTexImage1D(), glTexImage2D(), glGetTexImage()
GL_STENCIL_CLEAR_VALUE, GL_STENCIL_FAIL, GL_STENCIL_FUNC, GL_STENCIL_PASS_DEPTH_FAIL, GL_STENCIL_PASS_DEPTH_PASS, GL_STENCIL_REF	glGet*()
GL_STENCIL_TEST	glEnable(), glIsEnabled(), glGet*()
GL_STENCIL_VALUE_MASK, GL_STENCIL_WRITEMASK	glGet*()
GL_STEREO	glGet*()
GL_SUBPIXEL_BITS	glGet*()

Constant	Associated Commands
GL_T	glTexGen*(), glGetTexGen*()
GL_TEXTURE	glMatrixMode()
GL_TEXTURE_1D	glTexImage1D(), glGetTexImage(), glTexParameter*(), glGetTexParameter*(), glGetTexLevelParameter*(), glEnable(), glIsEnabled(), glGet*()
GL_TEXTURE_2D	glTexImage2D(), glGetTexImage(), glTexParameter*(), glGetTexParameter*(), glGetTexLevelParameter*(), glEnable(), glIsEnabled(), glGet*()
GL_TEXTURE_BIT	glPushAttrib()
GL_TEXTURE_BORDER	glGetTexParameter*(), glGetTexLevelParameter*()
GL_TEXTURE_BORDER_COLOR	glTexParameter*(), glGetTexParameter*(), glGetTexLevelParameter*()
GL_TEXTURE_COMPONENTS	glGetTexParameter*(), glGetTexLevelParameter*()
GL_TEXTURE_ENV, GL_TEXTURE_ENV_COLOR, GL_TEXTURE_ENV_MODE	glTexEnv*(), glGetTexEnv*()
GL_TEXTURE_GEN_MODE	glTexGen*()
GL_TEXTURE_GEN_Q, GL_TEXTURE_GEN_R, GL_TEXTURE_GEN_S, GL_TEXTURE_GEN_T	glEnable(), glIsEnabled(), glGet*()
GL_TEXTURE_HEIGHT	glGetTexParameter*(), glGetTexLevelParameter*()
GL_TEXTURE_MAG_FILTER	glTexParameter*(), glGetTexParameter*(), glGetTexLevelParameter*()
GL_TEXTURE_MATRIX	glGet*()
GL_TEXTURE_MIN_FILTER	glTexParameter*(), glGetTexParameter*(), glGetTexLevelParameter*()
GL_TEXTURE_STACK_DEPTH	glGet*()

Constant	Associated Commands
GL_TEXTURE_WIDTH	glGetTexParameter*(), glGetTexLevelParameter*()
GL_TEXTURE_WRAP_S, GL_TEXTURE_WRAP_T	glTexParameter*(), glGetTexParameter*(), glGetTexLevelParameter*()
GL_TRANSFORM_BIT	glPushAttrib()
GL_TRIANGLES, GL_TRIANGLE_FAN, GL_TRIANGLE_STRIP	glBegin()
GL_TRUE	glColorMask(), glGet*(), glIsEnabled(), glIsList()
GL_UNPACK_ALIGNMENT, GL_UNPACK_LSB_FIRST, GL_UNPACK_ROW_LENGTH, GL_UNPACK_SKIP_PIXELS, GL_UNPACK_SKIP_ROWS, GL_UNPACK_SWAP_BYTES	glPixelStore*(), glGet*()
GL_UNSIGNED_BYTE, GL_UNSIGNED_INT, GL_UNSIGNED_SHORT	glCallLists(), glDrawPixels(), glReadPixels(), glTexImage1D(), glTexImage2D(), glGetTexImage()
GL_VENDOR, GL_VERSION	glGetString()
GL_VIEWPORT	glGet*()
GL_VIEWPORT_BIT	glPushAttrib()
GL_XOR	glLogicOp()
GL_ZERO	glBlendFunc(), glStencilOp()
GL_ZOOM_X, GL_ZOOM_Y	glGet*()

Chapter 5

OpenGL Reference Pages

This chapter contains the reference pages, in alphabetical order, for all the OpenGL commands. Each reference page may describe more than one related command, as shown in the following list of pages. The OpenGL Utility Library routines and those comprising the OpenGL extension to the X Window System are described in the following chapters.

glAccum	glGenLists	glNewList, glEndList
glAlphaFunc	glGet	glNormal
glBegin, glEnd	glGetClipPlane	glOrtho
glBitmap	glGetError	glPassThrough
glBlendFunc	glGetLight	glPixelMap
glCallList	glGetMap	glPixelStore
glCallLists	glGetMaterial	glPixelTransfer
glClear	glGetPixelMap	glPixelZoom
glClearAccum	glGetPolygonStipple	glPointSize
glClearColor	glGetString	glPolygonMode
glClearDepth	glGetTexEnv	glPolygonStipple
glClearIndex	glGetTexGen	glPushAttrib, glPopAttrib
glClearStencil	glGetTexImage	glPushMatrix, glPopMatrix
glClipPlane	glGetTexLevelParameter	glPushName, glPopName
glColor	glGetTexParameter	glRasterPos
glColorMask	glHint	glReadBuffer
glColorMaterial	glIndex	glReadPixels
glCopyPixels	glIndexMask	glRect
glCullFace	glInitNames	glRenderMode
glDeleteLists	glIsEnabled	glRotate
glDepthFunc	glIsList	glScale
glDepthMask	glLight	glScissor
glDepthRange	glLightModel	glSelectBuffer
glDrawBuffer	glLineStipple	glShadeModel
glDrawPixels	glLineWidth	glStencilFunc
glEdgeFlag	glListBase	glStencilMask
glEnable, glDisable	glLoadIdentity	glStencilOp
glEvalCoord	glLoadMatrix	glTexCoord
glEvalMesh	glLoadName	glTexEnv
glEvalPoint	glLogicOp	glTexGen
glFeedbackBuffer	glMap1	glTexImage1D
glFinish	glMap2	glTexImage2D
glFlush	glMapGrid	glTexParameter
glFog	glMaterial	glTranslate
glFrontFace	glMatrixMode	glVertex
glFrustum	glMultMatrix	glViewport

NAME

glAccum – operate on the accumulation buffer

C SPECIFICATION

void **glAccum**(GLenum *op*,
                  GLfloat *value*)

PARAMETERS

op   Specifies the accumulation buffer operation. Symbolic constants **GL_ACCUM**, **GL_LOAD**, **GL_ADD**, **GL_MULT**, and **GL_RETURN** are accepted.

value Specifies a floating-point value used in the accumulation buffer operation. *op* determines how *value* is used.

DESCRIPTION

The accumulation buffer is an extended-range color buffer. Images are not rendered into it. Rather, images rendered into one of the color buffers are added to the contents of the accumulation buffer after rendering. Effects such as antialiasing (of points, lines, and polygons), motion blur, and depth of field can be created by accumulating images generated with different transformation matrices.

Each pixel in the accumulation buffer consists of red, green, blue, and alpha values. The number of bits per component in the accumulation buffer depends on the implementation. You can examine this number by calling **glGetIntegerv** four times, with arguments **GL_ACCUM_RED_BITS**, **GL_ACCUM_GREEN_BITS**, **GL_ACCUM_BLUE_BITS**, and **GL_ACCUM_ALPHA_BITS**, respectively. Regardless of the number of bits per component, however, the range of values stored by each component is [-1, 1]. The accumulation buffer pixels are mapped one-to-one with frame buffer pixels.

glAccum operates on the accumulation buffer. The first argument, *op*, is a symbolic constant that selects an accumulation buffer operation. The second argument, *value*, is a floating-point value to be used in that operation. Five operations are specified: **GL_ACCUM**, **GL_LOAD**, **GL_ADD**, **GL_MULT**, and **GL_RETURN**.

All accumulation buffer operations are limited to the area of the current scissor box and are applied identically to the red, green, blue, and alpha components of each pixel. The contents of an accumulation buffer pixel component are undefined if the **glAccum** operation results in a value outside the range [-1,1].

The operations are as follows:

GL_ACCUM

Obtains R, G, B, and A values from the buffer currently selected for reading (see **glReadBuffer**). Each component value is divided by $2^n - 1$, where n is the number of bits allocated to each color component in the currently selected buffer. The result is a floating-point value in the range [0,1], which is multiplied by *value* and added to the corresponding pixel component in the accumulation buffer, thereby updating the accumulation buffer.

GL_LOAD

Similar to **GL_ACCUM**, except that the current value in the accumulation buffer is not used in the calculation of the new value. That is, the R, G, B, and A values from the currently selected buffer are divided by $2^n - 1$, multiplied by *value*, and then stored in the corresponding accumulation buffer cell, overwriting the current value.

GL_ADD Adds *value* to each R, G, B, and A in the accumulation buffer.

GL_MULT

Multiplies each R, G, B, and A in the accumulation buffer by *value* and returns the scaled component to its corresponding accumulation buffer location.

GL_RETURN

Transfers accumulation buffer values to the color buffer or buffers currently selected for writing. Each R, G, B, and A component is multiplied by *value*, then multiplied by $2^n - 1$, clamped to the range $[0, 2^n - 1]$, and stored in the corresponding display buffer cell. The only fragment operations that are applied to this transfer are pixel ownership, scissor, dithering, and color writemasks.

The accumulation buffer is cleared by specifying R, G, B, and A values to set it to with the **glClearAccum** directive, and issuing a **glClear** command with the accumulation buffer enabled.

NOTES

Only those pixels within the current scissor box are updated by any **glAccum** operation.

ERRORS

GL_INVALID_ENUM is generated if *op* is not an accepted value.

GL_INVALID_OPERATION is generated if there is no accumulation buffer.

GL_INVALID_OPERATION is generated if **glAccum** is called between a call to **glBegin** and the corresponding call to **glEnd**.

ASSOCIATED GETS

glGet with argument GL_ACCUM_RED_BITS
glGet with argument GL_ACCUM_GREEN_BITS
glGet with argument GL_ACCUM_BLUE_BITS
glGet with argument GL_ACCUM_ALPHA_BITS

SEE ALSO

glBlendFunc, **glClear**, **glClearAccum**, **glCopyPixels**, **glGet**, **glLogicOp**, **glPixelStore**, **glPixelTransfer**, **glReadPixels**, **glReadBuffer**, **glScissor**, **glStencilOp**

NAME

glAlphaFunc – specify the alpha test function

C SPECIFICATION

void **glAlphaFunc**(GLenum *func*,
                      GLclampf *ref*)

PARAMETERS

func   Specifies the alpha comparison function. Symbolic constants **GL_NEVER**, **GL_LESS**, **GL_EQUAL**, **GL_LEQUAL**, **GL_GREATER**, **GL_NOTEQUAL**, **GL_GEQUAL**, and **GL_ALWAYS** are accepted. The default function is **GL_ALWAYS**.

ref   Specifies the reference value that incoming alpha values are compared to. This value is clamped to the range 0 through 1, where 0 represents the lowest possible alpha value and 1 the highest possible value. The default reference is 0.

DESCRIPTION

The alpha test discards fragments depending on the outcome of a comparison between the incoming fragment's alpha value and a constant reference value. **glAlphaFunc** specifies the reference and comparison function. The comparison is performed only if alpha testing is enabled. (See **glEnable** and **glDisable** of **GL_ALPHA_TEST**.)

func and *ref* specify the conditions under which the pixel is drawn. The incoming alpha value is compared to *ref* using the function specified by *func*. If the comparison passes, the incoming fragment is drawn, conditional on subsequent stencil and depth buffer tests. If the comparison fails, no change is made to the frame buffer at that pixel location.

The comparison functions are as follows:

GL_NEVER   Never passes.

GL_LESS   Passes if the incoming alpha value is less than the reference value.

GL_EQUAL   Passes if the incoming alpha value is equal to the reference value.

GL_LEQUAL   Passes if the incoming alpha value is less than or equal to the reference value.

GL_GREATER   Passes if the incoming alpha value is greater than the reference value.

GL_NOTEQUAL   Passes if the incoming alpha value is not equal to the reference value.

GL_GEQUAL   Passes if the incoming alpha value is greater than or equal to the reference value.

GL_ALWAYS   Always passes.

glAlphaFunc operates on all pixel writes, including those resulting from the scan conversion of points, lines, polygons, and bitmaps, and from pixel draw and copy operations. **glAlphaFunc** does not affect screen clear operations.

NOTES

Alpha testing is done only in RGBA mode.

ERRORS

GL_INVALID_ENUM is generated if *func* is not an accepted value.

GL_INVALID_OPERATION is generated if **glAlphaFunc** is called between a call to **glBegin** and the corresponding call to **glEnd**.

ASSOCIATED GETS

glGet with argument GL_ALPHA_TEST_FUNC
glGet with argument GL_ALPHA_TEST_REF
glIsEnabled with argument GL_ALPHA_TEST

SEE ALSO

glBlendFunc, **glClear**, **glDepthFunc**, **glEnable**, **glStencilFunc**

NAME

      glBegin, **glEnd** – delimit the vertices of a primitive or a group of like primitives

C SPECIFICATION

      void **glBegin**(GLenum *mode*)

PARAMETERS

      mode Specifies the primitive or primitives that will be created from vertices presented between **glBegin** and the subsequent **glEnd**. Ten symbolic constants are accepted: GL_POINTS, GL_LINES, GL_LINE_STRIP, GL_LINE_LOOP, GL_TRIANGLES, GL_TRIANGLE_STRIP, GL_TRIANGLE_FAN, GL_QUADS, GL_QUAD_STRIP, and GL_POLYGON.

C SPECIFICATION

      void **glEnd**(void)

DESCRIPTION

      glBegin and **glEnd** delimit the vertices that define a primitive or a group of like primitives. **glBegin** accepts a single argument that specifies which of ten ways the vertices are interpreted. Taking n as an integer count starting at one, and N as the total number of vertices specified, the interpretations are as follows:

GL_POINTS

      Treats each vertex as a single point. Vertex n defines point n. N points are drawn.

GL_LINES

      Treates each pair of vertices as an independent line segment. Vertices $2n-1$ and $2n$ define line n. $N/2$ lines are drawn.

GL_LINE_STRIP

      Draws a connected group of line segments from the first vertex to the last. Vertices n and $n+1$ define line n. $N-1$ lines are drawn.

GL_LINE_LOOP

      Draws a connected group of line segments from the first vertex to the last, then back to the first. Vertices n and $n+1$ define line n. The last line, however, is defined by vertices N and 1. N lines are drawn.

GL_TRIANGLES

      Treats each triplet of vertices as an independent triangle. Vertices $3n-2$, $3n-1$, and $3n$ define triangle n. $N/3$ triangles are drawn.

GL_TRIANGLE_STRIP

Draws a connected group of triangles. One triangle is defined for each vertex presented after the first two vertices. For odd n, vertices n, $n+1$, and $n+2$ define triangle n. For even n, vertices $n+1$, n, and $n+2$ define triangle n. $N-2$ triangles are drawn.

GL_TRIANGLE_FAN

Draws a connected group of triangles. One triangle is defined for each vertex presented after the first two vertices. Vertices 1, $n+1$, and $n+2$ define triangle n. $N-2$ triangles are drawn.

GL_QUADS

Treats each group of four vertices as an independent quadrilateral. Vertices $4n-3$, $4n-2$, $4n-1$, and $4n$ define quadrilateral n. $N/4$ quadrilaterals are drawn.

GL_QUAD_STRIP

Draws a connected group of quadrilaterals. One quadrilateral is defined for each pair of vertices presented after the first pair. Vertices $2n-1$, $2n$, $2n+2$, and $2n+1$ define quadrilateral n. $N/2-1$ quadrilaterals are drawn. Note that the order in which vertices are used to construct a quadrilateral from strip data is different from that used with independent data.

GL_POLYGON

Draws a single, convex polygon. Vertices 1 through N define this polygon.

Only a subset of GL commands can be used between **glBegin** and **glEnd**. The commands are **glVertex**, **glColor**, **glIndex**, **glNormal**, **glTexCoord**, **glEvalCoord**, **glEvalPoint**, **glMaterial**, and **glEdgeFlag**. Also, it is acceptable to use **glCallList** or **glCallLists** to execute display lists that include only the preceding commands. If any other GL command is called between **glBegin** and **glEnd**, the error flag is set and the command is ignored.

Regardless of the value chosen for *mode*, there is no limit to the number of vertices that can be defined between **glBegin** and **glEnd**. Lines, triangles, quadrilaterals, and polygons that are incompletely specified are not drawn. Incomplete specification results when either too few vertices are provided to specify even a single primitive or when an incorrect multiple of vertices is specified. The incomplete primitive is ignored; the rest are drawn.

The minimum specification of vertices for each primitive is as follows: 1 for a point, 2 for a line, 3 for a triangle, 4 for a quadrilateral, and 3 for a polygon. Modes that require a certain multiple of vertices are GL_LINES (2), GL_TRIANGLES (3), GL_QUADS (4), and GL_QUAD_STRIP (2).

ERRORS

GL_INVALID_ENUM is generated if *mode* is set to an unaccepted value.

GL_INVALID_OPERATION is generated if a command other than **glVertex**, **glColor**, **glIndex**, **glNormal**, **glTexCoord**, **glEvalCoord**, **glEvalPoint**, **glMaterial**, **glEdgeFlag**, **glCallList**, or **glCallLists** is called between **glBegin** and the corresponding **glEnd**.

GL_INVALID_OPERATION is generated if **glEnd** is called before the corresponding **glBegin** is called.

SEE ALSO

glCallList, glCallLists, glColor, glEdgeFlag, glEvalCoord, glEvalPoint, glIndex, glMaterial, glNormal, glTexCoord, glVertex

NAME

glBitmap – draw a bitmap

C SPECIFICATION

void **glBitmap**(GLsizei *width*,
GLsizei *height*,
GLfloat *xorig*,
GLfloat *yorig*,
GLfloat *xmove*,
GLfloat *ymove*,
const GLubyte **bitmap*)

PARAMETERS

width, height
Specify the pixel width and height of the bitmap image.

xorig, yorig Specify the location of the origin in the bitmap image. The origin is measured from the lower left corner of the bitmap, with right and up being the positive axes.

xmove, ymove
Specify the *x* and *y* offsets to be added to the current raster position after the bitmap is drawn.

bitmap Specifies the address of the bitmap image.

DESCRIPTION

A bitmap is a binary image. When drawn, the bitmap is positioned relative to the current raster position, and frame buffer pixels corresponding to ones in the bitmap are written using the current raster color or index. Frame buffer pixels corresponding to zeros in the bitmap are not modified.

glBitmap takes seven arguments. The first pair specify the width and height of the bitmap image. The second pair specify the location of the bitmap origin relative to the lower left corner of the bitmap image. The third pair of arguments specify *x* and *y* offsets to be added to the current raster position after the bitmap has been drawn. The final argument is a pointer to the bitmap image itself.

The bitmap image is interpreted like image data for the **glDrawPixels** command, with *width* and *height* corresponding to the width and height arguments of that command, and with *type* set to **GL_BITMAP** and *format* set to **GL_COLOR_INDEX**.

Modes specified using **glPixelStore** affect the interpretation of bitmap image data; modes specified using **glPixelTransfer** do not.

If the current raster position is invalid, **glBitmap** is ignored. Otherwise, the lower left corner of the bitmap image is positioned at the window coordinates

$$x_w = \lfloor x_r - x_o \rfloor$$

$$y_w = \lfloor y_r - y_o \rfloor$$

where (x_r, y_r) is the raster position and (x_o, y_o) is the bitmap origin. Fragments are then generated for each pixel corresponding to a one in the bitmap image. These fragments are generated using the current raster z coordinate, color or color index, and current raster texture coordinates. They are then treated just as if they had been generated by a point, line, or polygon, including texture mapping, fogging, and all per-fragment operations such as alpha and depth testing.

After the bitmap has been drawn, the x and y coordinates of the current raster position are offset by *xmove* and *ymove*. No change is made to the z coordinate of the current raster position, or to the current raster color, index, or texture coordinates.

ERRORS

GL_INVALID_VALUE is generated if *width* or *height* is negative.

GL_INVALID_OPERATION is generated if **glBitmap** is called between a call to **glBegin** and the corresponding call to **glEnd**.

ASSOCIATED GETS

glGet with argument GL_CURRENT_RASTER_POSITION
glGet with argument GL_CURRENT_RASTER_COLOR
glGet with argument GL_CURRENT_RASTER_INDEX
glGet with argument GL_CURRENT_RASTER_TEXTURE_COORDS
glGet with argument GL_CURRENT_RASTER_POSITION_VALID

SEE ALSO

glDrawPixels, glRasterPos, glPixelStore, glPixelTransfer

NAME

glBlendFunc – specify pixel arithmetic

C SPECIFICATION

void **glBlendFunc**(GLenum *sfactor*,
                         GLenum *dfactor*)

PARAMETERS

sfactor Specifies how the red, green, blue, and alpha source-blending factors are computed. Nine symbolic constants are accepted: **GL_ZERO, GL_ONE, GL_DST_COLOR, GL_ONE_MINUS_DST_COLOR, GL_SRC_ALPHA, GL_ONE_MINUS_SRC_ALPHA, GL_DST_ALPHA, GL_ONE_MINUS_DST_ALPHA,** and **GL_SRC_ALPHA_SATURATE.**

dfactor Specifies how the red, green, blue, and alpha destination blending factors are computed. Eight symbolic constants are accepted: **GL_ZERO, GL_ONE, GL_SRC_COLOR, GL_ONE_MINUS_SRC_COLOR, GL_SRC_ALPHA, GL_ONE_MINUS_SRC_ALPHA, GL_DST_ALPHA,** and **GL_ONE_MINUS_DST_ALPHA.**

DESCRIPTION

In RGB mode, pixels can be drawn using a function that blends the incoming (source) RGBA values with the RGBA values that are already in the frame buffer (the destination values). By default, blending is disabled. Use **glEnable** and **glDisable** with argument **GL_BLEND** to enable and disable blending.

glBlendFunc defines the operation of blending when it is enabled. *sfactor* specifies which of nine methods is used to scale the source color components. *dfactor* specifies which of eight methods is used to scale the destination color components. The eleven possible methods are described in the table below. Each method defines four scale factors, one each for red, green, blue, and alpha.

In the table and in subsequent equations, source and destination color components are referred to as (R_s,G_s,B_s,A_s) and (R_d,G_d,B_d,A_d). They are understood to have integer values between zero and (k_R,k_G,k_B,k_A), where

$$k_c = 2^{m_c}-1$$

and (m_R,m_G,m_B,m_A) is the number of red, green, blue, and alpha bitplanes.

Source and destination scale factors are referred to as (s_R,s_G,s_B,s_A) and (d_R,d_G,d_B,d_A). The scale factors described in the table, denoted (f_R,f_G,f_B,f_A), represent either source or destination factors. All scale factors have range [0,1].

parameter	$(f_R,\ f_G,\ f_B,\ f_A)$
GL_ZERO	$(0, 0, 0, 0)$
GL_ONE	$(1, 1, 1, 1)$
GL_SRC_COLOR	$(R_s/k_R,\ G_s/k_G,\ B_s/k_B,\ A_s/k_A)$
GL_ONE_MINUS_SRC_COLOR	$(1, 1, 1, 1) - (R_s/k_R,\ G_s/k_G,\ B_s/k_B,\ A_s/k_A)$
GL_DST_COLOR	$(R_d/k_R,\ G_d/k_G,\ B_d/k_B,\ A_d/k_A)$
GL_ONE_MINUS_DST_COLOR	$(1, 1, 1, 1) - (R_d/k_R,\ G_d/k_G,\ B_d/k_B,\ A_d/k_A)$
GL_SRC_ALPHA	$(A_s/k_A,\ A_s/k_A,\ A_s/k_A,\ A_s/k_A)$
GL_ONE_MINUS_SRC_ALPHA	$(1, 1, 1, 1) - (A_s/k_A,\ A_s/k_A,\ A_s/k_A,\ A_s/k_A)$
GL_DST_ALPHA	$(A_d/k_A,\ A_d/k_A,\ A_d/k_A,\ A_d/k_A)$
GL_ONE_MINUS_DST_ALPHA	$(1, 1, 1, 1) - (A_d/k_A,\ A_d/k_A,\ A_d/k_A,\ A_d/k_A)$
GL_SRC_ALPHA_SATURATE	$(i, i, i, 1)$

In the table,

$$i = \min(A_s,\ k_A - A_d)\ /\ k_A$$

To determine the blended RGBA values of a pixel when drawing in RGB mode, the system uses the following equations:

$$R_d = \min(k_R,\ R_s s_R + R_d d_R)$$
$$G_d = \min(k_G,\ G_s s_G + G_d d_G)$$
$$B_d = \min(k_B,\ B_s s_B + B_d d_B)$$
$$A_d = \min(k_A,\ A_s s_A + A_d d_A)$$

Despite the apparent precision of the above equations, blending arithmetic is not exactly specified, because blending operates with imprecise integer color values. However, a blend factor that should be equal to one is guaranteed not to modify its multiplicand, and a blend factor equal to zero reduces its multiplicand to zero. Thus, for example, when *sfactor* is **GL_SRC_ALPHA**, *dfactor* is **GL_ONE_MINUS_SRC_ALPHA**, and A_s is equal to k_A, the equations reduce to simple replacement:

$$R_d = R_s$$
$$G_d = G_s$$
$$B_d = B_s$$
$$A_d = A_s$$

EXAMPLES

Transparency is best implemented using blend function (**GL_SRC_ALPHA**, **GL_ONE_MINUS_SRC_ALPHA**) with primitives sorted from farthest to nearest. Note that this transparency calculation does not require the presence of alpha bitplanes in the frame buffer.

Blend function (GL_SRC_ALPHA, GL_ONE_MINUS_SRC_ALPHA) is also useful for rendering antialiased points and lines in arbitrary order.

Polygon antialiasing is optimized using blend function (GL_SRC_ALPHA_SATURATE, GL_ONE) with polygons sorted from nearest to farthest. (See the **glEnable**, **glDisable** reference page and the GL_POLYGON_SMOOTH argument for information on polygon antialiasing.) Destination alpha bitplanes, which must be present for this blend function to operate correctly, store the accumulated coverage.

NOTES

Incoming (source) alpha is correctly thought of as a material opacity, ranging from 1.0 (K_A), representing complete opacity, to 0.0 (0), representing completely transparency.

When more than one color buffer is enabled for drawing, blending is done separately for each enabled buffer, using for destination color the contents of that buffer. (See **glDrawBuffer**.)

Blending affects only RGB rendering. It is ignored by color index renderers.

ERRORS

GL_INVALID_ENUM is generated if either *sfactor* or *dfactor* is not an accepted value.

GL_INVALID_OPERATION is generated if **glBlendFunc** is called between a call to **glBegin** and the corresponding call to **glEnd**.

ASSOCIATED GETS

glGet with argument GL_BLEND_SRC
glGet with argument GL_BLEND_DST
glIsEnabled with argument GL_BLEND

SEE ALSO

glAlphaFunc, glClear, glDrawBuffer, glEnable, glLogicOp, glStencilFunc

NAME

glCallList – execute a display list

C SPECIFICATION

void **glCallList**(GLuint *list*)

PARAMETERS

list Specifies the integer name of the display list to be executed.

DESCRIPTION

glCallList causes the named display list to be executed. The commands saved in the display list are executed in order, just as if they were called without using a display list. If *list* has not been defined as a display list, **glCallList** is ignored.

glCallList can appear inside a display list. To avoid the possibility of infinite recursion resulting from display lists calling one another, a limit is placed on the nesting level of display lists during display-list execution. This limit is at least 64, and it depends on the implementation.

GL state is not saved and restored across a call to **glCallList**. Thus, changes made to GL state during the execution of a display list remain after execution of the display list is completed. Use **glPushAttrib**, **glPopAttrib**, **glPushMatrix**, and **glPopMatrix** to preserve GL state across **glCallList** calls.

NOTES

Display lists can be executed between a call to **glBegin** and the corresponding call to **glEnd**, as long as the display list includes only commands that are allowed in this interval.

ASSOCIATED GETS

glGet with argument GL_MAX_LIST_NESTING
glIsList

SEE ALSO

glCallLists, **glDeleteLists**, **glGenLists**, **glNewList**, **glPushAttrib**, **glPushMatrix**

NAME

glCallLists – execute a list of display lists

C SPECIFICATION

void **glCallLists**(GLsizei *n*,
                          GLenum *type*,
                          const GLvoid **lists*)

PARAMETERS

n   Specifies the number of display lists to be executed.

type Specifies the type of values in *lists*. Symbolic constants **GL_BYTE**, **GL_UNSIGNED_BYTE**, **GL_SHORT**, **GL_UNSIGNED_SHORT**, **GL_INT**, **GL_UNSIGNED_INT**, **GL_FLOAT**, **GL_2_BYTES**, **GL_3_BYTES**, and **GL_4_BYTES** are accepted.

lists Specifies the address of an array of name offsets in the display list. The pointer type is void because the offsets can be bytes, shorts, ints, or floats, depending on the value of *type*.

DESCRIPTION

glCallLists causes each display list in the list of names passed as *lists* to be executed. As a result, the commands saved in each display list are executed in order, just as if they were called without using a display list. Names of display lists that have not been defined are ignored.

glCallLists provides an efficient means for executing display lists. *n* allows lists with various name formats to be accepted. The formats are as follows:

GL_BYTE	*lists* is treated as an array of signed bytes, each in the range -128 through 127.
GL_UNSIGNED_BYTE	*lists* is treated as an array of unsigned bytes, each in the range 0 through 255.
GL_SHORT	*lists* is treated as an array of signed two-byte integers, each in the range -32768 through 32767.
GL_UNSIGNED_SHORT	*lists* is treated as an array of unsigned two-byte integers, each in the range 0 through 65535.
GL_INT	*lists* is treated as an array of signed four-byte integers.

GL_UNSIGNED_INT	*lists* is treated as an array of unsigned four-byte integers.
GL_FLOAT	*lists* is treated as an array of four-byte floating-point values.
GL_2_BYTES	*lists* is treated as an array of unsigned bytes. Each pair of bytes specifies a single display-list name. The value of the pair is computed as 256 times the unsigned value of the first byte plus the unsigned value of the second byte.
GL_3_BYTES	*lists* is treated as an array of unsigned bytes. Each triplet of bytes specifies a single display-list name. The value of the triplet is [computed] as 65536 times the unsigned value of the first [byte, plus 25]6 times the unsigned value of the second byte [plus the u]nsigned value of the third byte.
GL_4_BYTES	*lists* is treat[ed as an arra]y of unsigned bytes. Each quadruplet [of bytes spe]cifies a single display-list name. The value [of the quadr]uplet is computed as 16777216 times the [unsigned val]ue of the first byte, plus 65536 times the [unsigned val]ue of the second byte, plus 256 times the [unsigned va]lue of the third byte, plus the unsigned [value of the] fourth byte.

The list of display list names is not r[eturn]ed. Rather, *n* specifies how many names are to be taken from *lists*.

An additional level of indirection is made available with the **glListBase** command, which specifies a signed offset that is added to each display-list name specified in *lists* before that display list is executed.

glCallLists can appear inside a display list. To avoid the possibility of infinite recursion resulting from display lists calling one another, a limit is placed on the nesting level of display lists during display-list execution. This limit must be at least 64, and it depends on the implementation.

GL state is not saved and restored across a call to **glCallLists**. Thus, changes made to GL state during the execution of the display lists remain after execution is completed. Use **glPushAttrib**, **glPopAttrib**, **glPushMatrix**, and **glPopMatrix** to preserve GL state across **glCallLists** calls.

NOTES

Display lists can be executed between a call to **glBegin** and the corresponding call to **glEnd**, as long as the display list includes only commands that are allowed in this interval.

ASSOCIATED GETS

glGet with argument **GL_LIST_BASE**
glGet with argument **GL_MAX_LIST_NESTING**
glIsList

SEE ALSO

glCallList, glDeleteLists, glGenLists, glListBase, glNewList, glPushAttrib, glPush-Matrix

NAME

glClear – clear buffers within the viewport

C SPECIFICATION

void **glClear**(GLbitfield *mask*)

PARAMETERS

mask Bitwise OR of masks that indicate the buffers to be cleared. The four masks are GL_COLOR_BUFFER_BIT, GL_DEPTH_BUFFER_BIT, GL_ACCUM_BUFFER_BIT, and GL_STENCIL_BUFFER_BIT.

DESCRIPTION

glClear sets the bitplane area of the viewport to values previously selected by **glClearColor**, **glClearIndex**, **glClearDepth**, **glClearStencil**, and **glClearAccum**. Multiple color buffers can be cleared simultaneously by selecting more than one buffer at a time using **glDrawBuffer**.

The pixel ownership test, the scissor test, dithering, and the buffer writemasks affect the operation of **glClear**. The scissor box bounds the cleared region. Alpha function, blend function, logical operation, stenciling, texture mapping, and z-buffering are ignored by **glClear**.

glClear takes a single argument that is the bitwise OR of several values indicating which buffer is to be cleared.

The values are as follows:

GL_COLOR_BUFFER_BIT — Indicates the buffers currently enabled for color writing.

GL_DEPTH_BUFFER_BIT — Indicates the depth buffer.

GL_ACCUM_BUFFER_BIT — Indicates the accumulation buffer.

GL_STENCIL_BUFFER_BIT — Indicates the stencil buffer.

The value to which each buffer is cleared depends on the setting of the clear value for that buffer.

NOTES

If a buffer is not present, then a **glClear** directed at that buffer has no effect.

ERRORS

GL_INVALID_VALUE is generated if any bit other than the four defined bits is set in *mask*.

GL_INVALID_OPERATION is generated if **glClear** is called between a call to **glBegin** and the corresponding call to **glEnd**.

ASSOCIATED GETS

glGet with argument GL_ACCUM_CLEAR_VALUE
glGet with argument GL_DEPTH_CLEAR_VALUE
glGet with argument GL_INDEX_CLEAR_VALUE
glGet with argument GL_COLOR_CLEAR_VALUE
glGet with argument GL_STENCIL_CLEAR_VALUE

SEE ALSO

glClearAccum, glClearColor, glClearDepth, glClearIndex, glClearStencil, glDrawBuffer, glScissor

NAME

glClearAccum – specify clear values for the accumulation buffer

C SPECIFICATION

void **glClearAccum**(GLfloat *red*,
                      GLfloat *green*,
                      GLfloat *blue*,
                      GLfloat *alpha*)

PARAMETERS

red, green, blue, alpha

Specify the red, green, blue, and alpha values used when the accumulation buffer is cleared. The default values are all zero.

DESCRIPTION

glClearAccum specifies the red, green, blue, and alpha values used by **glClear** to clear the accumulation buffer.

Values specified by **glClearAccum** are clamped to the range [-1,1].

ERRORS

GL_INVALID_OPERATION is generated if **glClearAccum** is called between a call to **glBegin** and the corresponding call to **glEnd**.

ASSOCIATED GETS

glGet with argument GL_ACCUM_CLEAR_VALUE

SEE ALSO

glClear

NAME

glClearColor – specify clear values for the color buffers

C SPECIFICATION

void **glClearColor**(GLclampf *red*,
                    GLclampf *green*,
                    GLclampf *blue*,
                    GLclampf *alpha*)

PARAMETERS

red, green, blue, alpha

Specify the red, green, blue, and alpha values used when the color buffers are cleared. The default values are all zero.

DESCRIPTION

glClearColor specifies the red, green, blue, and alpha values used by **glClear** to clear the color buffers. Values specified by **glClearColor** are clamped to the range [0,1].

ERRORS

GL_INVALID_OPERATION is generated if **glClearColor** is called between a call to **glBegin** and the corresponding call to **glEnd**.

ASSOCIATED GETS

glGet with argument GL_COLOR_CLEAR_VALUE

SEE ALSO

glClear

glClearDepth

NAME

glClearDepth – specify the clear value for the depth buffer

C SPECIFICATION

void **glClearDepth**(GLclampd *depth*)

PARAMETERS

depth Specifies the depth value used when the depth buffer is cleared.

DESCRIPTION

glClearDepth specifies the depth value used by **glClear** to clear the depth buffer. Values specified by **glClearDepth** are clamped to the range [0,1].

ERRORS

GL_INVALID_OPERATION is generated if **glClearDepth** is called between a call to **glBegin** and the corresponding call to **glEnd**.

ASSOCIATED GETS

glGet with argument GL_DEPTH_CLEAR_VALUE

SEE ALSO

glClear

NAME

glClearIndex – specify the clear value for the color index buffers

C SPECIFICATION

void **glClearIndex**(GLfloat c)

PARAMETERS

c Specifies the index used when the color index buffers are cleared. The default value is zero.

DESCRIPTION

glClearIndex specifies the index used by **glClear** to clear the color index buffers. c is not clamped. Rather, c is converted to a fixed-point value with unspecified precision to the right of the binary point. The integer part of this value is then masked with 2^m-1, where m is the number of bits in a color index stored in the frame buffer.

ERRORS

GL_INVALID_OPERATION is generated if **glClearIndex** is called between a call to **glBegin** and the corresponding call to **glEnd**.

ASSOCIATED GETS

glGet with argument **GL_INDEX_CLEAR_VALUE**
glGet with argument **GL_INDEX_BITS**

SEE ALSO

glClear

NAME

glClearStencil – specify the clear value for the stencil buffer

C SPECIFICATION

void **glClearStencil**(GLint *s*)

PARAMETERS

s Specifies the index used when the stencil buffer is cleared. The default value is zero.

DESCRIPTION

glClearStencil specifies the index used by **glClear** to clear the stencil buffer. *s* is masked with 2^m-1, where *m* is the number of bits in the stencil buffer.

ERRORS

GL_INVALID_OPERATION is generated if **glClearStencil** is called between a call to **glBegin** and the corresponding call to **glEnd**.

ASSOCIATED GETS

glGet with argument GL_STENCIL_CLEAR_VALUE
glGet with argument GL_STENCIL_BITS

SEE ALSO

glClear

NAME

glClipPlane – specify a plane against which all geometry is clipped

C SPECIFICATION

void **glClipPlane**(GLenum *plane*,
                      const GLdouble **equation*)

PARAMETERS

plane   Specifies which clipping plane is being positioned. Symbolic names of the
form **GL_CLIP_PLANE***i*, where *i* is an integer between 0 and
GL_MAX_CLIP_PLANES –1, are accepted.

equation Specifies the address of an array of four double-precision floating-point
values. These values are interpreted as a plane equation.

DESCRIPTION

Geometry is always clipped against the boundaries of a six-plane frustum in *x*, *y*, and
z. **glClipPlane** allows the specification of additional planes, not necessarily perpen-
dicular to the *x*, *y*, or *z* axis, against which all geometry is clipped. Up to
GL_MAX_CLIP_PLANES planes can be specified, where **GL_MAX_CLIP_PLANES** is
at least six in all implementations. Because the resulting clipping region is the
intersection of the defined half-spaces, it is always convex.

glClipPlane specifies a half-space using a four-component plane equation. When
glClipPlane is called, *equation* is transformed by the inverse of the modelview
matrix and stored in the resulting eye coordinates. Subsequent changes to the
modelview matrix have no effect on the stored plane-equation components. If the
dot product of the eye coordinates of a vertex with the stored plane equation components is positive or zero, the vertex is *in* with respect to that clipping plane. Otherwise, it is *out*.

Clipping planes are enabled and disabled with **glEnable** and **glDisable**, and called
with the argument **GL_CLIP_PLANE***i*, where *i* is the plane number.

By default, all clipping planes are defined as (0,0,0,0) in eye coordinates and are disabled.

NOTES

It is always the case that **GL_CLIP_PLANE***i* = **GL_CLIP_PLANE0** + *i*.

ERRORS

GL_INVALID_ENUM is generated if *plane* is not an accepted value.

GL_INVALID_OPERATION is generated if **glClipPlane** is called between a call to **glBegin** and the corresponding call to **glEnd**.

ASSOCIATED GETS

glGetClipPlane
glIsEnabled with argument GL_CLIP_PLANE*i*

SEE ALSO

glEnable

NAME

glColor3b, glColor3d, glColor3f, glColor3i, glColor3s, glColor3ub, glColor3ui, glColor3us, glColor4b, glColor4d, glColor4f, glColor4i, glColor4s, glColor4ub, glColor4ui, glColor4us, glColor3bv, glColor3dv, glColor3fv, glColor3iv, glColor3sv, glColor3ubv, glColor3uiv, glColor3usv, glColor4bv, glColor4dv, glColor4fv, glColor4iv, glColor4sv, glColor4ubv, glColor4uiv, glColor4usv
– set the current color

C SPECIFICATION

```
void glColor3b( GLbyte red,
                GLbyte green,
                GLbyte blue )
void glColor3d( GLdouble red,
                GLdouble green,
                GLdouble blue )
void glColor3f( GLfloat red,
                GLfloat green,
                GLfloat blue )
void glColor3i( GLint red,
                GLint green,
                GLint blue )
void glColor3s( GLshort red,
                GLshort green,
                GLshort blue )
void glColor3ub( GLubyte red,
                GLubyte green,
                GLubyte blue )
void glColor3ui( GLuint red,
                GLuint green,
                GLuint blue )
void glColor3us( GLushort red,
                GLushort green,
                GLushort blue )
void glColor4b( GLbyte red,
                GLbyte green,
                GLbyte blue,
                GLbyte alpha )
void glColor4d( GLdouble red,
                GLdouble green,
                GLdouble blue,
                GLdouble alpha )
```

void **glColor4f**(GLfloat *red,*
             GLfloat *green,*
             GLfloat *blue,*
             GLfloat *alpha*)
void **glColor4i**(GLint *red,*
             GLint *green,*
             GLint *blue,*
             GLint *alpha*)
void **glColor4s**(GLshort *red,*
             GLshort *green,*
             GLshort *blue,*
             GLshort *alpha*)
void **glColor4ub**(GLubyte *red,*
              GLubyte *green,*
              GLubyte *blue,*
              GLubyte *alpha*)
void **glColor4ui**(GLuint *red,*
             GLuint *green,*
             GLuint *blue,*
             GLuint *alpha*)
void **glColor4us**(GLushort *red,*
              GLushort *green,*
              GLushort *blue,*
              GLushort *alpha*)

PARAMETERS

red, green, blue

Specify new red, green, and blue values for the current color.

alpha   Specifies a new alpha value for the current color. Included only in the four-argument **glColor4** command.

C SPECIFICATION

void **glColor3bv**(const GLbyte **v*)
void **glColor3dv**(const GLdouble **v*)
void **glColor3fv**(const GLfloat **v*)
void **glColor3iv**(const GLint **v*)
void **glColor3sv**(const GLshort **v*)
void **glColor3ubv**(const GLubyte **v*)
void **glColor3uiv**(const GLuint **v*)
void **glColor3usv**(const GLushort **v*)
void **glColor4bv**(const GLbyte **v*)
void **glColor4dv**(const GLdouble **v*)
void **glColor4fv**(const GLfloat **v*)

void **glColor4iv**(const GLint *v)
void **glColor4sv**(const GLshort *v)
void **glColor4ubv**(const GLubyte *v)
void **glColor4uiv**(const GLuint *v)
void **glColor4usv**(const GLushort *v)

PARAMETERS

v   Specifies a pointer to an array that contains red, green, blue, and (sometimes) alpha values.

DESCRIPTION

The GL stores both a current single-valued color index and a current four-valued RGBA color. **glColor** sets a new four-valued RGBA color. **glColor** has two major variants: **glColor3** and **glColor4**. **glColor3** variants specify new red, green, and blue values explicitly, and set the current alpha value to 1.0 implicitly. **glColor4** variants specify all four color components explicitly.

glColor3b, **glColor4b**, **glColor3s**, **glColor4s**, **glColor3i**, and **glColor4i** take three or four unsigned byte, short, or long integers as arguments. When **v** is appended to the name, the color commands can take a pointer to an array of such values.

Current color values are stored in floating-point format, with unspecified mantissa and exponent sizes. Unsigned integer color components, when specified, are linearly mapped to floating-point values such that the largest representable value maps to 1.0 (full intensity), and zero maps to 0.0 (zero intensity). Signed integer color components, when specified, are linearly mapped to floating-point values such that the most positive representable value maps to 1.0, and the most negative representable value maps to −1.0. Floating-point values are mapped directly.

Neither floating-point nor signed integer values are clamped to the range [0,1] before updating the current color. However, color components are clamped to this range before they are interpolated or written into a color buffer.

NOTES

The current color can be updated at any time. In particular, **glColor** can be called between a call to **glBegin** and the corresponding call to **glEnd**.

ASSOCIATED GETS

glGet with argument **GL_CURRENT_COLOR**
glGet with argument **GL_RGBA_MODE**

SEE ALSO

glIndex

NAME

glColorMask – enable and disable writing of frame buffer color components

C SPECIFICATION

void **glColorMask**(GLboolean *red*,
        GLboolean *green*,
        GLboolean *blue*,
        GLboolean *alpha*)

PARAMETERS

red, green, blue, alpha

    Specify whether red, green, blue, and alpha can or cannot be written into the frame buffer. The default values are all **GL_TRUE**, indicating that the color components can be written.

DESCRIPTION

glColorMask specifies whether the individual color components in the frame buffer can or cannot be written. If *red* is **GL_FALSE**, for example, no change is made to the red component of any pixel in any of the color buffers, regardless of the drawing operation attempted.

Changes to individual bits of components cannot be controlled. Rather, changes are either enabled or disabled for entire color components.

ERRORS

GL_INVALID_OPERATION is generated if **glColorMask** is called between a call to **glBegin** and the corresponding call to **glEnd**.

ASSOCIATED GETS

glGet with argument **GL_COLOR_WRITEMASK**
glGet with argument **GL_RGBA_MODE**

SEE ALSO

glColor, **glIndex**, **glIndexMask**, **glDepthMask**, **glStencilMask**

NAME

glColorMaterial – cause a material color to track the current color

C SPECIFICATION

void **glColorMaterial**(GLenum *face*,
GLenum *mode*)

PARAMETERS

face Specifies whether front, back, or both front and back material parameters should track the current color. Accepted values are **GL_FRONT**, **GL_BACK**, and **GL_FRONT_AND_BACK**. The default value is **GL_FRONT_AND_BACK**.

mode

Specifies which of several material parameters track the current color. Accepted values are **GL_EMISSION**, **GL_AMBIENT**, **GL_DIFFUSE**, **GL_SPECULAR**, and **GL_AMBIENT_AND_DIFFUSE**. The default value is **GL_AMBIENT_AND_DIFFUSE**.

DESCRIPTION

glColorMaterial specifies which material parameters track the current color. When **GL_COLOR_MATERIAL** is enabled, the material parameter or parameters specified by *mode*, of the material or materials specified by *face*, track the current color at all times.
GL_COLOR_MATERIAL is enabled and disabled using the commands **glEnable** and **glDisable**, called with **GL_COLOR_MATERIAL** as their argument. By default, it is disabled.

NOTES

glColorMaterial allows a subset of material parameters to be changed for each vertex using only the **glColor** command, without calling **glMaterial**. If only such a subset of parameters is to be specified for each vertex, **glColorMaterial** is preferred over calling **glMaterial**.

ERRORS

GL_INVALID_ENUM is generated if *face* or *mode* is not an accepted value.

GL_INVALID_OPERATION is generated if **glColorMaterial** is called between a call to **glBegin** and the corresponding call to **glEnd**.

ASSOCIATED GETS

  glIsEnabled with argument GL_COLOR_MATERIAL
  glGet with argument GL_COLOR_MATERIAL_PARAMETER
  glGet with argument GL_COLOR_MATERIAL_FACE

SEE ALSO

  glColor, glEnable, glLight, glLightModel, glMaterial

NAME

glCopyPixels – copy pixels in the frame buffer

C SPECIFICATION

void **glCopyPixels**(GLint *x*,
GLint *y*,
GLsizei *width*,
GLsizei *height*,
GLenum *type*)

PARAMETERS

x, *y*

Specify the window coordinates of the lower left corner of the rectangular region of pixels to be copied.

width, *height*

Specify the dimensions of the rectangular region of pixels to be copied. Both must be nonnegative.

type

Specifies whether color values, depth values, or stencil values are to be copied. Symbolic constants **GL_COLOR**, **GL_DEPTH**, and **GL_STENCIL** are accepted.

DESCRIPTION

glCopyPixels copies a screen-aligned rectangle of pixels from the specified frame buffer location to a region relative to the current raster position. Its operation is well defined only if the entire pixel source region is within the exposed portion of the window. Results of copies from outside the window, or from regions of the window that are not exposed, are hardware dependent and undefined.

x and *y* specify the window coordinates of the lower left corner of the rectangular region to be copied. *width* and *height* specify the dimensions of the rectangular region to be copied. Both *width* and *height* must not be negative.

Several parameters control the processing of the pixel data while it is being copied. These parameters are set with three commands: **glPixelTransfer**, **glPixelMap**, and **glPixelZoom**. This reference page describes the effects on **glCopyPixels** of most, but not all, of the parameters specified by these three commands.

glCopyPixels copies values from each pixel with the lower left-hand corner at $(x + i, y + j)$ for $0 \leq i < width$ and $0 \leq j < height$. This pixel is said to be the *i*th pixel in the *j*th row. Pixels are copied in row order from the lowest to the highest row, left to right in each row.

type specifies whether color, depth, or stencil data is to be copied. The details of the transfer for each data type are as follows:

GL_COLOR   Indices or RGBA colors are read from the buffer currently specified as the read source buffer (see **glReadBuffer**). If the GL is in color index mode, each index that is read from this buffer is converted to a fixed-point format with an unspecified number of bits to the right of the binary point. Each index is then shifted left by **GL_INDEX_SHIFT** bits, and added to **GL_INDEX_OFFSET**. If **GL_INDEX_SHIFT** is negative, the shift is to the right. In either case, zero bits fill otherwise unspecified bit locations in the result. If **GL_MAP_COLOR** is true, the index is replaced with the value that it references in lookup table **GL_PIXEL_MAP_I_TO_I**. Whether the lookup replacement of the index is done or not, the integer part of the index is then ANDed with 2^b-1, where b is the number of bits in a color index buffer.

If the GL is in RGBA mode, the red, green, blue, and alpha components of each pixel that is read are converted to an internal floating-point format with unspecified precision. The conversion maps the largest representable component value to 1.0, and component value zero to 0.0. The resulting floating-point color values are then multiplied by **GL_c_SCALE** and added to **GL_c_BIAS**, where *c* is **RED**, **GREEN**, **BLUE**, and **ALPHA** for the respective color components. The results are clamped to the range [0,1]. If **GL_MAP_COLOR** is true, each color component is scaled by the size of lookup table **GL_PIXEL_MAP_c_TO_c**, then replaced by the value that it references in that table. *c* is **R**, **G**, **B**, or **A**, respectively.

The resulting indices or RGBA colors are then converted to fragments by attaching the current raster position *z* coordinate and texture coordinates to each pixel, then assigning window coordinates (x_r+i, y_r+j), where (x_r, y_r) is the current raster position, and the pixel was the *i*th pixel in the *j*th row. These pixel fragments are then treated just like the fragments generated by rasterizing points, lines, or polygons. Texture mapping, fog, and all the fragment operations are applied before the fragments are written to the frame buffer.

GL_DEPTH   Depth values are read from the depth buffer and converted directly to an internal floating-point format with unspecified precision. The resulting floating-point depth value is then multiplied by **GL_DEPTH_SCALE** and added to **GL_DEPTH_BIAS**. The result is clamped to the range [0,1].

The resulting depth components are then converted to fragments by attaching the current raster position color or color index and texture coordinates to each pixel, then assigning window coordinates (x_r+i, y_r+j), where (x_r, y_r) is the current raster position, and the pixel was the ith pixel in the jth row. These pixel fragments are then treated just like the fragments generated by rasterizing points, lines, or polygons. Texture mapping, fog, and all the fragment operations are applied before the fragments are written to the frame buffer.

GL_STENCIL   Stencil indices are read from the stencil buffer and converted to an internal fixed-point format with an unspecified number of bits to the right of the binary point. Each fixed-point index is then shifted left by **GL_INDEX_SHIFT** bits, and added to **GL_INDEX_OFFSET**. If **GL_INDEX_SHIFT** is negative, the shift is to the right. In either case, zero bits fill otherwise unspecified bit locations in the result. If **GL_MAP_STENCIL** is true, the index is replaced with the value that it references in lookup table **GL_PIXEL_MAP_S_TO_S**. Whether the lookup replacement of the index is done or not, the integer part of the index is then ANDed with 2^b-1, where b is the number of bits in the stencil buffer. The resulting stencil indices are then written to the stencil buffer such that the index read from the ith location of the jth row is written to location (x_r+i, y_r+j), where (x_r, y_r) is the current raster position. Only the pixel ownership test, the scissor test, and the stencil writemask affect these writes.

The rasterization described thus far assumes pixel zoom factors of 1.0. If **glPixelZoom** is used to change the x and y pixel zoom factors, pixels are converted to fragments as follows. If (x_r, y_r) is the current raster position, and a given pixel is in the ith location in the jth row of the source pixel rectangle, then fragments are generated for pixels whose centers are in the rectangle with corners at

$$(x_r+zoom_x i, \ y_r+zoom_y j)$$

and

$$(x_r+zoom_x(i+1), \ y_r+zoom_y(j+1))$$

where $zoom_x$ is the value of **GL_ZOOM_X** and $zoom_y$ is the value of **GL_ZOOM_Y**.

EXAMPLES

To copy the color pixel in the lower left corner of the window to the current raster position, use

```
glCopyPixels(0, 0, 1, 1, GL_COLOR);
```

NOTES

Modes specified by **glPixelStore** have no effect on the operation of **glCopyPixels**.

ERRORS

GL_INVALID_ENUM is generated if *type* is not an accepted value.

GL_INVALID_VALUE is generated if either *width* or *height* is negative.

GL_INVALID_OPERATION is generated if *type* is **GL_DEPTH** and there is no depth buffer.

GL_INVALID_OPERATION is generated if *type* is **GL_STENCIL** and there is no stencil buffer.

GL_INVALID_OPERATION is generated if **glCopyPixels** is called between a call to **glBegin** and the corresponding call to **glEnd**.

ASSOCIATED GETS

glGet with argument GL_CURRENT_RASTER_POSITION
glGet with argument GL_CURRENT_RASTER_POSITION_VALID

SEE ALSO

glDepthFunc, glDrawBuffer, glDrawPixels, glPixelMap, glPixelTransfer, glPixelZoom, glRasterPos, glReadBuffer, glReadPixels, glStencilFunc

NAME

glCullFace – specify whether front- or back-facing facets can be culled

C SPECIFICATION

void **glCullFace**(GLenum *mode*)

PARAMETERS

mode Specifies whether front- or back-facing facets are candidates for culling. Symbolic constants **GL_FRONT** and **GL_BACK** are accepted. The default value is **GL_BACK**.

DESCRIPTION

glCullFace specifies whether front- or back-facing facets are culled (as specified by *mode*) when facet culling is enabled. Facet culling is enabled and disabled using the **glEnable** and **glDisable** commands with the argument GL_CULL_FACE. Facets include triangles, quadrilaterals, polygons, and rectangles.

glFrontFace specifies which of the clockwise and counterclockwise facets are front-facing and back-facing. See **glFrontFace**.

ERRORS

GL_INVALID_ENUM is generated if *mode* is not an accepted value.

GL_INVALID_OPERATION is generated if **glCullFace** is called between a call to **glBegin** and the corresponding call to **glEnd**.

ASSOCIATED GETS

glIsEnabled with argument GL_CULL_FACE
glGet with argument GL_CULL_FACE_MODE

SEE ALSO

glEnable, **glFrontFace**

NAME

> **glDeleteLists** – delete a contiguous group of display lists

C SPECIFICATION

> void **glDeleteLists**(GLuint *list*,
>   GLsizei *range*)

PARAMETERS

> *list*   Specifies the integer name of the first display list to delete.
>
> *range* Specifies the number of display lists to delete.

DESCRIPTION

> **glDeleteLists** causes a contiguous group of display lists to be deleted. *list* is the name of the first display list to be deleted, and *range* is the number of display lists to delete. All display lists d with $list \leq d \leq list + range - 1$ are deleted.
>
> All storage locations allocated to the specified display lists are freed, and the names are available for reuse at a later time. Names within the range that do not have an associated display list are ignored. If *range* is zero, nothing happens.

ERRORS

> GL_INVALID_VALUE is generated if *range* is negative.
>
> GL_INVALID_OPERATION is generated if **glDeleteLists** is called between a call to **glBegin** and the corresponding call to **glEnd**.

SEE ALSO

> glCallList, glCallLists, glGenList, glIsList, glNewList

NAME

glDepthFunc – specify the value used for depth buffer comparisons

C SPECIFICATION

void **glDepthFunc**(GLenum *func*)

PARAMETERS

func Specifies the depth comparison function. Symbolic constants **GL_NEVER**, **GL_LESS**, **GL_EQUAL**, **GL_LEQUAL**, **GL_GREATER**, **GL_NOTEQUAL**, **GL_GEQUAL**, and **GL_ALWAYS** are accepted. The default value is **GL_LESS**.

DESCRIPTION

glDepthFunc specifies the function used to compare each incoming pixel z value with the z value present in the depth buffer. The comparison is performed only if depth testing is enabled. (See **glEnable** and **glDisable** of GL_DEPTH_TEST.)

func specifies the conditions under which the pixel will be drawn. The comparison functions are as follows:

GL_NEVER	Never passes.
GL_LESS	Passes if the incoming z value is less than the stored z value.
GL_EQUAL	Passes if the incoming z value is equal to the stored z value.
GL_LEQUAL	Passes if the incoming z value is less than or equal to the stored z value.
GL_GREATER	Passes if the incoming z value is greater than the stored z value.
GL_NOTEQUAL	Passes if the incoming z value is not equal to the stored z value.
GL_GEQUAL	Passes if the incoming z value is greater than or equal to the stored z value.
GL_ALWAYS	Always passes.

The default value of *func* is **GL_LESS**. Initially, depth testing is disabled.

ERRORS

GL_INVALID_ENUM is generated if *func* is not an accepted value.

GL_INVALID_OPERATION is generated if **glDepthFunc** is called between a call to **glBegin** and the corresponding call to **glEnd**.

ASSOCIATED GETS

glGet with argument **GL_DEPTH_FUNC**

glIsEnabled with argument **GL_DEPTH_TEST**

SEE ALSO

glDepthRange, glEnable

NAME

glDepthMask – enable or disable writing into the depth buffer

C SPECIFICATION

void **glDepthMask**(GLboolean *flag*)

PARAMETERS

flag   Specifies whether the depth buffer is enabled for writing. If *flag* is zero, depth buffer writing is disabled. Otherwise, it is enabled. Initially, depth buffer writing is enabled.

DESCRIPTION

glDepthMask specifies whether the depth buffer is enabled for writing. If *flag* is zero, depth buffer writing is disabled. Otherwise, it is enabled. Initially, depth buffer writing is enabled.

ERRORS

GL_INVALID_OPERATION is generated if **glDepthMask** is called between a call to **glBegin** and the corresponding call to **glEnd**.

ASSOCIATED GETS

glGet with argument **GL_DEPTH_WRITEMASK**

SEE ALSO

glColorMask, **glDepthFunc**, **glDepthRange**, **glIndexMask**, **glStencilMask**

NAME

glDepthRange – specify the mapping of *z* values from normalized device coordinates to window coordinates

C SPECIFICATION

void **glDepthRange**(GLclampd *near,*
                               GLclampd *far*)

PARAMETERS

near   Specifies the mapping of the near clipping plane to window coordinates. The default value is 0.

far   Specifies the mapping of the far clipping plane to window coordinates. The default value is 1.

DESCRIPTION

After clipping and division by *w*, *z* coordinates range from –1.0 to 1.0, corresponding to the near and far clipping planes. **glDepthRange** specifies a linear mapping of the normalized *z* coordinates in this range to window *z* coordinates. Regardless of the actual depth buffer implementation, window coordinate depth values are treated as though they range from 0.0 through 1.0 (like color components). Thus, the values accepted by **glDepthRange** are both clamped to this range before they are accepted.

The default mapping of 0,1 maps the near plane to 0 and the far plane to 1. With this mapping, the depth buffer range is fully utilized.

NOTES

It is not necessary that *near* be less than *far*. Reverse mappings such as 1,0 are acceptable.

ERRORS

GL_INVALID_OPERATION is generated if **glDepthRange** is called between a call to **glBegin** and the corresponding call to **glEnd**.

ASSOCIATED GETS

glGet with argument **GL_DEPTH_RANGE**

SEE ALSO

glDepthFunc, **glViewport**

NAME

glDrawBuffer – specify which color buffers are to be drawn into

C SPECIFICATION

void **glDrawBuffer**(GLenum *mode*)

PARAMETERS

mode Specifies up to four color buffers to be drawn into. Symbolic constants
GL_NONE, **GL_FRONT_LEFT**, **GL_FRONT_RIGHT**, **GL_BACK_LEFT**,
GL_BACK_RIGHT, **GL_FRONT**, **GL_BACK**, **GL_LEFT**, **GL_RIGHT**,
GL_FRONT_AND_BACK, and **GL_AUX***i*, where *i* is between 0 and
GL_AUX_BUFFERS −1, are accepted. The default value is **GL_FRONT** for
single-buffered contexts, and **GL_BACK** for double-buffered contexts.

DESCRIPTION

When colors are written to the frame buffer, they are written into the color buffers
specified by **glDrawBuffer**. The specifications are as follows:

GL_NONE	No color buffers are written.
GL_FRONT_LEFT	Only the front left color buffer is written.
GL_FRONT_RIGHT	Only the front right color buffer is written.
GL_BACK_LEFT	Only the back left color buffer is written.
GL_BACK_RIGHT	Only the back right color buffer is written.
GL_FRONT	Only the front left and front right color buffers are written. If there is no front right color buffer, only the front left color buffer is written.
GL_BACK	Only the back left and back right color buffers are written. If there is no back right color buffer, only the back left color buffer is written.
GL_LEFT	Only the front left and back left color buffers are written. If there is no back left color buffer, only the front left color buffer is written.
GL_RIGHT	Only the front right and back right color buffers are written. If there is no back right color buffer, only the front right color buffer is written.

GL_FRONT_AND_BACK   All the front and back color buffers (front left, front right, back left, back right) are written. If there are no back color buffers, only the front left and front right color buffers are written. If there are no right color buffers, only the front left and back left color buffers are written. If there are no right or back color buffers, only the front left color buffer is written.

GL_AUX*i*   Only auxiliary color buffer *i* is written.

If more than one color buffer is selected for drawing, then blending or logical operations are computed and applied independently for each color buffer and can produce different results in each buffer.

Monoscopic contexts include only *left* buffers, and stereoscopic contexts include both *left* and *right* buffers. Likewise, single-buffered contexts include only *front* buffers, and double-buffered contexts include both *front* and *back* buffers. The context is selected at GL initialization.

NOTES

It is always the case that **GL_AUX***i* = **GL_AUX0** + *i*.

ERRORS

GL_INVALID_ENUM is generated if *mode* is not an accepted value.

GL_INVALID_OPERATION is generated if none of the buffers indicated by *mode* exists.

GL_INVALID_OPERATION is generated if **glDrawBuffer** is called between a call to **glBegin** and the corresponding call to **glEnd**.

ASSOCIATED GETS

glGet with argument **GL_DRAW_BUFFER**
glGet with argument **GL_AUX_BUFFERS**

SEE ALSO

glBlendFunc, glColorMask, glIndexMask, glLogicOp, glReadSource

NAME

glDrawPixels – write a block of pixels to the frame buffer

C SPECIFICATION

void **glDrawPixels**(GLsizei *width*,
GLsizei *height*,
GLenum *format*,
GLenum *type*,
const GLvoid **pixels*)

PARAMETERS

width, height

Specify the dimensions of the pixel rectangle that will be written into the frame buffer.

format Specifies the format of the pixel data. Symbolic constants **GL_COLOR_INDEX**, **GL_STENCIL_INDEX**, **GL_DEPTH_COMPONENT**, **GL_RGBA**, **GL_RED**, **GL_GREEN**, **GL_BLUE**, **GL_ALPHA**, **GL_RGB**, **GL_LUMINANCE**, and **GL_LUMINANCE_ALPHA** are accepted.

type Specifies the data type for *pixels*. Symbolic constants **GL_UNSIGNED_BYTE**, **GL_BYTE**, **GL_BITMAP**, **GL_UNSIGNED_SHORT**, **GL_SHORT**, **GL_UNSIGNED_INT**, **GL_INT**, and **GL_FLOAT** are accepted.

pixels Specifies a pointer to the pixel data.

DESCRIPTION

glDrawPixels reads pixel data from memory and writes it into the frame buffer relative to the current raster position. Use **glRasterPos** to set the current raster position, and use **glGet** with argument **GL_CURRENT_RASTER_POSITION** to query the raster position.

Several parameters define the encoding of pixel data in memory and control the processing of the pixel data before it is placed in the frame buffer. These parameters are set with four commands: **glPixelStore**, **glPixelTransfer**, **glPixelMap**, and **glPixelZoom**. This reference page describes the effects on **glDrawPixels** of many, but not all, of the parameters specified by these four commands.

Data is read from *pixels* as a sequence of signed or unsigned bytes, signed or unsigned shorts, signed or unsigned integers, or single-precision floating-point values, depending on *type*. Each of these bytes, shorts, integers, or floating-point values is interpreted as one color or depth component, or one index, depending on *format*. Indices are always treated individually. Color components are treated as

101

groups of one, two, three, or four values, again based on *format*. Both individual indices and groups of components are referred to as pixels. If *type* is **GL_BITMAP**, the data must be unsigned bytes, and *format* must be either **GL_COLOR_INDEX** or **GL_STENCIL_INDEX**. Each unsigned byte is treated as eight 1-bit pixels, with bit ordering determined by **GL_UNPACK_LSB_FIRST** (see **glPixelStore**).

width×height pixels are read from memory, starting at location *pixels*. By default, these pixels are taken from adjacent memory locations, except that after all *width* pixels are read, the read pointer is advanced to the next four-byte boundary. The four-byte row alignment is specified by **glPixelStore** with argument **GL_UNPACK_ALIGNMENT**, and it can be set to one, two, four, or eight bytes. Other pixel store parameters specify different read pointer advancements, both before the first pixel is read, and after all *width* pixels are read. Refer to the **glPixel-Store** reference page for details on these options.

The *width×height* pixels that are read from memory are each operated on in the same way, based on the values of several parameters specified by **glPixelTransfer** and **glPixelMap**. The details of these operations, as well as the target buffer into which the pixels are drawn, are specific to the format of the pixels, as specified by *format*. *format* can assume one of eleven symbolic values:

GL_COLOR_INDEX

Each pixel is a single value, a color index. It is converted to fixed-point format, with an unspecified number of bits to the right of the binary point, regardless of the memory data type. Floating-point values convert to true fixed-point values. Signed and unsigned integer data is converted with all fraction bits set to zero. Bitmap data convert to either 0.0 or 1.0.

Each fixed-point index is then shifted left by **GL_INDEX_SHIFT** bits and added to **GL_INDEX_OFFSET**. If **GL_INDEX_SHIFT** is negative, the shift is to the right. In either case, zero bits fill otherwise unspecified bit locations in the result.

If the GL is in RGBA mode, the resulting index is converted to an RGBA pixel using the **GL_PIXEL_MAP_I_TO_R**, **GL_PIXEL_MAP_I_TO_G**, **GL_PIXEL_MAP_I_TO_B**, and **GL_PIXEL_MAP_I_TO_A** tables. If the GL is in color index mode, and if **GL_MAP_COLOR** is true, the index is replaced with the value that it references in lookup table **GL_PIXEL_MAP_I_TO_I**. Whether the lookup replacement of the index is done or not, the integer part of the index is then ANDed with 2^b-1, where *b* is the number of bits in a color index buffer.

The resulting indices or RGBA colors are then converted to fragments by attaching the current raster position z coordinate and texture coordinates to each pixel, then assigning x and y window coordinates to the nth fragment such that

$$x_n = x_r + n \bmod \textit{width}$$

$$y_n = y_r + \lfloor n/\textit{width} \rfloor$$

where (x_r, y_r) is the current raster position. These pixel fragments are then treated just like the fragments generated by rasterizing points, lines, or polygons. Texture mapping, fog, and all the fragment operations are applied before the fragments are written to the frame buffer.

GL_STENCIL_INDEX

Each pixel is a single value, a stencil index. It is converted to fixed-point format, with an unspecified number of bits to the right of the binary point, regardless of the memory data type. Floating-point values convert to true fixed-point values. Signed and unsigned integer data is converted with all fraction bits set to zero. Bitmap data convert to either 0.0 or 1.0.

Each fixed-point index is then shifted left by **GL_INDEX_SHIFT** bits, and added to **GL_INDEX_OFFSET**. If **GL_INDEX_SHIFT** is negative, the shift is to the right. In either case, zero bits fill otherwise unspecified bit locations in the result. If **GL_MAP_STENCIL** is true, the index is replaced with the value that it references in lookup table **GL_PIXEL_MAP_S_TO_S**. Whether the lookup replacement of the index is done or not, the integer part of the index is then ANDed with $2^b - 1$, where b is the number of bits in the stencil buffer. The resulting stencil indices are then written to the stencil buffer such that the nth index is written to location

$$x_n = x_r + n \bmod \textit{width}$$

$$y_n = y_r + \lfloor n/\textit{width} \rfloor$$

where (x_r, y_r) is the current raster position. Only the pixel ownership test, the scissor test, and the stencil writemask affect these writes.

GL_DEPTH_COMPONENT

Each pixel is a single-depth component. Floating-point data is converted directly to an internal floating-point format with unspecified precision. Signed integer data is mapped linearly to the internal floating-point format such that the most positive representable integer value maps to 1.0, and the most negative representable value maps to -1.0. Unsigned integer data is mapped similarly: the largest integer value maps to 1.0, and zero maps to 0.0. The resulting floating-point depth value is then multiplied by **GL_DEPTH_SCALE** and added to **GL_DEPTH_BIAS**. The result is clamped to the range [0,1].

The resulting depth components are then converted to fragments by attaching the current raster position color or color index and texture coordinates to each pixel, then assigning x and y window coordinates to the nth fragment such that

$$x_n = x_r + n \bmod width$$

$$y_n = y_r + \lfloor n/width \rfloor$$

where (x_r, y_r) is the current raster position. These pixel fragments are then treated just like the fragments generated by rasterizing points, lines, or polygons. Texture mapping, fog, and all the fragment operations are applied before the fragments are written to the frame buffer.

GL_RGBA

Each pixel is a four-component group: red first, followed by green, followed by blue, followed by alpha. Floating-point values are converted directly to an internal floating-point format with unspecified precision. Signed integer values are mapped linearly to the internal floating-point format such that the most positive representable integer value maps to 1.0, and the most negative representable value maps to -1.0. Unsigned integer data is mapped similarly: the largest integer value maps to 1.0, and zero maps to 0.0. The resulting floating-point color values are then multiplied by **GL_c_SCALE** and added to **GL_c_BIAS**, where c is **RED**, **GREEN**, **BLUE**, and **ALPHA** for the respective color components. The results are clamped to the range [0,1].

If **GL_MAP_COLOR** is true, each color component is scaled by the size of lookup table **GL_PIXEL_MAP_c_TO_c**, then replaced by the value that it references in that table. c is **R**, **G**, **B**, or **A**, respectively.

The resulting RGBA colors are then converted to fragments by attaching the current raster position z coordinate and texture coordinates to each pixel, then assigning x and y window coordinates to the nth fragment such that

$$x_n = x_r + n \bmod width$$

$$y_n = y_r + \lfloor n/width \rfloor$$

where (x_r, y_r) is the current raster position. These pixel fragments are then treated just like the fragments generated by rasterizing points, lines, or polygons. Texture mapping, fog, and all the fragment operations are applied before the fragments are written to the frame buffer.

GL_RED

Each pixel is a single red component. This component is converted to the internal floating-point format in the same way as the red component of an RGBA pixel is, then it is converted to an RGBA pixel with green and blue set to 0.0, and alpha set to 1.0. After this conversion, the pixel is treated just as if it had been read as an RGBA pixel.

GL_GREEN

Each pixel is a single green component. This component is converted to the internal floating-point format in the same way as the green component of an RGBA pixel is, then it is converted to an RGBA pixel with red and blue set to 0.0, and alpha set to 1.0. After this conversion, the pixel is treated just as if it had been read as an RGBA pixel.

GL_BLUE

Each pixel is a single blue component. This component is converted to the internal floating-point format in the same way as the blue component of an RGBA pixel is, then it is converted to an RGBA pixel with red and green set to 0.0, and alpha set to 1.0. After this conversion, the pixel is treated just as if it had been read as an RGBA pixel.

GL_ALPHA

Each pixel is a single alpha component. This component is converted to the internal floating-point format in the same way as the alpha component of an RGBA pixel is, then it is converted to an RGBA pixel with red, green, and blue set to 0.0. After this conversion, the pixel is treated just as if it had been read as an RGBA pixel.

GL_RGB

Each pixel is a three-component group: red first, followed by green, followed by blue. Each component is converted to the internal floating-point format in the same way as the red, green, and blue components of an RGBA pixel are. The color triple is converted to an RGBA pixel with alpha set to 1.0. After this conversion, the pixel is treated just as if it had been read as an RGBA pixel.

GL_LUMINANCE

Each pixel is a single luminance component. This component is converted to the internal floating-point format in the same way as the red component of an RGBA pixel is, then it is converted to an RGBA pixel with red, green, and blue set to the converted luminance value, and alpha set to 1.0. After this conversion, the pixel is treated just as if it had been read as an RGBA pixel.

GL_LUMINANCE_ALPHA

Each pixel is a two-component group: luminance first, followed by alpha. The two components are converted to the internal floating-point format in the same way as the red component of an RGBA pixel is, then they are converted to an RGBA pixel with red, green, and blue set to the converted luminance value, and alpha set to the converted alpha value. After this conversion, the pixel is treated just as if it had been read as an RGBA pixel.

The following table summarizes the meaning of the valid constants for the *type* parameter:

type	*corresponding type*
GL_UNSIGNED_BYTE	unsigned 8-bit integer
GL_BYTE	signed 8-bit integer
GL_BITMAP	single bits in unsigned 8-bit integers
GL_UNSIGNED_SHORT	unsigned 16-bit integer
GL_SHORT	signed 16-bit integer
GL_UNSIGNED_INT	unsigned 32-bit integer
GL_INT	32-bit integer
GL_FLOAT	single-precision floating-point

The rasterization described thus far assumes pixel zoom factors of 1.0. If **glPixel-Zoom** is used to change the x and y pixel zoom factors, pixels are converted to fragments as follows. If (x_r, y_r) is the current raster position, and a given pixel is in the nth column and mth row of the pixel rectangle, then fragments are generated for pixels whose centers are in the rectangle with corners at

$$(x_r + zoom_x n, \ y_r + zoom_y m)$$

$$(x_r + zoom_x(n+1), \ y_r + zoom_y(m+1))$$

where $zoom_x$ is the value of **GL_ZOOM_X** and $zoom_y$ is the value of **GL_ZOOM_Y**.

ERRORS

GL_INVALID_VALUE is generated if either *width* or *height* is negative.

GL_INVALID_ENUM is generated if *format* or *type* is not one of the accepted values.

GL_INVALID_OPERATION is generated if *format* is **GL_RED**, **GL_GREEN**, **GL_BLUE**, **GL_ALPHA**, **GL_RGB**, **GL_RGBA**, **GL_LUMINANCE**, or **GL_LUMINANCE_ALPHA**, and the GL is in color index mode.

GL_INVALID_ENUM is generated if *type* is **GL_BITMAP** and *format* is not either **GL_COLOR_INDEX** or **GL_STENCIL_INDEX**.

GL_INVALID_OPERATION is generated if *format* is **GL_STENCIL_INDEX** and there is no stencil buffer.

GL_INVALID_OPERATION is generated if **glDrawPixels** is called between a call to **glBegin** and the corresponding call to **glEnd**.

ASSOCIATED GETS

glGet with argument **GL_CURRENT_RASTER_POSITION**
glGet with argument **GL_CURRENT_RASTER_POSITION_VALID**

SEE ALSO

glAlphaFunc, **glBlendFunc**, **glCopyPixels**, **glDepthFunc**, **glLogicOp**, **glPixelMap**, **glPixelStore**, **glPixelTransfer**, **glPixelZoom**, **glRasterPos**, **glReadPixels**, **glScissor**, **glStencilFunc**

NAME

glEdgeFlag, glEdgeFlagv – flag edges as either boundary or nonboundary

C SPECIFICATION

void **glEdgeFlag**(GLboolean *flag*)

PARAMETERS

flag Specifics the current edge flag value, either true or false.

C SPECIFICATION

void **glEdgeFlagv**(const GLboolean **flag*)

PARAMETERS

flag Specifies a pointer to an array that contains a single Boolean element, which replaces the current edge flag value.

DESCRIPTION

Each vertex of a polygon, separate triangle, or separate quadrilateral specified between a **glBegin/glEnd** pair is marked as the start of either a boundary or non-boundary edge. If the current edge flag is true when the vertex is specified, the vertex is marked as the start of a boundary edge. Otherwise, the vertex is marked as the start of a nonboundary edge. **glEdgeFlag** sets the edge flag to true if *flag* is nonzero, false otherwise.

The vertices of connected triangles and connected quadrilaterals are always marked as boundary, regardless of the value of the edge flag.

Boundary and nonboundary edge flags on vertices are significant only if **GL_POLYGON_MODE** is set to **GL_POINT** or **GL_LINE**. See **glPolygonMode**.

Initially, the edge flag bit is true.

NOTES

The current edge flag can be updated at any time. In particular, **glEdgeFlag** can be called between a call to **glBegin** and the corresponding call to **glEnd**.

ASSOCIATED GETS

glGet with argument **GL_EDGE_FLAG**

SEE ALSO

glBegin, **glPolygonMode**

NAME

glEnable, glDisable – enable or disable GL capabilities

C SPECIFICATION

void **glEnable**(GLenum *cap*)

PARAMETERS

cap Specifies a symbolic constant indicating a GL capability.

C SPECIFICATION

void **glDisable**(GLenum *cap*)

PARAMETERS

cap Specifies a symbolic constant indicating a GL capability.

DESCRIPTION

glEnable and **glDisable** enable and disable various capabilities. Use **glIsEnabled** or **glGet** to determine the current setting of any capability.

Both **glEnable** and **glDisable** take a single argument, *cap*, which can assume one of the following values:

GL_ALPHA_TEST   If enabled, do alpha testing. See **glAlphaFunc**.

GL_AUTO_NORMAL   If enabled, compute surface normal vectors analytically when either **GL_MAP2_VERTEX_3** or **GL_MAP2_VERTEX_4** is used to generate vertices. See **glMap2**.

GL_BLEND   If enabled, blend the incoming RGBA color values with the values in the color buffers. See **glBlendFunc**.

GL_CLIP_PLANE*i*   If enabled, clip geometry against user-defined clipping plane *i*. See **glClipPlane**.

GL_COLOR_MATERIAL   If enabled, have one or more material parameters track the current color. See **glColorMaterial**.

GL_CULL_FACE   If enabled, cull polygons based on their winding in window coordinates. See **glCullFace**.

GL_DEPTH_TEST   If enabled, do depth comparisons and update the depth buffer. See **glDepthFunc** and **glDepthRange**.

GL_DITHER   If enabled, dither color components or indices before they are written to the color buffer.

GL_FOG	If enabled, blend a fog color into the posttexturing color. See **glFog**.
GL_LIGHT*i*	If enabled, include light *i* in the evaluation of the lighting equation. See **glLightModel** and **glLight**.
GL_LIGHTING	If enabled, use the current lighting parameters to compute the vertex color or index. Otherwise, simply associate the current color or index with each vertex. See **glMaterial**, **glLightModel**, and **glLight**.
GL_LINE_SMOOTH	If enabled, draw lines with correct filtering. Otherwise, draw aliased lines. See **glLineWidth**.
GL_LINE_STIPPLE	If enabled, use the current line stipple pattern when drawing lines. See **glLineStipple**.
GL_LOGIC_OP	If enabled, apply the currently selected logical operation to the incoming and color buffer indices. See **glLogicOp**.
GL_MAP1_COLOR_4	If enabled, calls to **glEvalCoord1**, **glEvalMesh1**, and **glEvalPoint1** will generate RGBA values. See **glMap1**.
GL_MAP1_INDEX	If enabled, calls to **glEvalCoord1**, **glEvalMesh1**, and **glEvalPoint1** will generate color indices. See **glMap1**.
GL_MAP1_NORMAL	If enabled, calls to **glEvalCoord1**, **glEvalMesh1**, and **glEvalPoint1** will generate normals. See **glMap1**.
GL_MAP1_TEXTURE_COORD_1	If enabled, calls to **glEvalCoord1**, **glEvalMesh1**, and **glEvalPoint1** will generate *s* texture coordinates. See **glMap1**.
GL_MAP1_TEXTURE_COORD_2	If enabled, calls to **glEvalCoord1**, **glEvalMesh1**, and **glEvalPoint1** will generate *s* and *t* texture coordinates. See **glMap1**.
GL_MAP1_TEXTURE_COORD_3	If enabled, calls to **glEvalCoord1**, **glEvalMesh1**, and **glEvalPoint1** will generate *s*, *t*, and *r* texture coordinates. See **glMap1**.
GL_MAP1_TEXTURE_COORD_4	If enabled, calls to **glEvalCoord1**, **glEvalMesh1**, and **glEvalPoint1** will generate *s*, *t*, *r*, and *q* texture coordinates. See **glMap1**.

GL_MAP1_VERTEX_3 If enabled, calls to **glEvalCoord1**, **glEvalMesh1**, and **glEvalPoint1** will generate will generate x, y, and z vertex coordinates. See **glMap1**.

GL_MAP1_VERTEX_4 If enabled, calls to **glEvalCoord1**, **glEvalMesh1**, and **glEvalPoint1** will generate homogeneous x, y, z, and w vertex coordinates. See **glMap1**.

GL_MAP2_COLOR_4 If enabled, calls to **glEvalCoord2**, **glEvalMesh2**, and **glEvalPoint2** will generate RGBA values. See **glMap2**.

GL_MAP2_INDEX If enabled, calls to **glEvalCoord2**, **glEvalMesh2**, and **glEvalPoint2** will generate color indices. See **glMap2**.

GL_MAP2_NORMAL If enabled, calls to **glEvalCoord2**, **glEvalMesh2**, and **glEvalPoint2** will generate normals. See **glMap2**.

GL_MAP2_TEXTURE_COORD_1

If enabled, calls to **glEvalCoord2**, **glEvalMesh2**, and **glEvalPoint2** will generate s texture coordinates. See **glMap2**.

GL_MAP2_TEXTURE_COORD_2

If enabled, calls to **glEvalCoord2**, **glEvalMesh2**, and **glEvalPoint2** will generate s and t texture coordinates. See **glMap2**.

GL_MAP2_TEXTURE_COORD_3

If enabled, calls to **glEvalCoord2**, **glEvalMesh2**, and **glEvalPoint2** will generate s, t, and r texture coordinates. See **glMap2**.

GL_MAP2_TEXTURE_COORD_4

If enabled, calls to **glEvalCoord2**, **glEvalMesh2**, and **glEvalPoint2** will generate s, t, r, and q texture coordinates. See **glMap2**.

GL_MAP2_VERTEX_3 If enabled, calls to **glEvalCoord2**, **glEvalMesh2**, and **glEvalPoint2** will generate will generate x, y, and z vertex coordinates. See **glMap2**.

GL_MAP2_VERTEX_4 If enabled, calls to **glEvalCoord2**, **glEvalMesh2**, and **glEvalPoint2** will generate homogeneous x, y, z, and w vertex coordinates. See **glMap2**.

GL_NORMALIZE If enabled, normal vectors specified with **glNormal** are scaled to unit length after transformation. See **glNormal**.

GL_POINT_SMOOTH	If enabled, draw points with proper filtering. Otherwise, draw aliased points. See **glPointSize**.
GL_POLYGON_SMOOTH	If enabled, draw polygons with proper filtering. Otherwise, draw aliased polygons. See **glPolygonMode**.
GL_POLYGON_STIPPLE	If enabled, use the current polygon stipple pattern when rendering polygons. See **glPolygonStipple**.
GL_SCISSOR_TEST	If enabled, discard fragments that are outside the scissor rectangle. See **glScissor**.
GL_STENCIL_TEST	If enabled, do stencil testing and update the stencil buffer. See **glStencilFunc** and **glStencilOp**.
GL_TEXTURE_1D	If enabled, one-dimensional texturing is performed (unless two-dimensional texturing is also enabled). See **glTexImage1D**.
GL_TEXTURE_2D	If enabled, two-dimensional texturing is performed. See **glTexImage2D**.
GL_TEXTURE_GEN_Q	If enabled, the q texture coordinate is computed using the texture generation function defined with **glTexGen**. Otherwise, the current q texture coordinate is used. See **glTexGen**.
GL_TEXTURE_GEN_R	If enabled, the r texture coordinate is computed using the texture generation function defined with **glTexGen**. Otherwise, the current r texture coordinate is used. See **glTexGen**.
GL_TEXTURE_GEN_S	If enabled, the s texture coordinate is computed using the texture generation function defined with **glTexGen**. Otherwise, the current s texture coordinate is used. See **glTexGen**.
GL_TEXTURE_GEN_T	If enabled, the t texture coordinate is computed using the texture generation function defined with **glTexGen**. Otherwise, the current t texture coordinate is used. See **glTexGen**.

ERRORS

GL_INVALID_ENUM is generated if *cap* is not one of the values listed above.

GL_INVALID_OPERATION is generated if **glEnable** is called between a call to **glBegin** and the corresponding call to **glEnd**.

SEE ALSO

glAlphaFunc, glBlendFunc, glClipPlane, glColorMaterial, glCullFace, glDepthFunc, glDepthRange, glFog, glGet, glIsEnabled, glLight, glLightModel, glLineWidth, glLineStipple, glLogicOp, glMap1, glMap2, glMaterial, glNormal, glPointSize, glPolygonMode, glPolygonStipple, glScissor, glStencilFunc, glStencilOp, glTexGen, glTexImage1D, glTexImage2D

NAME

glEvalCoord1d, glEvalCoord1f, glEvalCoord2d, glEvalCoord2f, glEvalCoord1dv, glEvalCoord1fv, glEvalCoord2dv, glEvalCoord2fv – evaluate enabled one- and two-dimensional maps

C SPECIFICATION

void **glEvalCoord1d**(GLdouble u)
void **glEvalCoord1f**(GLfloat u)
void **glEvalCoord2d**(GLdouble u,
                GLdouble v)
void **glEvalCoord2f**(GLfloat u,
                GLfloat v)

PARAMETERS

u Specifies a value that is the domain coordinate u to the basis function defined in a previous **glMap1** or **glMap2** command.

v Specifies a value that is the domain coordinate v to the basis function defined in a previous **glMap2** command. This argument is not present in an **glEvalCoord1** command.

C SPECIFICATION

void **glEvalCoord1dv**(const GLdouble *u)
void **glEvalCoord1fv**(const GLfloat *u)
void **glEvalCoord2dv**(const GLdouble *u)
void **glEvalCoord2fv**(const GLfloat *u)

PARAMETERS

u Specifies a pointer to an array containing either one or two domain coordinates. The first coordinate is u. The second coordinate is v, which is present only in **glEvalCoord2** versions.

DESCRIPTION

glEvalCoord1 evaluates enabled one-dimensional maps at argument u. **glEvalCoord2** does the same for two-dimensional maps using two domain values, u and v. Maps are defined with **glMap1** and **glMap2** and enabled and disabled with **glEnable** and **glDisable**.

When one of the **glEvalCoord** commands is issued, all currently enabled maps of the indicated dimension are evaluated. Then, for each enabled map, it is as if the corresponding GL command was issued with the computed value. That is, if **GL_MAP1_INDEX** or **GL_MAP2_INDEX** is enabled, a **glIndex** command is simulated. If **GL_MAP1_COLOR_4** or **GL_MAP2_COLOR_4** is enabled, a **glColor** command is simulated. If **GL_MAP1_NORMAL** or **GL_MAP2_NORMAL** is enabled, a normal vector is produced, and if any of GL_MAP1_TEXTURE_COORD_1, GL_MAP1_TEXTURE_COORD_2, GL_MAP1_TEXTURE_COORD_3, GL_MAP1_TEXTURE_COORD_4, GL_MAP2_TEXTURE_COORD_1, GL_MAP2_TEXTURE_COORD_2, GL_MAP2_TEXTURE_COORD_3, or GL_MAP2_TEXTURE_COORD_4 is enabled, then an appropriate **glTexCoord** command is simulated.

The GL uses evaluated values instead of current values for those evaluations that are enabled, and current values otherwise, for color, color index, normal, and texture coordinates. However, the evaluated values do not update the current values. Thus, if **glVertex** commands are interspersed with **glEvalCoord** commands, the color, normal, and texture coordinates associated with the **glVertex** commands are not affected by the values generated by the **glEvalCoord** commands, but rather only by the most recent **glColor**, **glIndex**, **glNormal**, and **glTexCoord** commands.

No commands are issued for maps that are not enabled. If more than one texture evaluation is enabled for a particular dimension (for example, GL_MAP2_TEXTURE_COORD_1 and GL_MAP2_TEXTURE_COORD_2), then only the evaluation of the map that produces the larger number of coordinates (in this case, GL_MAP2_TEXTURE_COORD_2) is carried out. GL_MAP1_VERTEX_4 overrides GL_MAP1_VERTEX_3, and GL_MAP2_VERTEX_4 overrides GL_MAP2_VERTEX_3, in the same manner. If neither a three- nor four-component vertex map is enabled for the specified dimension, the **glEvalCoord** command is ignored.

If automatic normal generation is enabled, by calling **glEnable** with argument GL_AUTO_NORMAL, **glEvalCoord2** generates surface normals analytically, regardless of the contents or enabling of the GL_MAP2_NORMAL map. Let

$$\mathbf{m} = \frac{\partial \mathbf{p}}{\partial \mathbf{u}} \times \frac{\partial \mathbf{p}}{\partial \mathbf{v}}$$

Then the generated normal **n** is

$$\mathbf{n} = \frac{\mathbf{m}}{||\mathbf{m}||}$$

If automatic normal generation is disabled, the corresponding normal map GL_MAP2_NORMAL, if enabled, is used to produce a normal. If neither automatic normal generation nor a normal map is enabled, no normal is generated for **glEvalCoord2** commands.

ASSOCIATED GETS

glIsEnabled with argument GL_MAP1_VERTEX_3
glIsEnabled with argument GL_MAP1_VERTEX_4
glIsEnabled with argument GL_MAP1_INDEX

glIsEnabled with argument GL_MAP1_COLOR_4
glIsEnabled with argument GL_MAP1_NORMAL
glIsEnabled with argument GL_MAP1_TEXTURE_COORD_1
glIsEnabled with argument GL_MAP1_TEXTURE_COORD_2
glIsEnabled with argument GL_MAP1_TEXTURE_COORD_3
glIsEnabled with argument GL_MAP1_TEXTURE_COORD_4
glIsEnabled with argument GL_MAP2_VERTEX_3
glIsEnabled with argument GL_MAP2_VERTEX_4
glIsEnabled with argument GL_MAP2_INDEX
glIsEnabled with argument GL_MAP2_COLOR_4
glIsEnabled with argument GL_MAP2_NORMAL
glIsEnabled with argument GL_MAP2_TEXTURE_COORD_1
glIsEnabled with argument GL_MAP2_TEXTURE_COORD_2
glIsEnabled with argument GL_MAP2_TEXTURE_COORD_3
glIsEnabled with argument GL_MAP2_TEXTURE_COORD_4
glIsEnabled with argument GL_AUTO_NORMAL
glGetMap

SEE ALSO

glBegin, glColor, glEnable, glEvalMesh, glEvalPoint, glIndex, glMap1, glMap2, glMapGrid, glNormal, glTexCoord, glVertex

NAME

glEvalMesh1, **glEvalMesh2** – compute a one- or two-dimensional grid of points or lines

C SPECIFICATION

void **glEvalMesh1**(GLenum *mode,*
                     GLint *i1,*
                     GLint *i2*)

PARAMETERS

mode In **glEvalMesh1**, specifies whether to compute a one-dimensional mesh of points or lines. Symbolic constants **GL_POINT** and **GL_LINE** are accepted.

i1, i2 Specify the first and last integer values for grid domain variable *i.*

C SPECIFICATION

void **glEvalMesh2**(GLenum *mode,*
                     GLint *i1,*
                     GLint *i2,*
                     GLint *j1,*
                     GLint *j2*)

PARAMETERS

mode In **glEvalMesh2**, specifies whether to compute a two-dimensional mesh of points, lines, or polygons. Symbolic constants **GL_POINT**, **GL_LINE**, and **GL_FILL** are accepted.

i1, i2 Specify the first and last integer values for grid domain variable *i.*

j1, j2 Specify the first and last integer values for grid domain variable *j.*

DESCRIPTION

glMapGrid and **glEvalMesh** are used in tandem to efficiently generate and evaluate a series of evenly spaced map domain values. **glEvalMesh** steps through the integer domain of a one- or two-dimensional grid, whose range is the domain of the evaluation maps specified by **glMap1** and **glMap2**. *mode* determines whether the resulting vertices are connected as points, lines, or filled polygons.

In the one-dimensional case, **glEvalMesh1**, the mesh is generated as if the following code fragment were executed:

```
glBegin (type) ;
for (i = i1; i <= i2; i += 1)
    glEvalCoord1 (i·Δu + u₁)
glEnd () ;
```

where

$$\Delta u = (u_2 - u_1)/n$$

and n, u_1, and u_2 are the arguments to the most recent **glMapGrid1** command. *type* is **GL_POINTS** if *mode* is **GL_POINT**, or **GL_LINES** if *mode* is **GL_LINE**. The one absolute numeric requirement is that if $i = n$, then the value computed from $i \cdot \Delta u + u_1$ is exactly u_2.

In the two-dimensional case, **glEvalMesh2**, let

$$\Delta u = (u_2 - u_1)/n$$

$$\Delta v = (v_2 - v_1)/m,$$

where n, u_1, u_2, m, v_1, and v_2 are the arguments to the most recent **glMapGrid2** command. Then, if *mode* is **GL_FILL**, the **glEvalMesh2** command is equivalent to:

```
for (j = j1;  j < j2; j += 1) {
    glBegin (GL_QUAD_STRIP) ;
    for (i = i1; i <= i2; i += 1) {
        glEvalCoord2 (i·Δu + u₁, j·Δv + v₁) ;
        glEvalCoord2 (i·Δu + u₁, (j+1)·Δv + v₁) ;
    }
    glEnd () ;
}
```

If *mode* is **GL_LINE**, then a call to **glEvalMesh2** is equivalent to:

```
for (j = j1;   j <= j2; j += 1) {
    glBegin(GL_LINE_STRIP);
    for (i = i1;  i <= i2; i += 1)
        glEvalCoord2(i·Δu + u₁, j·Δv + v₁);
    glEnd();
}
for (i = i1;   i <= i2; i += 1) {
    glBegin(GL_LINE_STRIP);
    for (j = j1;  j <= j1; j += 1)
        glEvalCoord2(i·Δu + u₁, j·Δv + v₁);
    glEnd();
}
```

And finally, if *mode* is **GL_POINT**, then a call to **glEvalMesh2** is equivalent to:

```
glBegin(GL_POINTS);
for (j = j1;   j <= j2; j += 1) {
    for (i = i1;  i <= i2; i += 1) {
        glEvalCoord2(i·Δu + u₁, j·Δv + v₁);
    }
}
glEnd();
```

In all three cases, the only absolute numeric requirements are that if $i = n$, then the value computed from $i \cdot \Delta u + u_1$ is exactly u_2, and if $j = m$, then the value computed from $j \cdot \Delta v + v_1$ is exactly v_2.

ERRORS

GL_INVALID_ENUM is generated if *mode* is not an accepted value.

GL_INVALID_OPERATION is generated if **glEvalMesh** is called between a call to **glBegin** and the corresponding call to **glEnd**.

ASSOCIATED GETS

glGet with argument **GL_MAP1_GRID_DOMAIN**
glGet with argument **GL_MAP2_GRID_DOMAIN**
glGet with argument **GL_MAP1_GRID_SEGMENTS**
glGet with argument **GL_MAP2_GRID_SEGMENTS**

SEE ALSO

glBegin, glEvalCoord, glEvalPoint, glMap1, glMap2, glMapGrid

NAME

glEvalPoint1, glEvalPoint2 – generate and evaluate a single point in a mesh

C SPECIFICATION

void **glEvalPoint1**(GLint i)
void **glEvalPoint2**(GLint i,
                    GLint j)

PARAMETERS

i Specifies the integer value for grid domain variable i.

j Specifies the integer value for grid domain variable j (**glEvalPoint2** only).

DESCRIPTION

glMapGrid and **glEvalMesh** are used in tandem to efficiently generate and evaluate a series of evenly spaced map domain values. **glEvalPoint** can be used to evaluate a single grid point in the same gridspace that is traversed by **glEvalMesh**. Calling **glEvalPoint1** is equivalent to calling

$$\text{glEvalCoord1}\,(i \cdot \Delta u\; +\; u_1)\,;$$

where

$$\Delta u = (u_2 - u_1)/n$$

and n, u_1, and u_2 are the arguments to the most recent **glMapGrid1** command. The one absolute numeric requirement is that if $i = n$, then the value computed from $i \cdot \Delta u + u_1$ is exactly u_2.

In the two-dimensional case, **glEvalPoint2**, let

$$\Delta u = (u_2 - u_1)/n$$

$$\Delta v = (v_2 - v_1)/m$$

where n, u_1, u_2, m, v_1, and v_2 are the arguments to the most recent **glMapGrid2** command. Then the **glEvalPoint2** command is equivalent to calling

$$\text{glEvalCoord2}\,(i \cdot \Delta u\; +\; u_1,\; j \cdot \Delta v\; +\; v_1)\,;$$

The only absolute numeric requirements are that if $i = n$, then the value computed from $i \cdot \Delta u + u_1$ is exactly u_2, and if $j = m$, then the value computed from $j \cdot \Delta v + v_1$ is exactly v_2.

ASSOCIATED GETS

glGet with argument GL_MAP1_GRID_DOMAIN
glGet with argument GL_MAP2_GRID_DOMAIN
glGet with argument GL_MAP1_GRID_SEGMENTS
glGet with argument GL_MAP2_GRID_SEGMENTS

SEE ALSO

glEvalCoord, glEvalMesh, glMap1, glMap2, glMapGrid

NAME

glFeedbackBuffer – controls feedback mode

C SPECIFICATION

void **glFeedbackBuffer**(GLsizei *size*,
GLenum *type*,
GLfloat **buffer*)

PARAMETERS

size   Specifies the maximum number of values that can be written into *buffer*.

type   Specifies a symbolic constant that describes the information that will be returned for each vertex. **GL_2D**, **GL_3D**, **GL_3D_COLOR**, **GL_3D_COLOR_TEXTURE**, and **GL_4D_COLOR_TEXTURE** are accepted.

buffer Returns the feedback data.

DESCRIPTION

The **glFeedbackBuffer** function controls feedback. Feedback, like selection, is a GL mode. The mode is selected by calling **glRenderMode** with **GL_FEEDBACK**. When the GL is in feedback mode, no pixels are produced by rasterization. Instead, information about primitives that would have been rasterized is fed back to the application using the GL.

glFeedbackBuffer has three arguments: *buffer* is a pointer to an array of floating-point values into which feedback information is placed. *size* indicates the size of the array. *type* is a symbolic constant describing the information that is fed back for each vertex. **glFeedbackBuffer** must be issued before feedback mode is enabled (by calling **glRenderMode** with argument **GL_FEEDBACK**). Setting **GL_FEEDBACK** without establishing the feedback buffer, or calling **glFeedbackBuffer** while the GL is in feedback mode, is an error.

The GL is taken out of feedback mode by calling **glRenderMode** with a parameter value other than **GL_FEEDBACK**. When this is done while the GL is in feedback mode, **glRenderMode** returns the number of entries placed in the feedback array. The returned value never exceeds *size*. If the feedback data required more room than was available in *buffer*, **glRenderMode** returns a negative value.

While in feedback mode, each primitive that would be rasterized generates a block of values that get copied into the feedback array. If doing so would cause the number of entries to exceed the maximum, the block is partially written so as to fill the array (if there is any room left at all), and an overflow flag is set. Each block begins with a code indicating the primitive type, followed by values that describe the primitive's vertices and associated data. Entries are also written for bitmaps and pixel rectangles. Feedback occurs after polygon culling and **glPolyMode** interpretation of polygons has taken place, so polygons that are culled are not returned in the feedback buffer. It can also occur after polygons with more than three edges are broken up into triangles, if the GL implementation renders polygons by performing this decomposition.

The **glPassThrough** command can be used to insert a marker into the feedback buffer. See **glPassThrough**.

Following is the grammar for the blocks of values written into the feedback buffer. Each primitive is indicated with a unique identifying value followed by some number of vertices. Polygon entries include an integer value indicating how many vertices follow. A vertex is fed back as some number of floating-point values, as determined by *type*. Colors are fed back as four values in RGBA mode and one value in color index mode.

> feedbackList ← feedbackItem feedbackList | feedbackItem
>
> feedbackItem ← point | lineSegment | polygon | bitmap | pixelRectangle | passThru
>
> point ← **GL_POINT_TOKEN** vertex
>
> lineSegment ← **GL_LINE_TOKEN** vertex vertex | **GL_LINE_RESET_TOKEN** vertex vertex
>
> polygon ← **GL_POLYGON_TOKEN** n polySpec
>
> polySpec ← polySpec vertex | vertex vertex vertex
>
> bitmap ← **GL_BITMAP_TOKEN** vertex
>
> pixelRectangle ← **GL_DRAW_PIXEL_TOKEN** vertex | **GL_COPY_PIXEL_TOKEN** vertex
>
> passThru ← **GL_PASS_THROUGH_TOKEN** value
>
> vertex ← 2d | 3d | 3dColor | 3dColorTexture | 4dColorTexture
>
> 2d ← value value
>
> 3d ← value value value
>
> 3dColor ← value value value color
>
> 3dColorTexture ← value value value color tex
>
> 4dColorTexture ← value value value value color tex
>
> color ← rgba | index
>
> rgba ← value value value value
>
> index ← value
>
> tex ← value value value value

value is a floating-point number, and *n* is a floating-point integer giving the number of vertices in the polygon. GL_POINT_TOKEN, GL_LINE_TOKEN, GL_LINE_RESET_TOKEN, GL_POLYGON_TOKEN, GL_BITMAP_TOKEN, GL_DRAW_PIXEL_TOKEN, GL_COPY_PIXEL_TOKEN and GL_PASS_THROUGH_TOKEN are symbolic floating-point constants. GL_LINE_RESET_TOKEN is returned whenever the line stipple pattern is reset. The data returned as a vertex depends on the feedback *type*.

The following table gives the correspondence between *type* and the number of values per vertex. *k* is 1 in color index mode and 4 in RGBA mode.

type	coordinates	color	texture	total number of values
GL_2D	x, y			2
GL_3D	x, y, z			3
GL_3D_COLOR	x, y, z	k		3+k
GL_3D_COLOR_TEXTURE	x, y, z,	k	4	7+k
GL_4D_COLOR_TEXTURE	x, y, z, w	k	4	8+k

Feedback vertex coordinates are in window coordinates, except *w*, which is in clip coordinates. Feedback colors are lighted, if lighting is enabled. Feedback texture coordinates are generated, if texture coordinate generation is enabled. They are always transformed by the texture matrix.

NOTES

glFeedbackBuffer, when used in a display list, is not compiled into the display list but rather is executed immediately.

ERRORS

GL_INVALID_ENUM is generated if *type* is not an accepted value.

GL_INVALID_VALUE is generated if *size* is negative.

GL_INVALID_OPERATION is generated if **glFeedbackBuffer** is called while the render mode is GL_FEEDBACK, or if **glRenderMode** is called with argument GL_FEEDBACK before **glFeedbackBuffer** is called at least once.

GL_INVALID_OPERATION is generated if **glFeedbackBuffer** is called between a call to **glBegin** and the corresponding call to **glEnd**.

ASSOCIATED GETS

glGet with argument GL_RENDER_MODE

SEE ALSO

glBegin, glLineStipple, glPassThrough, glPolygonMode, glRenderMode, glSelectBuffer

NAME

glFinish – block until all GL execution is complete

C SPECIFICATION

void **glFinish**(void *void*)

DESCRIPTION

glFinish does not return until the effects of all previously called GL commands are complete. Such effects include all changes to GL state, all changes to connection state, and all changes to the frame buffer contents.

NOTES

glFinish requires a round trip to the server.

ERRORS

GL_INVALID_OPERATION is generated if **glFinish** is called between a call to **glBegin** and the corresponding call to **glEnd**.

SEE ALSO

glFlush, glXWaitGL, glXWaitX

NAME

glFlush – force execution of GL commands in finite time

C SPECIFICATION

void **glFlush**(void *void*)

DESCRIPTION

Different GL implementations buffer commands in several different locations, including network buffers and the graphics accelerator itself. **glFlush** empties all of these buffers, causing all issued commands to be executed as quickly as they are accepted by the actual rendering engine. Though this execution may not be completed in any particular time period, it does complete in finite time.

Because any GL program might be executed over a network, or on an accelerator that buffers commands, all programs should call **glFlush** whenever they count on having all of their previously issued commands completed. For example, call **glFlush** before waiting for user input that depends on the generated image.

NOTES

glFlush can return at any time. It does not wait until the execution of all previously issued OpenGL commands is complete.

ERRORS

GL_INVALID_OPERATION is generated if **glFlush** is called between a call to **glBegin** and the corresponding call to **glEnd**.

SEE ALSO

glFinish

NAME

glFogf, **glFogi**, **glFogfv**, **glFogiv** – specify fog parameters

C SPECIFICATION

void **glFogf**(GLenum *pname*,
                GLfloat *param*)
void **glFogi**(GLenum *pname*,
               GLint *param*)

PARAMETERS

pname Specifies a single-valued fog parameter. **GL_FOG_MODE**, **GL_FOG_DENSITY**, **GL_FOG_START**, **GL_FOG_END**, and **GL_FOG_INDEX** are accepted.

param Specifies the value that *pname* will be set to.

C SPECIFICATION

void **glFogfv**(GLenum *pname*,
                const GLfloat **params*)
void **glFogiv**(GLenum *pname*,
                const GLint **params*)

PARAMETERS

pname Specifies a fog parameter. **GL_FOG_MODE**, **GL_FOG_DENSITY**, **GL_FOG_START**, **GL_FOG_END**, **GL_FOG_INDEX**, and **GL_FOG_COLOR** are accepted.

params Specifies the value or values to be assigned to *pname*. **GL_FOG_COLOR** requires an array of four values. All other parameters accept an array containing only a single value.

DESCRIPTION

Fog is enabled and disabled with **glEnable** and **glDisable** using the argument **GL_FOG**. While enabled, fog affects rasterized geometry, bitmaps, and pixel blocks, but not buffer clear operations.

glFog assigns the value or values in *params* to the fog parameter specified by *pname*. The accepted values for *pname* are as follows:

GL_FOG_MODE   *params* is a single integer or floating-point value that specifies the equation to be used to compute the fog blend factor, *f*. Three symbolic constants are accepted: **GL_LINEAR**, **GL_EXP**, and **GL_EXP2**. The equations corresponding to these symbolic constants are defined below. The default fog mode is **GL_EXP**.

GL_FOG_DENSITY   *params* is a single integer or floating-point value that specifies *density*, the fog density used in both exponential fog equations. The default fog density is 1.0.

GL_FOG_START   *params* is a single integer or floating-point value that specifies *start*, the near distance used in the linear fog equation. The default near distance is 0.0.

GL_FOG_END   *params* is a single integer or floating-point value that specifies *end*, the far distance used in the linear fog equation. The default far distance is 1.0.

GL_FOG_INDEX   *params* is a single integer or floating-point value that specifies i_f, the fog color index. The default fog index is 0.0.

GL_FOG_COLOR   *params* contains four integer or floating-point values that specify C_f, the fog color. Integer values are mapped linearly such that the most positive representable value maps to 1.0, and the most negative representable value maps to –1.0. Floating-point values are mapped directly. After conversion, all color components are clamped to the range [0,1]. The default fog color is (0,0,0,0).

Fog blends a fog color with each rasterized pixel fragment's posttexturing color using a blending factor *f*. Factor *f* is computed in one of three ways, depending on the fog mode. Let *z* be the distance in eye coordinates from the origin to the fragment being fogged. The equation for **GL_LINEAR** fog is

$$f = \frac{end - z}{end - start}$$

The equation for **GL_EXP** fog is

$$f = e^{(-density \cdot z)}$$

The equation for **GL_EXP2** fog is

$$f = e^{-(density \cdot z)^2}$$

Regardless of the fog mode, *f* is clamped to the range [0,1] after it is computed. Then, if the GL is in RGBA color mode, the fragment's color C_r is replaced by

$$C_{r'} = fC_r + (1-f)C_f$$

In color index mode, the fragment's color index i_r is replaced by

$$i_{r'} = i_r + (1-f)i_f$$

ERRORS

GL_INVALID_ENUM is generated if *pname* is not an accepted value.

GL_INVALID_OPERATION is generated if **glFog** is called between a call to **glBegin** and the corresponding call to **glEnd**.

ASSOCIATED GETS

glIsEnabled with argument GL_FOG
glGet with argument GL_FOG_COLOR
glGet with argument GL_FOG_INDEX
glGet with argument GL_FOG_DENSITY
glGet with argument GL_FOG_START
glGet with argument GL_FOG_END
glGet with argument GL_FOG_MODE

SEE ALSO

glEnable

NAME

glFrontFace – define front- and back-facing polygons

C SPECIFICATION

void **glFrontFace**(GLenum *mode*)

PARAMETERS

mode Specifies the orientation of front-facing polygons. **GL_CW** and **GL_CCW** are accepted. The default value is **GL_CCW**.

DESCRIPTION

In a scene composed entirely of opaque closed surfaces, back-facing polygons are never visible. Eliminating these invisible polygons has the obvious benefit of speeding up the rendering of the image. Elimination of back-facing polygons is enabled and disabled with **glEnable** and **glDisable** using argument **GL_CULL_FACE**.

The projection of a polygon to window coordinates is said to have clockwise winding if an imaginary object following the path from its first vertex, its second vertex, and so on, to its last vertex, and finally back to its first vertex, moves in a clockwise direction about the interior of the polygon. The polygon's winding is said to be counterclockwise if the imaginary object following the same path moves in a counterclockwise direction about the interior of the polygon. **glFrontFace** specifies whether polygons with clockwise winding in window coordinates, or counterclockwise winding in window coordinates, are taken to be front-facing. Passing **GL_CCW** to *mode* selects counterclockwise polygons as front-facing; **GL_CW** selects clockwise polygons as front-facing. By default, counterclockwise polygons are taken to be front-facing.

ERRORS

GL_INVALID_ENUM is generated if *mode* is not an accepted value.

GL_INVALID_OPERATION is generated if **glFrontFace** is called between a call to **glBegin** and the corresponding call to **glEnd**.

ASSOCIATED GETS

glGet with argument **GL_FRONT_FACE**

SEE ALSO

glCullFace, glLightModel

NAME

glFrustum – multiply the current matrix by a perspective matrix

C SPECIFICATION

void **glFrustum**(GLdouble *left,*
GLdouble *right,*
GLdouble *bottom,*
GLdouble *top,*
GLdouble *near,*
GLdouble *far*)

PARAMETERS

left, right
Specify the coordinates for the left and right vertical clipping planes.

bottom, top
Specify the coordinates for the bottom and top horizontal clipping planes.

near, far Specify the distances to the near and far depth clipping planes. Both distances must be positive.

DESCRIPTION

glFrustum describes a perspective matrix that produces a perspective projection. (*left, bottom, –near*) and (*right, top, –near*) specify the points on the near clipping plane that are mapped to the lower left and upper right corners of the window, respectively, assuming that the eye is located at (0, 0, 0). *–far* specifies the location of the far clipping plane. Both *near* and *far* must be positive. The corresponding matrix is

$$\begin{bmatrix} \dfrac{2\,near}{right-left} & 0 & A & 0 \\ 0 & \dfrac{2\,near}{top-bottom} & B & 0 \\ 0 & 0 & C & D \\ 0 & 0 & -1 & 0 \end{bmatrix}$$

$$A = \frac{right+left}{right-left}$$

$$B = \frac{top+bottom}{top-bottom}$$

$$C = -\frac{far+near}{far-near}$$

$$D = -\frac{2\ far\ near}{far-near}$$

The current matrix is multiplied by this matrix with the result replacing the current matrix. That is, if M is the current matrix and F is the frustum perspective matrix, then M is replaced with M • F.

Use **glPushMatrix** and **glPopMatrix** to save and restore the current matrix stack.

NOTES

Depth buffer precision is affected by the values specified for *near* and *far*. The greater the ratio of *far* to *near* is, the less effective the depth buffer will be at distinguishing between surfaces that are near each other. If

$$r = \frac{far}{near}$$

roughly $\log_2 r$ bits of depth buffer precision are lost. Because *r* approaches infinity as *near* approaches zero, *near* must never be set to zero.

ERRORS

GL_INVALID_VALUE is generated if *near* or *far* is not positive.

GL_INVALID_OPERATION is generated if **glFrustum** is called between a call to **glBegin** and the corresponding call to **glEnd**.

ASSOCIATED GETS

glGet with argument GL_MATRIX_MODE
glGet with argument GL_MODELVIEW_MATRIX
glGet with argument GL_PROJECTION_MATRIX
glGet with argument GL_TEXTURE_MATRIX

SEE ALSO

glOrtho, glMatrixMode, glMultMatrix, glPushMatrix, glViewport

NAME

glGenLists – generate a contiguous set of empty display lists

C SPECIFICATION

GLuint **glGenLists**(GLsizei *range*)

PARAMETERS

range   Specifies the number of contiguous empty display lists to be generated.

DESCRIPTION

glGenLists has one argument, *range*. It returns an integer *n* such that *range* contiguous empty display lists, named *n*, *n+1*, ..., *n+range* –1, are created. If *range* is zero, if there is no group of *range* contiguous names available, or if any error is generated, no display lists are generated, and zero is returned.

ERRORS

GL_INVALID_VALUE is generated if *range* is negative.

GL_INVALID_OPERATION is generated if **glGenLists** is called between a call to **glBegin** and the corresponding call to **glEnd**.

ASSOCIATED GETS

glIsList

SEE ALSO

glCallList, glCallLists, glDeleteLists, glNewList

NAME

glGetBooleanv, glGetDoublev, glGetFloatv, glGetIntegerv – return the value or values of a selected parameter

C SPECIFICATION

void **glGetBooleanv**(GLenum *pname,*
                            GLboolean **params*)
void **glGetDoublev**(GLenum *pname,*
                            GLdouble **params*)
void **glGetFloatv**(GLenum *pname,*
                        GLfloat **params*)
void **glGetIntegerv**(GLenum *pname,*
                        GLint **params*)

PARAMETERS

pname Specifies the parameter value to be returned. The symbolic constants in the list below are accepted.

params Returns the value or values of the specified parameter.

DESCRIPTION

These four commands return values for simple state variables in GL. *pname* is a symbolic constant indicating the state variable to be returned, and *params* is a pointer to an array of the indicated type in which to place the returned data.

Type conversion is performed if *params* has a different type than the state variable value being requested. If **glGetBooleanv** is called, a floating-point or integer value is converted to **GL_FALSE** if and only if it is zero. Otherwise, it is converted to **GL_TRUE**. If **glGetIntegerv** is called, Boolean values are returned as **GL_TRUE** or **GL_FALSE**, and most floating-point values are rounded to the nearest integer value. Floating-point colors and normals, however, are returned with a linear mapping that maps 1.0 to the most positive representable integer value, and −1.0 to the most negative representable integer value. If **glGetFloatv** or **glGetDoublev** is called, Boolean values are returned as **GL_TRUE** or **GL_FALSE**, and integer values are converted to floating-point values.

The following symbolic constants are accepted by *pname*:

GL_ACCUM_ALPHA_BITS

params returns one value, the number of alpha bitplanes in the accumulation buffer.

GL_ACCUM_BLUE_BITS *params* returns one value, the number of blue bitplanes in the accumulation buffer.

GL_ACCUM_CLEAR_VALUE
params returns four values: the red, green, blue, and alpha values used to clear the accumulation buffer. Integer values, if requested, are linearly mapped from the internal floating-point representation such that 1.0 returns the most positive representable integer value, and −1.0 returns the most negative representable integer value. See **glClearAccum**.

GL_ACCUM_GREEN_BITS
params returns one value, the number of green bitplanes in the accumulation buffer.

GL_ACCUM_RED_BITS   *params* returns one value, the number of red bitplanes in the accumulation buffer.

GL_ALPHA_BIAS   *params* returns one value, the alpha bias factor used during pixel transfers. See **glPixelTransfer**.

GL_ALPHA_BITS   *params* returns one value, the number of alpha bitplanes in each color buffer.

GL_ALPHA_SCALE   *params* returns one value, the alpha scale factor used during pixel transfers. See **glPixelTransfer**.

GL_ALPHA_TEST_FUNC   *params* returns one value, the symbolic name of the alpha test function. See **glAlphaFunc**.

GL_ALPHA_TEST_REF   *params* returns one value, the reference value for the alpha test. See **glAlphaFunc**. An integer value, if requested, is linearly mapped from the internal floating-point representation such that 1.0 returns the most positive representable integer value, and −1.0 returns the most negative representable integer value.

GL_ATTRIB_STACK_DEPTH
params returns one value, the depth of the attribute stack. If the stack is empty, zero is returned. See **glPushAttrib**.

GL_AUTO_NORMAL   *params* returns a single Boolean value indicating whether 2-D map evaluation automatically generates surface normals. See **glMap2**.

GL_AUX_BUFFERS   *params* returns one value, the number of auxiliary color buffers.

GL_BLEND   *params* returns a single Boolean value indicating whether blending is enabled. See **glBlendFunc**.

GL_BLEND_DST	*params* returns one value, the symbolic constant identifying the destination blend function. See **glBlendFunc**.
GL_BLEND_SRC	*params* returns one value, the symbolic constant identifying the source blend function. See **glBlendFunc**.
GL_BLUE_BIAS	*params* returns one value, the blue bias factor used during pixel transfers. See **glPixelTransfer**.
GL_BLUE_BITS	*params* returns one value, the number of blue bitplanes in each color buffer.
GL_BLUE_SCALE	*params* returns one value, the blue scale factor used during pixel transfers. See **glPixelTransfer**.

GL_COLOR_CLEAR_VALUE

> *params* returns four values: the red, green, blue, and alpha values used to clear the color buffers. Integer values, if requested, are linearly mapped from the internal floating-point representation such that 1.0 returns the most positive representable integer value, and −1.0 returns the most negative representable integer value. See **glClearColor**.

GL_COLOR_MATERIAL	*params* returns a single Boolean value indicating whether one or more material parameters are tracking the current color. See **glColorMaterial**.

GL_COLOR_MATERIAL_FACE

> *params* returns one value, a symbolic constant indicating which materials have a parameter that is tracking the current color. See **glColorMaterial**.

GL_COLOR_MATERIAL_PARAMETER

> *params* returns one value, a symbolic constant indicating which material parameters are tracking the current color. See **glColorMaterial**.

GL_COLOR_WRITEMASK

> *params* returns four Boolean values: the red, green, blue, and alpha write enables for the color buffers. See **glColorMask**.

GL_CULL_FACE	*params* returns a single Boolean value indicating whether polygon culling is enabled. See **glCullFace**.
GL_CULL_FACE_MODE	*params* returns one value, a symbolic constant indicating which polygon faces are to be culled. See **glCullFace**.

GL_CURRENT_COLOR   *params* returns four values: the red, green, blue, and alpha values of the current color. Integer values, if requested, are linearly mapped from the internal floating-point representation such that 1.0 returns the most positive representable integer value, and −1.0 returns the most negative representable integer value. See **glColor**.

GL_CURRENT_INDEX   *params* returns one value, the current color index. See **glIndex**.

GL_CURRENT_NORMAL *params* returns three values: the *x*, *y*, and *z* values of the current normal. Integer values, if requested, are linearly mapped from the internal floating-point representation such that 1.0 returns the most positive representable integer value, and −1.0 returns the most negative representable integer value. See **glNormal**.

GL_CURRENT_RASTER_COLOR

params returns four values: the red, green, blue, and alpha values of the current raster position. Integer values, if requested, are linearly mapped from the internal floating-point representation such that 1.0 returns the most positive representable integer value, and −1.0 returns the most negative representable integer value. See **glRasterPos**.

GL_CURRENT_RASTER_INDEX

params returns one value, the color index of the current raster position. See **glRasterPos**.

GL_CURRENT_RASTER_POSITION

params returns four values: the *x*, *y*, *z*, and *w* components of the current raster position. *x*, *y*, and *z* are in window coordinates, and *w* is in clip coordinates. See **glRasterPos**.

GL_CURRENT_RASTER_TEXTURE_COORDS

params returns four values: the *s*, *t*, *r*, and *q* current raster texture coordinates. See **glRasterPos** and **glTexCoord**.

GL_CURRENT_RASTER_POSITION_VALID

params returns a single Boolean value indicating whether the current raster position is valid. See **glRasterPos**.

GL_CURRENT_TEXTURE_COORDS

params returns four values: the *s*, *t*, *r*, and *q* current texture coordinates. See **glTexCoord**.

GL_DEPTH_BITS

params returns one value, the number of bitplanes in the depth buffer.

GL_DEPTH_CLEAR_VALUE

params returns one value, the value that is used to clear the depth buffer. Integer values, if requested, are linearly mapped from the internal floating-point representation such that 1.0 returns the most positive representable integer value, and −1.0 returns the most negative representable integer value. See **glClearDepth**.

GL_DEPTH_FUNC

params returns one value, the symbolic constant that indicates the depth comparison function. See **glDepth-Func**.

GL_DEPTH_RANGE

params returns two values: the near and far mapping limits for the depth buffer. Integer values, if requested, are linearly mapped from the internal floating-point representation such that 1.0 returns the most positive representable integer value, and −1.0 returns the most negative representable integer value. See **glDepthRange**.

GL_DEPTH_WRITEMASK

params returns a single Boolean value indicating if the depth buffer is enabled for writing. See **glDepthMask**.

GL_DOUBLEBUFFER

params returns a single Boolean value indicating whether double buffering is supported.

GL_DRAW_BUFFER

params returns one value, a symbolic constant indicating which buffers are being drawn to. See **glDrawBuffer**.

GL_EDGE_FLAG

params returns a single Boolean value indication whether the current edge flag is true or false. See **glEdgeFlag**.

GL_FOG_COLOR

params returns four values: the red, green, blue, and alpha components of the fog color. Integer values, if requested, are linearly mapped from the internal floating-point representation such that 1.0 returns the most positive representable integer value, and −1.0 returns the most negative representable integer value. See **glFog**.

GL_FOG_DENSITY	*params* returns one value, the fog density parameter. See **glFog**.
GL_FOG_END	*params* returns one value, the end factor for the linear fog equation. See **glFog**.
GL_FOG_INDEX	*params* returns one value, the fog color index. See **glFog**.
GL_FOG_MODE	*params* returns one value, a symbolic constant indicating which fog equation is selected. See **glFog**.
GL_FOG_START	*params* returns one value, the start factor for the linear fog equation. See **glFog**.
GL_FRONT_FACE	*params* returns one value, a symbolic constant indicating whether clockwise or counterclockwise polygon winding is treated as front-facing. See **glFrontFace**.
GL_GREEN_BIAS	*params* returns one value, the green bias factor used during pixel transfers.
GL_GREEN_BITS	*params* returns one value, the number of green bitplanes in each color buffer.
GL_GREEN_SCALE	*params* returns one value, the green scale factor used during pixel transfers. See **glPixelTransfer**.
GL_INDEX_BITS	*params* returns one value, the number of bitplanes in each color index buffer.
GL_INDEX_CLEAR_VALUE	*params* returns one value, the color index used to clear the color index buffers. See **glClearIndex**.
GL_INDEX_MODE	*params* returns a single Boolean value indicating whether the GL is in color index mode (true) or RGBA mode (false).
GL_INDEX_OFFSET	*params* returns one value, the offset added to color and stencil indices during pixel transfers. See **glPixelTransfer**.
GL_INDEX_SHIFT	*params* returns one value, the amount that color and stencil indices are shifted during pixel transfers. See **glPixelTransfer**.
GL_INDEX_WRITEMASK	*params* returns one value, a mask indicating which bitplanes of each color index buffer can be written. See **glIndexMask**.

GL_LIGHT_MODEL_AMBIENT

params returns four values: the red, green, blue, and alpha components of the ambient intensity of the entire scene. Integer values, if requested, are linearly mapped from the internal floating-point representation such that 1.0 returns the most positive representable integer value, and −1.0 returns the most negative representable integer value. See **glLightModel**.

GL_LIGHT_MODEL_LOCAL_VIEWER

params returns a single Boolean value indicating whether specular reflection calculations treat the viewer as being local to the scene. See **glLightModel**.

GL_LIGHT_MODEL_TWO_SIDE

params returns a single Boolean value indicating whether separate materials are used to compute lighting for front- and back-facing polygons. See **glLightModel**.

GL_LINE_STIPPLE_PATTERN

params returns one value, the 16-bit line stipple pattern. See **glLineStipple**.

GL_LINE_STIPPLE_REPEAT

params returns one value, the line stipple repeat factor. See **glLineStipple**.

GL_LINE_WIDTH

params returns one value, the line width as specified with **glLineWidth**.

GL_LINE_WIDTH_GRANULARITY

params returns one value, the width difference between adjacent supported widths for antialiased lines. See **glLineWidth**.

GL_LINE_WIDTH_RANGE

params returns two values: the smallest and largest supported widths for antialiased lines. See **glLineWidth**.

GL_LIST_BASE

params returns one value, the base offset added to all names in arrays presented to **glCallLists**. See **glListBase**.

GL_LIST_INDEX

params returns one value, the name of the display list currently under construction. Zero is returned if no display list is currently under construction. See **glNewList**.

GL_LIST_MODE   *params* returns one value, a symbolic constant indicating the construction mode of the display list currently being constructed. See **glNewList**.

GL_LOGIC_OP_MODE   *params* returns one value, a symbolic constant indicating the selected logical operation mode. See **glLogicOp**.

GL_MAP1_GRID_DOMAIN

params returns two values: the endpoints of the 1-D map's grid domain. See **glMapGrid**.

GL_MAP1_GRID_SEGMENTS

params returns one value, the number of partitions in the 1-D map's grid domain. See **glMapGrid**.

GL_MAP2_GRID_DOMAIN

params returns four values: the endpoints of the 2-D map's i and j grid domains. See **glMapGrid**.

GL_MAP2_GRID_SEGMENTS

params returns two values: the number of partitions in the 2-D map's i and j grid domains. See **glMapGrid**.

GL_MAP_COLOR   *params* returns a single Boolean value indicating if colors and color indices are to be replaced by table lookup during pixel transfers. See **glPixelTransfer**.

GL_MAP_STENCIL   *params* returns a single Boolean value indicating if stencil indices are to be replaced by table lookup during pixel transfers. See **glPixelTransfer**.

GL_MATRIX_MODE   *params* returns one value, a symbolic constant indicating which matrix stack is currently the target of all matrix operations. See **glMatrixMode**.

GL_MAX_ATTRIB_STACK_DEPTH

params returns one value, the maximum supported depth of the attribute stack. See **glPushAttrib**.

GL_MAX_CLIP_PLANES *params* returns one value, the maximum number of application-defined clipping planes. See **glClipPlane**.

GL_MAX_EVAL_ORDER   *params* returns one value, the maximum equation order supported by 1-D and 2-D evaluators. See **glMap1** and **glMap2**.

GL_MAX_LIGHTS
params returns one value, the maximum number of lights. See **glLight**.

GL_MAX_LIST_NESTING
params returns one value, the maximum recursion depth allowed during display-list traversal. See **glCallList**.

GL_MAX_MODELVIEW_STACK_DEPTH
params returns one value, the maximum supported depth of the modelview matrix stack. See **glPushMatrix**.

GL_MAX_NAME_STACK_DEPTH
params returns one value, the maximum supported depth of the selection name stack. See **glPushName**.

GL_MAX_PIXEL_MAP_TABLE
params returns one value, the maximum supported size of a **glPixelMap** lookup table. See **glPixelMap**.

GL_MAX_PROJECTION_STACK_DEPTH
params returns one value, the maximum supported depth of the projection matrix stack. See **glPushMatrix**.

GL_MAX_TEXTURE_SIZE
params returns one value, the maximum width or height of any texture image (without borders). See **glTexImage1D** and **glTexImage2D**.

GL_MAX_TEXTURE_STACK_DEPTH
params returns one value, the maximum supported depth of the texture matrix stack. See **glPushMatrix**.

GL_MAX_VIEWPORT_DIMS
params returns two values: the maximum supported width and height of the viewport. See **glViewport**.

GL_MODELVIEW_MATRIX
params returns sixteen values: the modelview matrix on the top of the modelview matrix stack. See **glPushMatrix**.

GL_MODELVIEW_STACK_DEPTH
params returns one value, the number of matrices on the modelview matrix stack. See **glPushMatrix**.

GL_NAME_STACK_DEPTH
params returns one value, the number of names on the selection name stack. See **glPushMatrix**.

GL_PACK_ALIGNMENT   *params* returns one value, the byte alignment used for writing pixel data to memory. See **glPixelStore**.

GL_PACK_LSB_FIRST   *params* returns a single Boolean value indicating whether single-bit pixels being written to memory are written first to the least significant bit of each unsigned byte. See **glPixelStore**.

GL_PACK_ROW_LENGTH

params returns one value, the row length used for writing pixel data to memory. See **glPixelStore**.

GL_PACK_SKIP_PIXELS   *params* returns one value, the number of pixel locations skipped before the first pixel is written into memory. See **glPixelStore**.

GL_PACK_SKIP_ROWS   *params* returns one value, the number of rows of pixel locations skipped before the first pixel is written into memory. See **glPixelStore**.

GL_PACK_SWAP_BYTES *params* returns a single Boolean value indicating whether the bytes of two-byte and four-byte pixel indices and components are swapped before being written to memory. See **glPixelStore**.

GL_PIXEL_MAP_A_TO_A_SIZE

params returns one value, the size of the alpha-to-alpha pixel translation table. See **glPixelMap**.

GL_PIXEL_MAP_B_TO_B_SIZE

params returns one value, the size of the blue-to-blue pixel translation table. See **glPixelMap**.

GL_PIXEL_MAP_G_TO_G_SIZE

params returns one value, the size of the green-to-green pixel translation table. See **glPixelMap**.

GL_PIXEL_MAP_I_TO_A_SIZE

params returns one value, the size of the index-to-alpha pixel translation table. See **glPixelMap**.

GL_PIXEL_MAP_I_TO_B_SIZE

params returns one value, the size of the index-to-blue pixel translation table. See **glPixelMap**.

GL_PIXEL_MAP_I_TO_G_SIZE

params returns one value, the size of the index-to-green pixel translation table. See **glPixelMap**.

GL_PIXEL_MAP_I_TO_I_SIZE
> *params* returns one value, the size of the index-to-index pixel translation table. See **glPixelMap**.

GL_PIXEL_MAP_I_TO_R_SIZE
> *params* returns one value, the size of the index-to-red pixel translation table. See **glPixelMap**.

GL_PIXEL_MAP_R_TO_R_SIZE
> *params* returns one value, the size of the red-to-red pixel translation table. See **glPixelMap**.

GL_PIXEL_MAP_S_TO_S_SIZE
> *params* returns one value, the size of the stencil-to-stencil pixel translation table. See **glPixelMap**.

GL_POINT_SIZE   *params* returns one value, the point size as specified by **glPointSize**.

GL_POINT_SIZE_GRANULARITY
> *params* returns one value, the size difference between adjacent supported sizes for antialiased points. See **glPointSize**.

GL_POINT_SIZE_RANGE *params* returns two values: the smallest and largest supported sizes for antialiased points. See **glPointSize**.

GL_POLYGON_MODE   *params* returns two values: symbolic constants indicating whether front-facing and back-facing polygons are rasterized as points, lines, or filled polygons. See **glPolygonMode**.

GL_PROJECTION_MATRIX
> *params* returns sixteen values: the projection matrix on the top of the projection matrix stack.
> See **glPushMatrix**.

GL_PROJECTION_STACK_DEPTH
> *params* returns one value, the number of matrices on the projection matrix stack. See **glPushMatrix**.

GL_READ_BUFFER   *params* returns one value, a symbolic constant indicating which color buffer is selected for reading.
> See **glReadPixels** and **glAccum**.

GL_RED_BIAS   *params* returns one value, the red bias factor used during pixel transfers.

GL_RED_BITS *params* returns one value, the number of red bitplanes in each color buffer.

GL_RED_SCALE *params* returns one value, the red scale factor used during pixel transfers. See **glPixelTransfer**.

GL_RENDER_MODE *params* returns one value, a symbolic constant indicating whether the GL is in render, select, or feedback mode. See **glRenderMode**.

GL_RGBA_MODE *params* returns a single Boolean value indicating whether the GL is in RGBA mode (true) or color index mode (false). See **glColor**.

GL_SCISSOR_BOX *params* returns four values: the *x* and *y* window coordinates of the scissor box, follow by its width and height. See **glScissor**.

GL_SHADE_MODEL *params* returns one value, a symbolic constant indicating whether the shading mode is flat or smooth. See **glShadeModel**.

GL_STENCIL_BITS *params* returns one value, the number of bitplanes in the stencil buffer.

GL_STENCIL_CLEAR_VALUE
params returns one value, the index to which the stencil bitplanes are cleared. See **glClearStencil**.

GL_STENCIL_FAIL *params* returns one value, a symbolic constant indicating what action is taken when the stencil test fails. See **glStencilOp**.

GL_STENCIL_FUNC *params* returns one value, a symbolic constant indicating what function is used to compare the stencil reference value with the stencil buffer value. See **glStencilFunc**.

GL_STENCIL_PASS_DEPTH_FAIL
params returns one value, a symbolic constant indicating what action is taken when the stencil test passes, but the depth test fails. See **glStencilOp**.

GL_STENCIL_PASS_DEPTH_PASS
params returns one value, a symbolic constant indicating what action is taken when the stencil test passes and the depth test passes. See **glStencilOp**.

GL_STENCIL_REF   *params* returns one value, the reference value that is compared with the contents of the stencil buffer. See **glStencilFunc**.

GL_STENCIL_VALUE_MASK

params returns one value, the mask that is used to mask both the stencil reference value and the stencil buffer value before they are compared. See **glStencilFunc**.

GL_STENCIL_WRITEMASK

params returns one value, the mask that controls writing of the stencil bitplanes. **glStencilMask**.

GL_STEREO   *params* returns a single Boolean value indicating whether stereo buffers (left and right) are supported.

GL_SUBPIXEL_BITS   *params* returns one value, an estimate of the number of bits of subpixel resolution that are used to position rasterized geometry in window coordinates.

GL_TEXTURE_ENV_COLOR

params returns four values: the red, green, blue, and alpha values of the texture environment color. Integer values, if requested, are linearly mapped from the internal floating-point representation such that 1.0 returns the most positive representable integer value, and −1.0 returns the most negative representable integer value. See **glTexEnv**.

GL_TEXTURE_ENV_MODE

params returns one value, a symbolic constant indicating what texture environment function is currently selected. See **glTexEnv**.

GL_TEXTURE_MATRIX   *params* returns sixteen values: the texture matrix on the top of the texture matrix stack. See **glPushMatrix**.

GL_TEXTURE_STACK_DEPTH

params returns one value, the maximum supported depth of the texture matrix stack. See **glPushMatrix**.

GL_UNPACK_ALIGNMENT

params returns one value, the byte alignment used for reading pixel data from memory. See **glPixelStore**.

GL_UNPACK_LSB_FIRST   *params* returns a single Boolean value indicating whether single-bit pixels being read from memory are read first from the least significant bit of each unsigned byte. See **glPixelStore**.

GL_UNPACK_ROW_LENGTH
> *params* returns one value, the row length used for reading pixel data from memory. See **glPixelStore**.

GL_UNPACK_SKIP_PIXELS
> *params* returns one value, the number of pixel locations skipped before the first pixel is read from memory. See **glPixelStore**.

GL_UNPACK_SKIP_ROWS
> *params* returns one value, the number of rows of pixel locations skipped before the first pixel is read from memory. See **glPixelStore**.

GL_UNPACK_SWAP_BYTES
> *params* returns a single Boolean value indicating whether the bytes of two-byte and four-byte pixel indices and components are swapped after being read from memory. See **glPixelStore**.

GL_VIEWPORT
> *params* returns four values: the x and y window coordinates of the viewport, follow by its width and height. See **glViewport**.

GL_ZOOM_X
> *params* returns one value, the x pixel zoom factor. See **glPixelZoom**.

GL_ZOOM_Y
> *params* returns one value, the y pixel zoom factor. See **glPixelZoom**.

Many of the Boolean parameters can also be queried more easily using **glIsEnabled**.

ERRORS

GL_INVALID_ENUM is generated if *pname* is not an accepted value.

GL_INVALID_OPERATION is generated if **glGet** is called between a call to **glBegin** and the corresponding call to **glEnd**.

SEE ALSO

glGetClipPlane, glGetError, glGetLight, glGetMap, glGetMaterial, glGetPixelMap, glGetPolygonStipple, glGetString, glGetTexEnv, glGetTexGen, glGetTexImage1D, glGetTexImage2D, glGetTexLevelParameter, glGetTexParameter, glIsEnabled

NAME

glGetClipPlane – return the coefficients of the specified clipping plane

C SPECIFICATION

void **glGetClipPlane**(GLenum *plane*,
                        GLdouble **equation*)

PARAMETERS

plane   Specifies a clipping plane. The number of clipping planes depends on the implementation, but at least six clipping planes are supported. They are identified by symbolic names of the form **GL_CLIP_PLANE*i*** where $0 \le i <$ **GL_MAX_CLIP_PLANES**.

equation Returns four double-precision values that are the coefficients of the plane equation of *plane* in eye coordinates.

DESCRIPTION

glGetClipPlane returns in *plane* the four coefficients of the plane equation for *plane*.

NOTES

It is always the case that **GL_CLIP_PLANE*i*** = **GL_CLIP_PLANE0** + *i*.

If an error is generated, no change is made to the contents of *equation*.

ERRORS

GL_INVALID_ENUM is generated if *plane* is not an accepted value.

GL_INVALID_OPERATION is generated if **glGetClipPlane** is called between a call to **glBegin** and the corresponding call to **glEnd**.

SEE ALSO

glClipPlane

NAME

glGetError – return error information

C SPECIFICATION

GLenum **glGetError**(void *void*)

DESCRIPTION

glGetError returns the value of the error flag. Each detectable error is assigned a numeric code and symbolic name. When an error occurs, the error flag is set to the appropriate error code value. No other errors are recorded until **glGetError** is called, the error code is returned, and the flag is reset to **GL_NO_ERROR**. If a call to **glGetError** returns **GL_NO_ERROR**, there has been no detectable error since the last call to **glGetError**, or since the GL was initialized.

To allow for distributed implementations, there may be several error flags. If any single error flag has recorded an error, the value of that flag is returned and that flag is reset to **GL_NO_ERROR** when **glGetError** is called. If more than one flag has recorded an error, **glGetError** returns and clears an arbitrary error flag value. Thus, **glGetError** should always be called in a loop, until it returns **GL_NO_ERROR**, if all error flags are to be reset.

Initially, all error flags are set to **GL_NO_ERROR**.

The currently defined errors are as follows:

GL_NO_ERROR	No error has been recorded. The value of this symbolic constant is guaranteed to be zero.
GL_INVALID_ENUM	An unacceptable value is specified for an enumerated argument. The offending command is ignored, having no side effect other than to set the error flag.
GL_INVALID_VALUE	A numeric argument is out of range. The offending command is ignored, having no side effect other than to set the error flag.
GL_INVALID_OPERATION	The specified operation is not allowed in the current state. The offending command is ignored, having no side effect other than to set the error flag.
GL_STACK_OVERFLOW	This command would cause a stack overflow. The offending command is ignored, having no side effect other than to set the error flag.

GL_STACK_UNDERFLOW   This command would cause a stack underflow. The offending command is ignored, having no side effect other than to set the error flag.

GL_OUT_OF_MEMORY   There is not enough memory left to execute the command. The state of the GL is undefined, except for the state of the error flags, after this error is recorded.

When an error flag is set, results of a GL operation are undefined only if **GL_OUT_OF_MEMORY** has occurred. In all other cases, the command generating the error is ignored and has no effect on the GL state or frame buffer contents.

ERRORS

GL_INVALID_OPERATION is generated if **glGetError** is called between a call to **glBegin** and the corresponding call to **glEnd**.

NAME

glGetLightfv, **glGetLightiv** – return light source parameter values

C SPECIFICATION

void **glGetLightfv**(GLenum *light*,
                    GLenum *pname*,
                    GLfloat **params*)
void **glGetLightiv**(GLenum *light*,
                    GLenum *pname*,
                    GLint **params*)

PARAMETERS

light Specifies a light source. The number of possible lights depends on the implementation, but at least eight lights are supported. They are identified by symbolic names of the form **GL_LIGHT***i* where $0 \le i <$ **GL_MAX_LIGHTS**.

pname Specifies a light source parameter for *light*. Accepted symbolic names are **GL_AMBIENT**, **GL_DIFFUSE**, **GL_SPECULAR**, **GL_POSITION**, **GL_SPOT_DIRECTION**, **GL_SPOT_EXPONENT**, **GL_SPOT_CUTOFF**, **GL_CONSTANT_ATTENUATION**, **GL_LINEAR_ATTENUATION** , and **GL_QUADRATIC_ATTENUATION**.

params Returns the requested data.

DESCRIPTION

glGetLight returns in *params* the value or values of a light source parameter. *light* names the light and is a symbolic name of the form **GL_LIGHT***i* for $0 \le i <$ **GL_MAX_LIGHTS**, where **GL_MAX_LIGHTS** is an implementation dependent constant that is greater than or equal to eight. *pname* specifies one of ten light source parameters, again by symbolic name.

The parameters are as follows:

GL_AMBIENT *params* returns four integer or floating-point values representing the ambient intensity of the light source. Integer values, when requested, are linearly mapped from the internal floating-point representation such that 1.0 maps to the most positive representable integer value, and –1.0 maps to the most negative representable integer value. If the internal value is outside the range [–1,1], the corresponding integer return value is undefined.

GL_DIFFUSE   *params* returns four integer or floating-point values represent-
                     ing the diffuse intensity of the light source. Integer values,
                     when requested, are linearly mapped from the internal
                     floating-point representation such that 1.0 maps to the most
                     positive representable integer value, and –1.0 maps to the most
                     negative representable integer value. If the internal value is
                     outside the range [–1,1], the corresponding integer return
                     value is undefined.

GL_SPECULAR   *params* returns four integer or floating-point values represent-
                     ing the specular intensity of the light source. Integer values,
                     when requested, are linearly mapped from the internal
                     floating-point representation such that 1.0 maps to the most
                     positive representable integer value, and –1.0 maps to the most
                     negative representable integer value. If the internal value is
                     outside the range [–1,1], the corresponding integer return
                     value is undefined.

GL_POSITION   *params* returns four integer or floating-point values represent-
                     ing the position of the light source. Integer values, when
                     requested, are computed by rounding the internal floating-
                     point values to the nearest integer value. The returned values
                     are those maintained in eye coordinates. They will not be
                     equal to the values specified using **glLight**, unless the model-
                     view matrix was identity at the time **glLight** was called.

GL_SPOT_DIRECTION
                     params returns three integer or floating-point values represent-
                     ing the direction of the light source. Integer values, when
                     requested, are computed by rounding the internal floating-
                     point values to the nearest integer value. The returned values
                     are those maintained in eye coordinates. They will not be
                     equal to the values specified using **glLight**, unless the model-
                     view matrix was identity at the time **glLight** was called.
                     Although spot direction is normalized before being used in the
                     lighting equation, the returned values are the transformed ver-
                     sions of the specified values prior to normalization.

GL_SPOT_EXPONENT
                     params returns a single integer or floating-point value
                     representing the spot exponent of the light. An integer value,
                     when requested, is computed by rounding the internal
                     floating-point representation to the nearest integer.

GL_SPOT_CUTOFF *params* returns a single integer or floating-point value representing the spot cutoff angle of the light. An integer value, when requested, is computed by rounding the internal floating-point representation to the nearest integer.

GL_CONSTANT_ATTENUATION

params returns a single integer or floating-point value representing the constant (not distance related) attenuation of the light. An integer value, when requested, is computed by rounding the internal floating-point representation to the nearest integer.

GL_LINEAR_ATTENUATION

params returns a single integer or floating-point value representing the linear attenuation of the light. An integer value, when requested, is computed by rounding the internal floating-point representation to the nearest integer.

GL_QUADRATIC_ATTENUATION

params returns a single integer or floating-point value representing the quadratic attenuation of the light. An integer value, when requested, is computed by rounding the internal floating-point representation to the nearest integer.

NOTES

It is always the case that **GL_LIGHT**i = **GL_LIGHT0** + i.

If an error is generated, no change is made to the contents of *params*.

ERRORS

GL_INVALID_ENUM is generated if *light* or *pname* is not an accepted value.

GL_INVALID_OPERATION is generated if **glGetLight** is called between a call to **glBegin** and the corresponding call to **glEnd**.

SEE ALSO

glLight

NAME

glGetMapdv, glGetMapfv, glGetMapiv – return evaluator parameters

C SPECIFICATION

void **glGetMapdv**(GLenum *target*,
                    GLenum *query*,
                    GLdouble **v*)
void **glGetMapfv**(GLenum *target*,
                    GLenum *query*,
                    GLfloat **v*)
void **glGetMapiv**(GLenum *target*,
                    GLenum *query*,
                    GLint **v*)

PARAMETERS

target Specifies the symbolic name of a map. Accepted values are
          GL_MAP1_COLOR_4, **GL_MAP1_INDEX**, **GL_MAP1_NORMAL**,
          GL_MAP1_TEXTURE_COORD_1, **GL_MAP1_TEXTURE_COORD_2**,
          GL_MAP1_TEXTURE_COORD_3, **GL_MAP1_TEXTURE_COORD_4**,
          GL_MAP1_VERTEX_3, **GL_MAP1_VERTEX_4**, **GL_MAP2_COLOR_4** ,
          GL_MAP2_INDEX, **GL_MAP2_NORMAL**, **GL_MAP2_TEXTURE_COORD_1**,
          GL_MAP2_TEXTURE_COORD_2, **GL_MAP2_TEXTURE_COORD_3**,
          GL_MAP2_TEXTURE_COORD_4, **GL_MAP2_VERTEX_3**, and
          GL_MAP2_VERTEX_4.

query   Specifies which parameter to return. Symbolic names **GL_COEFF**,
          GL_ORDER, and **GL_DOMAIN** are accepted.

v   Returns the requested data.

DESCRIPTION

glMap1 and **glMap2** define evaluators. **glGetMap** returns evaluator parameters.
target chooses a map, *query* selects a specific parameter, and *v* points to storage where
the values will be returned.

The acceptable values for the *target* parameter are described in the **glMap1** and
glMap2 reference pages.

query can assume the following values:

GL_COEFF   *v* returns the control points for the evaluator function. One-
                      dimensional evaluators return *order* control points, and two-
                      dimensional evaluators return *uorder×vorder* control points. Each
                      control point consists of one, two, three, or four integer, single-
                      precision floating-point, or double-precision floating-point

values, depending on the type of the evaluator. Two-dimensional control points are returned in row-major order, incrementing the *uorder* index quickly, and the *vorder* index after each row. Integer values, when requested, are computed by rounding the internal floating-point values to the nearest integer values.

GL_ORDER   *v* returns the order of the evaluator function. One-dimensional evaluators return a single value, *order*. Two-dimensional evaluators return two values, *uorder* and *vorder*.

GL_DOMAIN   *v* returns the linear *u* and *v* mapping parameters. One-dimensional evaluators return two values, $u1$ and $u2$, as specified by **glMap1**. Two-dimensional evaluators return four values ($u1$, $u2$, $v1$, and $v2$) as specified by **glMap2**. Integer values, when requested, are computed by rounding the internal floating-point values to the nearest integer values.

NOTES

If an error is generated, no change is made to the contents of *v*.

ERRORS

GL_INVALID_ENUM is generated if either *target* or *query* is not an accepted value.

GL_INVALID_OPERATION is generated if **glGetMap** is called between a call to **glBegin** and the corresponding call to **glEnd**.

SEE ALSO

glEvalCoord, **glMap1**, **glMap2**

NAME

glGetMaterialfv, glGetMaterialiv – return material parameters

C SPECIFICATION

void **glGetMaterialfv**(GLenum *face*,
                     GLenum *pname*,
                     GLfloat **params*)
void **glGetMaterialiv**(GLenum *face*,
                     GLenum *pname*,
                     GLint **params*)

PARAMETERS

face   Specifies which of the two materials is being queried. **GL_FRONT** or **GL_BACK** are accepted, representing the front and back materials, respectively.

pname Specifies the material parameter to return. **GL_AMBIENT**, **GL_DIFFUSE**, **GL_SPECULAR**, **GL_EMISSION**, **GL_SHININESS**, and **GL_COLOR_INDEXES** are accepted.

params Returns the requested data.

DESCRIPTION

glGetMaterial returns in *params* the value or values of parameter *pname* of material *face*. Six parameters are defined:

GL_AMBIENT   *params* returns four integer or floating-point values representing the ambient reflectance of the material. Integer values, when requested, are linearly mapped from the internal floating-point representation such that 1.0 maps to the most positive representable integer value, and –1.0 maps to the most negative representable integer value. If the internal value is outside the range [–1,1], the corresponding integer return value is undefined.

GL_DIFFUSE   *params* returns four integer or floating-point values representing the diffuse reflectance of the material. Integer values, when requested, are linearly mapped from the internal floating-point representation such that 1.0 maps to the most positive representable integer value, and –1.0 maps to the most negative representable integer value. If the internal value is outside the range [–1,1], the corresponding integer return value is undefined.

GL_SPECULAR *params* returns four integer or floating-point values representing the specular reflectance of the material. Integer values, when requested, are linearly mapped from the internal floating-point representation such that 1.0 maps to the most positive representable integer value, and –1.0 maps to the most negative representable integer value. If the internal value is outside the range [–1,1], the corresponding integer return value is undefined.

GL_EMISSION *params* returns four integer or floating-point values representing the emitted light intensity of the material. Integer values, when requested, are linearly mapped from the internal floating-point representation such that 1.0 maps to the most positive representable integer value, and –1.0 maps to the most negative representable integer value. If the internal value is outside the range [–1,1], the corresponding integer return value is undefined.

GL_SHININESS *params* returns one integer or floating-point value representing the specular exponent of the material. Integer values, when requested, are computed by rounding the internal floating-point value to the nearest integer value.

GL_COLOR_INDEXES
params returns three integer or floating-point values representing the ambient, diffuse, and specular indices of the material. These indices are used only for color index lighting. (The other parameters are all used only for RGBA lighting.) Integer values, when requested, are computed by rounding the internal floating-point values to the nearest integer values.

NOTES

If an error is generated, no change is made to the contents of *params*.

ERRORS

GL_INVALID_ENUM is generated if *face* or *pname* is not an accepted value.

GL_INVALID_OPERATION is generated if **glGetMaterial** is called between a call to **glBegin** and the corresponding call to **glEnd**.

SEE ALSO

glMaterial

NAME

glGetPixelMapfv, glGetPixelMapuiv, glGetPixelMapusv – return the specified pixel map

C SPECIFICATION

```
void glGetPixelMapfv( GLenum map,
                      GLfloat *values )
void glGetPixelMapuiv( GLenum map,
                       GLuint *values )
void glGetPixelMapusv( GLenum map,
                       GLushort *values )
```

PARAMETERS

map   Specifies the name of the pixel map to return. Accepted values are
GL_PIXEL_MAP_I_TO_I, GL_PIXEL_MAP_S_TO_S,
GL_PIXEL_MAP_I_TO_R, GL_PIXEL_MAP_I_TO_G,
GL_PIXEL_MAP_I_TO_B, GL_PIXEL_MAP_I_TO_A,
GL_PIXEL_MAP_R_TO_R, GL_PIXEL_MAP_G_TO_G,
GL_PIXEL_MAP_B_TO_B, and GL_PIXEL_MAP_A_TO_A.

values Returns the pixel map contents.

DESCRIPTION

Please see the **glPixelMap** reference page for a description of the acceptable values for the *map* parameter. **glGetPixelMap** returns in *values* the contents of the pixel map specified in *map*. Pixel maps are used during the execution of **glReadPixels**, **glDrawPixels**, **glCopyPixels**, and **glTexImage** to map color indices, stencil indices, color components, and depth components to other values.

Unsigned integer values, if requested, are linearly mapped from the internal fixed or floating-point representation such that 1.0 maps to the largest representable integer value, and 0.0 maps to zero. Return unsigned integer values are undefined if the map value was not in the range [0,1].

To determine the required size of *map*, call **glGet** with the appropriate symbolic constant.

NOTES

If an error is generated, no change is made to the contents of *values*.

ERRORS

GL_INVALID_ENUM is generated if *map* is not an accepted value.

GL_INVALID_OPERATION is generated if **glGetPixelMap** is called between a call to **glBegin** and the corresponding call to **glEnd**.

ASSOCIATED GETS

glGet with argument GL_PIXEL_MAP_I_TO_I_SIZE
glGet with argument GL_PIXEL_MAP_S_TO_S_SIZE
glGet with argument GL_PIXEL_MAP_I_TO_R_SIZE
glGet with argument GL_PIXEL_MAP_I_TO_G_SIZE
glGet with argument GL_PIXEL_MAP_I_TO_B_SIZE
glGet with argument GL_PIXEL_MAP_I_TO_A_SIZE
glGet with argument GL_PIXEL_MAP_R_TO_R_SIZE
glGet with argument GL_PIXEL_MAP_G_TO_G_SIZE
glGet with argument GL_PIXEL_MAP_B_TO_B_SIZE
glGet with argument GL_PIXEL_MAP_A_TO_A_SIZE
glGet with argument GL_MAX_PIXEL_MAP_TABLE

SEE ALSO

glCopyPixels, **glDrawPixels**, **glPixelMap**, **glPixelTransfer**, **glReadPixels**, **glTexImage1D**, **glTexImage2D**

glGetPolygonStipple

NAME

glGetPolygonStipple – return the polygon stipple pattern

C SPECIFICATION

void **glGetPolygonStipple**(GLubyte *mask*)

PARAMETERS

mask Returns the stipple pattern.

DESCRIPTION

glGetPolygonStipple returns to *mask* a 32×32 polygon stipple pattern. The pattern is packed into memory as if **glReadPixels** with both *height* and *width* of 32, *type* of **GL_BITMAP**, and *format* of GL_COLOR_INDEX were called, and the stipple pattern were stored in an internal 32×32 color index buffer. Unlike **glReadPixels**, however, pixel transfer operations (shift, offset, pixel map) are not applied to the returned stipple image.

NOTES

If an error is generated, no change is made to the contents of *mask*.

ERRORS

GL_INVALID_OPERATION is generated if **glGetPolygonStipple** is called between a call to **glBegin** and the corresponding call to **glEnd**.

SEE ALSO

glPixelStore, glPixelTransfer, glPolygonStipple, glReadPixels

NAME

glGetString – returns a string describing the current GL connection

C SPECIFICATION

const GLubyte * **glGetString**(GLenum *name*)

PARAMETERS

name Specifies a symbolic constant, one of **GL_VENDOR**, **GL_RENDERER**, **GL_VERSION**, or **GL_EXTENSIONS**.

DESCRIPTION

glGetString returns a pointer to a static string describing some aspect of the current GL connection. *name* can be one of the following:

GL_VENDOR   Returns the company responsible for this GL implementation. This name does not change from release to release.

GL_RENDERER   Returns the name of the renderer. This name is typically specific to a particular configuration of a hardware platform. It does not change from release to release.

GL_VERSION   Returns a version or release number.

GL_EXTENSIONS   Returns a space-separated list of supported extensions to GL.

Because GL does not include queries for the performance characteristics of an implementation, it is expected that some applications will be written to recognize known platforms and will modify their GL usage based on known performance characteristics of these platforms. Strings **GL_VENDOR** and **GL_RENDERER** together uniquely specify a platform, and will not change from release to release. They should be used by such platform recognition algorithms.

The format and contents of the string that **glGetString** returns depend on the implementation, except that extension names will not include space characters and will be separated by space characters in the **GL_EXTENSIONS** string, and that all strings are null-terminated.

NOTES

If an error is generated, **glGetString** returns zero.

ERRORS

GL_INVALID_ENUM is generated if *name* is not an accepted value.

GL_INVALID_OPERATION is generated if **glGetString** is called between a call to **glBegin** and the corresponding call to **glEnd**.

NAME

glGetTexEnvfv, **glGetTexEnviv** – return texture environment parameters

C SPECIFICATION

void **glGetTexEnvfv**(GLenum *target*,
  GLenum *pname*,
  GLfloat **params*)
void **glGetTexEnviv**(GLenum *target*,
  GLenum *pname*,
  GLint **params*)

PARAMETERS

target Specifies a texture environment. Must be **GL_TEXTURE_ENV**.

pname

Specifies the symbolic name of a texture environment parameter. Accepted values are **GL_TEXTURE_ENV_MODE** and **GL_TEXTURE_ENV_COLOR**.

params

Returns the requested data.

DESCRIPTION

glGetTexEnv returns in *params* selected values of a texture environment that was specified with **glTexEnv**. *target* specifies a texture environment. Currently, only one texture environment is defined and supported: **GL_TEXTURE_ENV**.

pname names a specific texture environment parameter. The two parameters are as follows:

GL_TEXTURE_ENV_MODE

params returns the single-valued texture environment mode, a symbolic constant.

GL_TEXTURE_ENV_COLOR

params returns four integer or floating-point values that are the texture environment color. Integer values, when requested, are linearly mapped from the internal floating-point representation such that 1.0 maps to the most positive representable integer, and −1.0 maps to the most negative representable integer.

NOTES

If an error is generated, no change is made to the contents of *params*.

ERRORS

GL_INVALID_ENUM is generated if *target* or *pname* is not an accepted value.

GL_INVALID_OPERATION is generated if **glGetTexEnv** is called between a call to **glBegin** and the corresponding call to **glEnd**.

SEE ALSO

glTexEnv

NAME

glGetTexGendv, glGetTexGenfv, glGetTexGeniv – return texture coordinate generation parameters

C SPECIFICATION

void **glGetTexGendv**(GLenum *coord,*
                       GLenum *pname,*
                       GLdouble **params*)
void **glGetTexGenfv**(GLenum *coord,*
                       GLenum *pname,*
                       GLfloat **params*)
void **glGetTexGeniv**(GLenum *coord,*
                       GLenum *pname,*
                       GLint **params*)

PARAMETERS

coord   Specifies a texture coordinate. Must be **GL_S, GL_T, GL_R,** or **GL_Q.**

pname Specifies the symbolic name of the value(s) to be returned. Must be either **GL_TEXTURE_GEN_MODE** or the name of one of the texture generation plane equations: **GL_OBJECT_PLANE** or **GL_EYE_PLANE.**

params Returns the requested data.

DESCRIPTION

glGetTexGen returns in *params* selected parameters of a texture coordinate generation function that was specified using **glTexGen**. *coord* names one of the (s,t,r,q) texture coordinates, using the symbolic constant **GL_S, GL_T, GL_R,** or **GL_Q.**

pname specifies one of three symbolic names:

GL_TEXTURE_GEN_MODE   *params* returns the single-valued texture generation function, a symbolic constant.

GL_OBJECT_PLANE   *params* returns the four plane equation coefficients that specify object linear-coordinate generation. Integer values, when requested, are mapped directly from the internal floating-point representation.

GL_EYE_PLANE *params* returns the four plane equation coefficients that specify eye linear-coordinate generation. Integer values, when requested, are mapped directly from the internal floating-point representation. The returned values are those maintained in eye coordinates. They are not equal to the values specified using **glTexGen**, unless the modelview matrix was identity at the time **glTexGen** was called.

NOTES

If an error is generated, no change is made to the contents of *params*.

ERRORS

GL_INVALID_ENUM is generated if *coord* or *pname* is not an accepted value.

GL_INVALID_OPERATION is generated if **glGetTexGen** is called between a call to **glBegin** and the corresponding call to **glEnd**.

SEE ALSO

glTexGen

NAME

glGetTexImage – return a texture image

C SPECIFICATION

void **glGetTexImage**(GLenum *target*,
GLint *level*,
GLenum *format*,
GLenum *type*,
GLvoid **pixels*)

PARAMETERS

target   Specifies which texture is to be obtained. **GL_TEXTURE_1D** and **GL_TEXTURE_2D** are accepted.

level   Specifies the level-of-detail number of the desired image. Level 0 is the base image level. Level *n* is the *n*th mipmap reduction image.

format
Specifies a pixel format for the returned data. The supported formats are **GL_RED**, **GL_GREEN**, **GL_BLUE**, **GL_ALPHA**, **GL_RGB**, **GL_RGBA**, **GL_LUMINANCE**, and **GL_LUMINANCE_ALPHA**.

type   Specifies a pixel type for the returned data. The supported types are **GL_UNSIGNED_BYTE**, **GL_BYTE**, **GL_UNSIGNED_SHORT**, **GL_SHORT**, **GL_UNSIGNED_INT**, **GL_INT**, and **GL_FLOAT**.

pixels   Returns the texture image. Should be a pointer to an array of the type specified by *type*.

DESCRIPTION

glGetTexImage returns a texture image into *pixels*. *target* specifies whether the desired texture image is one specified by **glTexImage1D** (GL_TEXTURE_1D) or by **glTexImage2D** (GL_TEXTURE_2D). *level* specifies the level-of-detail number of the desired image. *format* and *type* specify the format and type of the desired image array. Please see the reference pages **glTexImage1D** and **glDrawPixels** for a description of the acceptable values for the *format* and *type* parameters, respectively.

Operation of **glGetTexImage** is best understood by considering the selected internal four-component texture image to be an RGBA color buffer the size of the image. The semantics of **glGetTexImage** are then identical to those of **glReadPixels** called with the same *format* and *type*, with *x* and *y* set to zero, *width* set to the width of the texture image (including border if one was specified), and *height* set to one for 1-D images, or to the height of the texture image (including border if one was specified) for 2-D images.

Because the internal texture image is an RGBA image, pixel formats **GL_COLOR_INDEX**, **GL_STENCIL_INDEX**, and **GL_DEPTH_COMPONENT** are not accepted, and pixel type **GL_BITMAP** is not accepted.

If the selected texture image does not contain four components, the following mappings are applied. Single-component textures are treated as RGBA buffers with red set to the single-component value, and green, blue, and alpha set to zero. Two-component textures are treated as RGBA buffers with red set to the value of component zero, alpha set to the value of component one, and green and blue set to zero. Finally, three-component textures are treated as RGBA buffers with red set to component zero, green set to component one, blue set to component two, and alpha set to zero.

To determine the required size of *pixels*, use **glGetTexLevelParameter** to ascertain the dimensions of the internal texture image, then scale the required number of pixels by the storage required for each pixel, based on *format* and *type*. Be sure to take the pixel storage parameters into account, especially **GL_PACK_ALIGNMENT**.

NOTES

If an error is generated, no change is made to the contents of *pixels*.

ERRORS

GL_INVALID_ENUM is generated if *target*, *format*, or *type* is not an accepted value.

GL_INVALID_VALUE is generated if *level* is less than zero or greater than $\log_2 max$, where max is the returned value of **GL_MAX_TEXTURE_SIZE**.

GL_INVALID_OPERATION is generated if **glGetTexImage** is called between a call to **glBegin** and the corresponding call to **glEnd**.

ASSOCIATED GETS

glGetTexLevelParameter with argument **GL_TEXTURE_WIDTH**
glGetTexLevelParameter with argument **GL_TEXTURE_HEIGHT**
glGetTexLevelParameter with argument **GL_TEXTURE_BORDER**
glGetTexLevelParameter with argument **GL_TEXTURE_COMPONENTS**
glGet with arguments **GL_PACK_ALIGNMENT** and others

SEE ALSO

glDrawPixels, **glReadPixels**, **glTexImage1D**, **glTexImage2D**

NAME

glGetTexLevelParameterfv, glGetTexLevelParameteriv – return texture parameter values for a specific level of detail

C SPECIFICATION

void **glGetTexLevelParameterfv**(GLenum *target*,
                                          GLint *level*,
                                          GLenum *pname*,
                                          GLfloat **params*)
void **glGetTexLevelParameteriv**(GLenum *target*,
                                          GLint *level*,
                                          GLenum *pname*,
                                          GLint **params*)

PARAMETERS

target Specifies the symbolic name of the target texture, either **GL_TEXTURE_1D** or **GL_TEXTURE_2D**.

level Specifies the level-of-detail number of the desired image. Level 0 is the base image level. Level *n* is the *n*th mipmap reduction image.

pname

  Specifies the symbolic name of a texture parameter. **GL_TEXTURE_WIDTH**, **GL_TEXTURE_HEIGHT**, **GL_TEXTURE_COMPONENTS**, and **GL_TEXTURE_BORDER** are accepted.

params

  Returns the requested data.

DESCRIPTION

glGetTexLevelParameter returns in *params* texture parameter values for a specific level-of-detail value, specified as *level*. *target* defines the target texture, either **GL_TEXTURE_1D** or **GL_TEXTURE_2D**, to specify one- or two-dimensional texturing. *pname* specifies the texture parameter whose value or values will be returned.

The accepted parameter names are as follows:

GL_TEXTURE_WIDTH

  params returns a single value, the width of the texture image. This value includes the border of the texture image.

GL_TEXTURE_HEIGHT

  params returns a single value, the height of the texture image. This value includes the border of the texture image.

GL_TEXTURE_COMPONENTS

params returns a single value, the number of components in the texture image.

GL_TEXTURE_BORDER

params returns a single value, the width in pixels of the border of the texture image.

NOTES

If an error is generated, no change is made to the contents of *params*.

ERRORS

GL_INVALID_ENUM is generated if *target* or *pname* is not an accepted value.

GL_INVALID_VALUE is generated if *level* is less than zero or greater than $\log_2 \text{max}$, where max is the returned value of **GL_MAX_TEXTURE_SIZE**.

GL_INVALID_OPERATION is generated if **glGetTexLevelParameter** is called between a call to **glBegin** and the corresponding call to **glEnd**.

SEE ALSO

glGetTexParameter, glTexImage1D, glTexImage2D, glTexParameter

NAME

glGetTexParameterfv, glGetTexParameteriv – return texture parameter values

C SPECIFICATION

```
void glGetTexParameterfv( GLenum target,
                          GLenum pname,
                          GLfloat *params )
void glGetTexParameteriv( GLenum target,
                          GLenum pname,
                          GLint *params )
```

PARAMETERS

target Specifies the symbolic name of the target texture. **GL_TEXTURE_1D** and **GL_TEXTURE_2D** are accepted.

pname
Specifies the symbolic name of a texture parameter. **GL_TEXTURE_MAG_FILTER**, **GL_TEXTURE_MIN_FILTER**, **GL_TEXTURE_WRAP_S**, **GL_TEXTURE_WRAP_T**, and **GL_TEXTURE_BORDER_COLOR** are accepted.

params
Returns the texture parameters.

DESCRIPTION

glGetTexParameter returns in *params* the value or values of the texture parameter specified as *pname*. *target* defines the target texture, either **GL_TEXTURE_1D** or **GL_TEXTURE_2D**, to specify one- or two-dimensional texturing. *pname* accepts the same symbols as **glTexParameter**, with the same interpretations:

GL_TEXTURE_MAG_FILTER	Returns the single-valued texture magnification filter, a symbolic constant.
GL_TEXTURE_MIN_FILTER	Returns the single-valued texture minification filter, a symbolic constant.
GL_TEXTURE_WRAP_S	Returns the single-valued wrapping function for texture coordinate *s*, a symbolic constant.
GL_TEXTURE_WRAP_T	Returns the single-valued wrapping function for texture coordinate *t*, a symbolic constant.

GL_TEXTURE_BORDER_COLOR   Returns four integer or floating-point numbers that comprise the RGBA color of the texture border. Floating-point values are returned in the range [0,1]. Integer values are returned as a linear mapping of the internal floating-point representation such that 1.0 maps to the most positive representable integer and −1.0 maps to the most negative representable integer.

NOTES

If an error is generated, no change is made to the contents of *params*.

ERRORS

GL_INVALID_ENUM is generated if *target* or *pname* is not an accepted value.

GL_INVALID_OPERATION is generated if **glGetTexParameter** is called between a call to **glBegin** and the corresponding call to **glEnd**.

SEE ALSO

glTexParameter

NAME

glHint – specify implementation-specific hints

C SPECIFICATION

void **glHint**(GLenum *target*,
            GLenum *mode*)

PARAMETERS

target   Specifies a symbolic constant indicating the behavior to be controlled.
**GL_FOG_HINT, GL_LINE_SMOOTH_HINT,
GL_PERSPECTIVE_CORRECTION_HINT, GL_POINT_SMOOTH_HINT**, and
GL_POLYGON_SMOOTH_HINT are accepted.

mode   Specifies a symbolic constant indicating the desired behavior. **GL_FASTEST**,
GL_NICEST, and **GL_DONT_CARE** are accepted.

DESCRIPTION

Certain aspects of GL behavior, when there is room for interpretation, can be
controlled with hints. A hint is specified with two arguments. *target* is a symbolic
constant indicating the behavior to be controlled, and *mode* is another symbolic
constant indicating the desired behavior. *mode* can be one of the following:

GL_FASTEST   The most efficient option should be chosen.

GL_NICEST   The most correct, or highest quality, option should be chosen.

GL_DONT_CARE   The client doesn't have a preference.

Though the implementation aspects that can be hinted are well defined, the
interpretation of the hints depends on the implementation. The hint aspects that
can be specified with *target*, along with suggested semantics, are as follows:

GL_FOG_HINT   Indicates the accuracy of fog calculation. If per-pixel fog calculation is not efficiently supported by the GL implementation,
hinting **GL_DONT_CARE** or **GL_FASTEST** can result in per-
vertex calculation of fog effects.

GL_LINE_SMOOTH_HINT
            Indicates the sampling quality of antialiased lines. Hinting
GL_NICEST can result in more pixel fragments being generated during rasterization, if a larger filter function is applied.

GL_PERSPECTIVE_CORRECTION_HINT
            Indicates the quality of color and texture coordinate interpola-
tion. If perspective-corrected parameter interpolation is not
efficiently supported by the GL implementation, hinting
GL_DONT_CARE or **GL_FASTEST** can result in simple linear
interpolation of colors and/or texture coordinates.

GL_POINT_SMOOTH_HINT
> Indicates the sampling quality of antialiased points. Hinting **GL_NICEST** can result in more pixel fragments being generated during rasterization, if a larger filter function is applied.

GL_POLYGON_SMOOTH_HINT
> Indicates the sampling quality of antialiased polygons. Hinting **GL_NICEST** can result in more pixel fragments being generated during rasterization, if a larger filter function is applied.

NOTES

The interpretation of hints depends on the implementation. **glHint** can be ignored.

ERRORS

GL_INVALID_ENUM is generated if either *target* or *mode* is not an accepted value.

GL_INVALID_OPERATION is generated if **glHint** is called between a call to **glBegin** and the corresponding call to **glEnd**.

NAME

glIndexd, glIndexf, glIndexi, glIndexs, glIndexdv, glIndexfv, glIndexiv, glIndexsv – set the current color index

C SPECIFICATION

void **glIndexd**(GLdouble *c*)
void **glIndexf**(GLfloat *c*)
void **glIndexi**(GLint *c*)
void **glIndexs**(GLshort *c*)

PARAMETERS

c Specifies the new value for the current color index.

C SPECIFICATION

void **glIndexdv**(const GLdouble **c*)
void **glIndexfv**(const GLfloat **c*)
void **glIndexiv**(const GLint **c*)
void **glIndexsv**(const GLshort **c*)

PARAMETERS

c Specifies a pointer to a one-element array that contains the new value for the current color index.

DESCRIPTION

glIndex updates the current (single-valued) color index. It takes one argument: the new value for the current color index.

The current index is stored as a floating-point value. Integer values are converted directly to floating-point values, with no special mapping.

Index values outside the representable range of the color index buffer are not clamped. However, before an index is dithered (if enabled) and written to the frame buffer, it is converted to fixed-point format. Any bits in the integer portion of the resulting fixed-point value that do not correspond to bits in the frame buffer are masked out.

NOTES

The current index can be updated at any time. In particular, **glIndex** can be called between a call to **glBegin** and the corresponding call to **glEnd**.

ASSOCIATED GETS

glGet with argument **GL_CURRENT_INDEX**

SEE ALSO

glColor

NAME

glIndexMask – control the writing of individual bits in the color index buffers

C SPECIFICATION

void **glIndexMask**(GLuint *mask*)

PARAMETERS

mask Specifies a bit mask to enable and disable the writing of individual bits in the color index buffers. Initially, the mask is all ones.

DESCRIPTION

glIndexMask controls the writing of individual bits in the color index buffers. The least significant n bits of *mask*, where n is the number of bits in a color index buffer, specify a mask. Wherever a one appears in the mask, the corresponding bit in the color index buffer (or buffers) is made writable. Where a zero appears, the bit is write-protected.

This mask is used only in color index mode, and it affects only the buffers currently selected for writing (see **glDrawBuffer**). Initially, all bits are enabled for writing.

ERRORS

GL_INVALID_OPERATION is generated if **glIndexMask** is called between a call to **glBegin** and the corresponding call to **glEnd**.

ASSOCIATED GETS

glGet with argument GL_INDEX_WRITEMASK

SEE ALSO

glColorMask, **glDepthMask**, **glDrawBuffer**, **glIndex**, **glStencilMask**

NAME

glInitNames – initialize the name stack

C SPECIFICATION

void **glInitNames**(void *void*)

DESCRIPTION

The name stack is used during selection mode to allow sets of rendering commands to be uniquely identified. It consists of an ordered set of unsigned integers. **glInitNames** causes the name stack to be initialized to its default empty state.

The name stack is always empty while the render mode is not **GL_SELECT**. Calls to **glInitNames** while the render mode is not **GL_SELECT** are ignored.

ERRORS

GL_INVALID_OPERATION is generated if **glInitNames** is called between a call to **glBegin** and the corresponding call to **glEnd**.

ASSOCIATED GETS

glGet with argument GL_NAME_STACK_DEPTH
glGet with argument GL_MAX_NAME_STACK_DEPTH

SEE ALSO

glLoadName, **glPushName**, **glRenderMode**, **glSelectBuffer**

NAME

glIsEnabled – test whether a capability is enabled

C SPECIFICATION

GLboolean **glIsEnabled**(GLenum *cap*)

PARAMETERS

cap Specifies a symbolic constant indicating a GL capability.

DESCRIPTION

glIsEnabled returns **GL_TRUE** if *cap* is an enabled capability and returns **GL_FALSE** otherwise. The following capabilities are accepted for *cap*:

GL_ALPHA_TEST	See **glAlphaFunc**.
GL_AUTO_NORMAL	See **glEvalCoord**.
GL_BLEND	See **glBlendFunc**.
GL_CLIP_PLANE*i*	See **glClipPlane**.
GL_COLOR_MATERIAL	See **glColorMaterial**.
GL_CULL_FACE	See **glCullFace**.
GL_DEPTH_TEST	See **glDepthFunc** and **glDepthRange**.
GL_DITHER	See **glEnable**.
GL_FOG	See **glFog**.
GL_LIGHT*i*	See **glLightModel** and **glLight**.
GL_LIGHTING	See **glMaterial**, **glLightModel**, and **glLight**.
GL_LINE_SMOOTH	See **glLineWidth**.
GL_LINE_STIPPLE	See **glLineStipple**.
GL_LOGIC_OP	See **glLogicOp**.
GL_MAP1_COLOR_4	See **glMap1**.
GL_MAP1_INDEX	See **glMap1**.
GL_MAP1_NORMAL	See **glMap1**.
GL_MAP1_TEXTURE_COORD_1	See **glMap1**.
GL_MAP1_TEXTURE_COORD_2	See **glMap1**.
GL_MAP1_TEXTURE_COORD_3	See **glMap1**.
GL_MAP1_TEXTURE_COORD_4	See **glMap1**.
GL_MAP1_VERTEX_3	See **glMap1**.
GL_MAP1_VERTEX_4	See **glMap1**.
GL_MAP2_COLOR_4	See **glMap2**.
GL_MAP2_INDEX	See **glMap2**.
GL_MAP2_NORMAL	See **glMap2**.
GL_MAP2_TEXTURE_COORD_1	See **glMap2**.
GL_MAP2_TEXTURE_COORD_2	See **glMap2**.

GL_MAP2_TEXTURE_COORD_3	See **glMap2**.
GL_MAP2_TEXTURE_COORD_4	See **glMap2**.
GL_MAP2_VERTEX_3	See **glMap2**.
GL_MAP2_VERTEX_4	See **glMap2**.
GL_NORMALIZE	See **glNormal**.
GL_POINT_SMOOTH	See **glPointSize**.
GL_POLYGON_SMOOTH	See **glPolygonMode**.
GL_POLYGON_STIPPLE	See **glPolygonStipple**.
GL_SCISSOR_TEST	See **glScissor**.
GL_STENCIL_TEST	See **glStencilFunc** and **glStencilOp**.
GL_TEXTURE_1D	See **glTexImage**.
GL_TEXTURE_2D	See **glTexImage**.
GL_TEXTURE_GEN_Q	See **glTexGen**.
GL_TEXTURE_GEN_R	See **glTexGen**.
GL_TEXTURE_GEN_S	See **glTexGen**.
GL_TEXTURE_GEN_T	See **glTexGen**.

NOTES

If an error is generated, **glIsEnabled** returns zero.

ERRORS

GL_INVALID_ENUM is generated if *cap* is not an accepted value.

GL_INVALID_OPERATION is generated if **glIsEnabled** is called between a call to **glBegin** and the corresponding call to **glEnd**.

SEE ALSO

glEnable

NAME

glIsList – test for display-list existence

C SPECIFICATION

GLboolean **glIsList**(GLuint *list*)

PARAMETERS

list Specifies a potential display-list name.

DESCRIPTION

glIsList returns **GL_TRUE** if *list* is the name of a display list and returns **GL_FALSE** otherwise.

ERRORS

GL_INVALID_OPERATION is generated if **glIsList** is called between a call to **glBegin** and the corresponding call to **glEnd**.

SEE ALSO

glCallList, **glCallLists**, **glDeleteLists**, **glGenLists**, **glNewList**

NAME

glLightf, glLighti, glLightfv, glLightiv – set light source parameters

C SPECIFICATION

void **glLightf**(GLenum *light*,
                GLenum *pname*,
                GLfloat *param*)
void **glLighti**(GLenum *light*,
                GLenum *pname*,
                GLint *param*)

PARAMETERS

light　Specifies a light. The number of lights is depends on the implementation, but at least eight lights are supported. They are identified by symbolic names of the form **GL_LIGHT**i where $0 \le i <$ **GL_MAX_LIGHTS**.

pname　Specifies a single-valued light source parameter for *light*. **GL_SPOT_EXPONENT, GL_SPOT_CUTOFF, GL_CONSTANT_ATTENUATION, GL_LINEAR_ATTENUATION** , and **GL_QUADRATIC_ATTENUATION** are accepted.

param　Specifies the value that parameter *pname* of light source *light* will be set to.

C SPECIFICATION

void **glLightfv**(GLenum *light*,
                GLenum *pname*,
                const GLfloat *params*)
void **glLightiv**(GLenum *light*,
                GLenum *pname*,
                const GLint *params*)

PARAMETERS

light　Specifies a light. The number of lights depends on the implementation, but at least eight lights are supported. They are identified by symbolic names of the form **GL_LIGHT**i where $0 \le i <$ **GL_MAX_LIGHTS**.

pname　Specifies a light source parameter for *light*. **GL_AMBIENT, GL_DIFFUSE, GL_SPECULAR, GL_POSITION, GL_SPOT_DIRECTION, GL_SPOT_EXPONENT, GL_SPOT_CUTOFF, GL_CONSTANT_ATTENUATION, GL_LINEAR_ATTENUATION,** and **GL_QUADRATIC_ATTENUATION** are accepted.

params Specifies a pointer to the value or values that parameter *pname* of light source *light* will be set to.

DESCRIPTION

glLight sets the values of individual light source parameters. *light* names the light and is a symbolic name of the form **GL_LIGHT**i, where $0 \le i < $ **GL_MAX_LIGHTS**. *pname* specifies one of ten light source parameters, again by symbolic name. *params* is either a single value or a pointer to an array that contains the new values.

Lighting calculation is enabled and disabled using **glEnable** and **glDisable** with argument **GL_LIGHTING**. When lighting is enabled, light sources that are enabled contribute to the lighting calculation. Light source *i* is enabled and disabled using **glEnable** and **glDisable** with argument **GL_LIGHT**i.

The ten light parameters are as follows:

GL_AMBIENT   *params* contains four integer or floating-point values that specify the ambient RGBA intensity of the light. Integer values are mapped linearly such that the most positive representable value maps to 1.0, and the most negative representable value maps to −1.0. Floating-point values are mapped directly. Neither integer nor floating-point values are clamped. The default ambient light intensity is (0.0, 0.0, 0.0, 1.0).

GL_DIFFUSE   *params* contains four integer or floating-point values that specify the diffuse RGBA intensity of the light. Integer values are mapped linearly such that the most positive representable value maps to 1.0, and the most negative representable value maps to −1.0. Floating-point values are mapped directly. Neither integer nor floating-point values are clamped. The default diffuse light intensity is (0.0, 0.0, 0.0, 1.0).

GL_SPECULAR   *params* contains four integer or floating-point values that specify the specular RGBA intensity of the light. Integer values are mapped linearly such that the most positive representable value maps to 1.0, and the most negative representable value maps to −1.0. Floating-point values are mapped directly. Neither integer nor floating-point values are clamped. The default specular light intensity is (0.0, 0.0, 0.0, 1.0).

GL_POSITION   *params* contains four integer or floating-point values that specify the position of the light in homogeneous object coordinates. Both integer and floating-point values are mapped directly. Neither integer nor floating-point values are clamped.

The position is transformed by the inverse of the modelview matrix when **glLight** is called, and it is stored in eye coordinates. If the *w* component of the position is 0.0, the light is treated as a directional source. Diffuse and specular lighting calculations take the light's direction, but not its actual position, into account, and attenuation is disabled. Otherwise, diffuse and specular lighting calculations are based on the actual location of the light in eye coordinates, and attenuation is enabled. The default position is (0,0,1,0); thus, the default light source is directional, parallel to, and in the direction of the −*z* axis.

GL_SPOT_DIRECTION

params contains three integer or floating-point values that specify the direction of the light in homogeneous object coordinates. Both integer and floating-point values are mapped directly. Neither integer nor floating-point values are clamped.

The spot direction is transformed by the inverse of the modelview matrix when **glLight** is called, and it is stored in eye coordinates. It is significant only when GL_SPOT_CUTOFF is not 180, which it is by default. The default direction is (0,0,−1).

GL_SPOT_EXPONENT

params is a single integer or floating-point value that specifies the intensity distribution of the light. Integer and floating-point values are mapped directly. Only values in the range [0,128] are accepted.

Effective light intensity is attenuated by the cosine of the angle between the direction of the light and the direction from the light to the vertex being lighted, raised to the power of the spot exponent. Thus, higher spot exponents result in a more focused light source, regardless of the spot cutoff angle (see next paragraph). The default spot exponent is 0, resulting in uniform light distribution.

GL_SPOT_CUTOFF *params* is a single integer or floating-point value that specifies the maximum spread angle of a light source. Integer and floating-point values are mapped directly. Only values in the range [0,90], and the special value 180, are accepted. If the angle between the direction of the light and the direction from the light to the vertex being lighted is greater than the spot cutoff angle, the light is completely masked.

Otherwise, its intensity is controlled by the spot exponent and the attenuation factors. The default spot cutoff is 180, resulting in uniform light distribution.

GL_CONSTANT_ATTENUATION

GL_LINEAR_ATTENUATION

GL_QUADRATIC_ATTENUATION

params is a single integer or floating-point value that specifies one of the three light attenuation factors. Integer and floating-point values are mapped directly. Only nonnegative values are accepted. If the light is positional, rather than directional, its intensity is attenuated by the reciprocal of the sum of: the constant factor, the linear factor times the distance between the light and the vertex being lighted, and the quadratic factor times the square of the same distance. The default attenuation factors are (1,0,0), resulting in no attenuation.

NOTES

It is always the case that **GL_LIGHT*i*** = **GL_LIGHT0** + *i*.

ERRORS

GL_INVALID_ENUM is generated if either *light* or *pname* is not an accepted value.

GL_INVALID_VALUE is generated if a spot exponent value is specified outside the range [0,180], or if spot cutoff is specified outside the range [0,90] (except for the special value 180), or if a negative attenuation factor is specified.

GL_INVALID_OPERATION is generated if **glLight** is called between a call to **glBegin** and the corresponding call to **glEnd**.

ASSOCIATED GETS

glGetLight
glIsEnabled with argument **GL_LIGHTING**

SEE ALSO

glColorMaterial, glLightModel, glMaterial

NAME

glLightModelf, glLightModeli, glLightModelfv, glLightModeliv – set the lighting model parameters

C SPECIFICATION

void **glLightModelf**(GLenum *pname*,
                       GLfloat *param*)
void **glLightModeli**(GLenum *pname*,
                       GLint *param*)

PARAMETERS

pname Specifies a single-valued lighting model parameter.
         GL_LIGHT_MODEL_LOCAL_VIEWER and
         GL_LIGHT_MODEL_TWO_SIDE are accepted.

param Specifies the value that *param* will be set to.

C SPECIFICATION

void **glLightModelfv**(GLenum *pname*,
                        const GLfloat **params*)
void **glLightModeliv**(GLenum *pname*,
                        const GLint **params*)

PARAMETERS

pname Specifies a lighting model parameter. **GL_LIGHT_MODEL_AMBIENT**,
         GL_LIGHT_MODEL_LOCAL_VIEWER, and
         GL_LIGHT_MODEL_TWO_SIDE are accepted.

params Specifies a pointer to the value or values that *params* will be set to.

DESCRIPTION

glLightModel sets the lighting model parameter. *pname* names a parameter and *params* gives the new value. There are three lighting model parameters:

GL_LIGHT_MODEL_AMBIENT

   params contains four integer or floating-point values that specify the ambient RGBA intensity of the entire scene. Integer values are mapped linearly such that the most positive representable value maps to 1.0, and the most negative representable value maps to –1.0. Floating-point values are mapped directly. Neither integer nor floating-point values are clamped. The default ambient scene intensity is (0.2, 0.2, 0.2, 1.0).

GL_LIGHT_MODEL_LOCAL_VIEWER

params is a single integer or floating-point value that specifies how specular reflection angles are computed. If *params* is 0 (or 0.0), specular reflections are computed from the origin of the eye coordinate system. Otherwise, reflection angles take the view direction to be parallel to and in the direction of the −z axis, regardless of the location of the vertex in eye coordinates. The default is false.

GL_LIGHT_MODEL_TWO_SIDE

params is a single integer or floating-point value that specifies whether one- or two-sided lighting calculations are done for polygons. It has no effect on the lighting calculations for points, lines, or bitmaps. If *params* is 0 (or 0.0), one-sided lighting is specified, and only the *front* material parameters are used in the lighting equation. Otherwise, two-sided lighting is specified. In this case, vertices of back-facing polygons are lighted using the *back* material parameters, and have their normals reversed before the lighting equation is evaluated. Vertices of front-facing polygons are always lighted using the *front* material parameters, with no change to their normals. The default is false.

In RGBA mode, the lighted color of a vertex is the sum of the material emission intensity, the product of the material ambient reflectance and the lighting model full-scene ambient intensity, and the contribution of each enabled light source. Each light source contributes the sum of three terms: ambient, diffuse, and specular. The ambient light source contribution is the product of the material ambient reflectance and the light's ambient intensity. The diffuse light source contribution is the product of the material diffuse reflectance, the light's diffuse intensity, and the dot product of the vertex's normal with the normalized vector from the vertex to the light source. The specular light source contribution is the product of the material specular reflectance, the light's specular intensity, and the dot product of the normalized vertex-to-eye and vertex-to-light vectors. All three light source contributions are attenuated equally based on the distance from the vertex to the light source and on light source direction, spread exponent, and spread cutoff angle. All dot products are replaced with zero if they evaluate to a negative value.

The alpha component of the resulting lighted color is set to the alpha value of the material diffuse reflectance.

ERRORS

GL_INVALID_ENUM is generated if *pname* is not an accepted value.

GL_INVALID_OPERATION is generated if **glLightModel** is called between a call to **glBegin** and the corresponding call to **glEnd**.

ASSOCIATED GETS

glGet with argument GL_LIGHT_MODEL_AMBIENT
glGet with argument GL_LIGHT_MODEL_LOCAL_VIEWER
glGet with argument GL_LIGHT_MODEL_TWO_SIDE
glIsEnabled with argument GL_LIGHTING

SEE ALSO

glLight, glMaterial

NAME

glLineStipple – specify the line stipple pattern

C SPECIFICATION

void **glLineStipple**(GLint *factor*,
                        GLushort *pattern*)

PARAMETERS

factor Specifies a multiplier for each bit in the line stipple pattern. If *factor* is 3, for example, each bit in the pattern will be used three times before the next bit in the pattern is used. *factor* is clamped to the range [1, 255] and defaults to one.

pattern Specifies a 16-bit integer whose bit pattern determines which fragments of a line will be drawn when the line is rasterized. Bit zero is used first, and the default pattern is all ones.

DESCRIPTION

Line stippling masks out certain fragments produced by rasterization; those fragments will not be drawn. The masking is achieved by using three parameters: the 16-bit line stipple pattern *pattern*, the repeat count *factor*, and an integer stipple counter *s*.

Counter *s* is reset to zero whenever **glBegin** is called, and before each line segment of a **glBegin(GL_LINES)/glEnd** sequence is generated. It is incremented after each fragment of a *width*–1, aliased line segment is generated, or after each *i* fragments of a *width*–*i* line segment are generated. The *i* fragments associated with count *s* are masked out if

$$\text{\textit{pattern} bit (\textit{s factor}) mod 16}$$

is zero, otherwise these fragments are sent to the frame buffer. Bit zero of *pattern* is the least significant bit.

Antialiased lines are treated as a sequence of 1×*width* rectangles for purposes of stippling. Rectangle *s* is rasterized or not based on the fragment rule described for aliased lines, counting rectangles rather than groups of fragments.

Line stippling is enabled or disabled using **glEnable** and **glDisable** with argument **GL_LINE_STIPPLE**. When enabled, the line stipple pattern is applied as described above. When disabled, it is as if the pattern were all ones. Initially, line stippling is disabled.

ERRORS

GL_INVALID_OPERATION is generated if **glLineStipple** is called between a call to **glBegin** and the corresponding call to **glEnd**.

ASSOCIATED GETS

glGet with argument **GL_LINE_STIPPLE_PATTERN**
glGet with argument **GL_LINE_STIPPLE_REPEAT**
glIsEnabled with argument **GL_LINE_STIPPLE**

SEE ALSO

glLineWidth, glPolygonStipple

NAME

glLineWidth – specify the width of rasterized lines

C SPECIFICATION

void **glLineWidth**(GLfloat *width*)

PARAMETERS

width   Specifies the width of rasterized lines. The default is 1.0.

DESCRIPTION

glLineWidth specifies the rasterized width of both aliased and antialiased lines. Using a line width other than 1.0 has different effects, depending on whether line antialiasing is enabled. Line antialiasing is controlled by calling **glEnable** and **glDisable** with argument **GL_LINE_SMOOTH**.

If line antialiasing is disabled, the actual width is determined by rounding the supplied width to the nearest integer. (If the rounding results in the value 0, it is as if the line width were 1.) If $|\Delta x| \geq |\Delta y|$, i pixels are filled in each column that is rasterized, where i is the rounded value of *width*. Otherwise, i pixels are filled in each row that is rasterized.

If antialiasing is enabled, line rasterization produces a fragment for each pixel square that intersects the region lying within the rectangle having width equal to the current line width, length equal to the actual length of the line, and centered on the mathematical line segment. The coverage value for each fragment is the window coordinate area of the intersection of the rectangular region with the corresponding pixel square. This value is saved and used in the final rasterization step.

Not all widths can be supported when line antialiasing is enabled. If an unsupported width is requested, the nearest supported width is used. Only width 1.0 is guaranteed to be supported; others depend on the implementation. The range of supported widths and the size difference between supported widths within the range can be queried by calling **glGet** with arguments **GL_LINE_WIDTH_RANGE** and **GL_LINE_WIDTH_GRANULARITY**.

NOTES

The line width specified by **glLineWidth** is always returned when **GL_LINE_WIDTH** is queried. Clamping and rounding for aliased and antialiased lines have no effect on the specified value.

ERRORS

GL_INVALID_VALUE is generated if *width* is less than or equal to zero.

GL_INVALID_OPERATION is generated if **glLineWidth** is called between a call to **glBegin** and the corresponding call to **glEnd**.

ASSOCIATED GETS

glGet with argument GL_LINE_WIDTH
glGet with argument GL_LINE_WIDTH_RANGE
glGet with argument GL_LINE_WIDTH_GRANULARITY
glIsEnabled with argument GL_LINE_SMOOTH

SEE ALSO

glEnable, **glLineSmooth**

NAME

glListBase – set the display-list base for **glCallLists**

C SPECIFICATION

void **glListBase**(GLuint *base*)

PARAMETERS

base Specifies an integer offset that will be added to **glCallLists** offsets to generate display-list names. Initial value is zero.

DESCRIPTION

glCallLists specifies an array of offsets. Display-list names are generated by adding *base* to each offset. Names that reference valid display lists are executed; the others are ignored.

ERRORS

GL_INVALID_OPERATION is generated if **glListBase** is called between a call to **glBegin** and the corresponding call to **glEnd**.

ASSOCIATED GETS

glGet with argument GL_LIST_BASE

SEE ALSO

glCallLists

NAME

glLoadIdentity – replace the current matrix with the identity matrix

C SPECIFICATION

void **glLoadIdentity**(void *void*)

DESCRIPTION

glLoadIdentity replaces the current matrix with the identity matrix. It is semantically equivalent to calling **glLoadMatrix** with the identity matrix

$$\begin{bmatrix} 1 & 0 & 0 & 0 \\ 0 & 1 & 0 & 0 \\ 0 & 0 & 1 & 0 \\ 0 & 0 & 0 & 1 \end{bmatrix}$$

but in some cases it is more efficient.

ERRORS

GL_INVALID_OPERATION is generated if **glLoadIdentity** is called between a call to **glBegin** and the corresponding call to **glEnd**.

ASSOCIATED GETS

glGet with argument GL_MATRIX_MODE
glGet with argument GL_MODELVIEW_MATRIX
glGet with argument GL_PROJECTION_MATRIX
glGet with argument GL_TEXTURE_MATRIX

SEE ALSO

glLoadMatrix, **glMatrixMode**, **glMultMatrix**, **glPushMatrix**

NAME

glLoadMatrixf, glLoadMatrixd – replace the current matrix with an arbitrary matrix

C SPECIFICATION

void **glLoadMatrixf**(const GLfloat *m)
void **glLoadMatrixd**(const GLdouble *m)

PARAMETERS

m   Specifies a pointer to a 4×4 matrix stored in column-major order as sixteen consecutive values.

DESCRIPTION

glLoadMatrix replaces the current matrix with the one specified in *m*. The current matrix is the projection matrix, modelview matrix, or texture matrix, determined by the current matrix mode (see **glMatrixMode**).

m points to a 4×4 matrix of single- or double-precision floating-point values stored in column-major order. That is, the matrix is stored as follows:

$$\begin{bmatrix} a_0 & a_4 & a_8 & a_{12} \\ a_1 & a_5 & a_9 & a_{13} \\ a_2 & a_6 & a_{10} & a_{14} \\ a_3 & a_7 & a_{11} & a_{15} \end{bmatrix}$$

ERRORS

GL_INVALID_OPERATION is generated if **glLoadMatrix** is called between a call to **glBegin** and the corresponding call to **glEnd**.

ASSOCIATED GETS

glGet with argument GL_MATRIX_MODE
glGet with argument GL_MODELVIEW_MATRIX
glGet with argument GL_PROJECTION_MATRIX
glGet with argument GL_TEXTURE_MATRIX

SEE ALSO

glLoadIdentity, glMatrixMode, glMultMatrix, glPushMatrix

NAME

glLoadName – load a name onto the name stack

C SPECIFICATION

void **glLoadName**(GLuint *name*)

PARAMETERS

name Specifies a name that will replace the top value on the name stack.

DESCRIPTION

The name stack is used during selection mode to allow sets of rendering commands to be uniquely identified. It consists of an ordered set of unsigned integers. **glLoad-Name** causes *name* to replace the value on the top of the name stack, which is initially empty.

The name stack is always empty while the render mode is not **GL_SELECT**. Calls to **glLoadName** while the render mode is not **GL_SELECT** are ignored.

ERRORS

GL_INVALID_OPERATION is generated if **glLoadName** is called while the name stack is empty.

GL_INVALID_OPERATION is generated if **glLoadName** is called between a call to **glBegin** and the corresponding call to **glEnd**.

ASSOCIATED GETS

glGet with argument **GL_NAME_STACK_DEPTH**
glGet with argument **GL_MAX_NAME_STACK_DEPTH**

SEE ALSO

glInitNames, **glPushName**, **glRenderMode**, **glSelectBuffer**

NAME

glLogicOp – specify a logical pixel operation for color index rendering

C SPECIFICATION

void **glLogicOp**(GLenum *opcode*)

PARAMETERS

opcode   Specifies a symbolic constant that selects a logical operation. The following symbols are accepted: **GL_CLEAR, GL_SET, GL_COPY, GL_COPY_INVERTED, GL_NOOP, GL_INVERT, GL_AND, GL_NAND, GL_OR, GL_NOR, GL_XOR, GL_EQUIV, GL_AND_REVERSE, GL_AND_INVERTED, GL_OR_REVERSE,** and **GL_OR_INVERTED.**

DESCRIPTION

glLogicOp specifies a logical operation that, when enabled, is applied between the incoming color index and the color index at the corresponding location in the frame buffer. The logical operation is enabled or disabled with **glEnable** and **glDisable** using the symbolic constant **GL_LOGIC_OP**.

opcode is a symbolic constant chosen from the list below. In the explanation of the logical operations, s represents the incoming color index and d represents the index in the frame buffer. Standard C-language operators are used. As these bitwise operators suggest, the logical operation is applied independently to each bit pair of the source and destination indices.

opcode	resulting value
GL_CLEAR	0
GL_SET	1
GL_COPY	s
GL_COPY_INVERTED	!s
GL_NOOP	d
GL_INVERT	!d
GL_AND	s & d
GL_NAND	!(s & d)
GL_OR	s | d
GL_NOR	!(s | d)
GL_XOR	s ^ d
GL_EQUIV	!(s ^ d)
GL_AND_REVERSE	s & !d
GL_AND_INVERTED	!s & d
GL_OR_REVERSE	s | !d
GL_OR_INVERTED	!s | d

NOTES

Logical pixel operations are not applied to RGBA color buffers.

When more than one color index buffer is enabled for drawing, logical operations are done separately for each enabled buffer, using for the destination index the contents of that buffer (see **glDrawBuffer**).

opcode must be one of the sixteen accepted values. Other values result in an error.

ERRORS

GL_INVALID_ENUM is generated if *opcode* is not an accepted value.

GL_INVALID_OPERATION is generated if **glLogicOp** is called between a call to **glBegin** and the corresponding call to **glEnd**.

ASSOCIATED GETS

glGet with argument GL_LOGIC_OP_MODE
glIsEnabled with argument GL_LOGIC_OP

SEE ALSO

glAlphaFunc, glBlendFunc, glDrawBuffer, glEnable, glStencilOp

NAME

glMap1d, glMap1f – define a one-dimensional evaluator

C SPECIFICATION

```
void glMap1d( GLenum target,
              GLdouble u1,
              GLdouble u2,
              GLint stride,
              GLint order,
              const GLdouble *points )
void glMap1f( GLenum target,
              GLfloat u1,
              GLfloat u2,
              GLint stride,
              GLint order,
              const GLfloat *points )
```

PARAMETERS

target Specifies the kind of values that are generated by the evaluator. Symbolic constants **GL_MAP1_VERTEX_3**, **GL_MAP1_VERTEX_4**, **GL_MAP1_INDEX**, **GL_MAP1_COLOR_4**, **GL_MAP1_NORMAL**, **GL_MAP1_TEXTURE_COORD_1**, **GL_MAP1_TEXTURE_COORD_2**, **GL_MAP1_TEXTURE_COORD_3**, and **GL_MAP1_TEXTURE_COORD_4** are accepted.

u1, u2

Specify a linear mapping of u, as presented to **glEvalCoord1**, to $\hat{u}$, the variable that is evaluated by the equations specified by this command.

stride Specifies the number of floats or doubles between the beginning of one control point and the beginning of the next one in the data structure referenced in *points*. This allows control points to be embedded in arbitrary data structures. The only constraint is that the values for a particular control point must occupy contiguous memory locations.

order Specifies the number of control points. Must be positive.

points Specifies a pointer to the array of control points.

DESCRIPTION

Evaluators provide a way to use polynomial or rational polynomial mapping to produce vertices, normals, texture coordinates, and colors. The values produced by an evaluator are sent to further stages of GL processing just as if they had been presented using **glVertex**, **glNormal**, **glTexCoord**, and **glColor** commands, except that the generated values do not update the current normal, texture coordinates, or color.

All polynomial or rational polynomial splines of any degree (up to the maximum degree supported by the GL implementation) can be described using evaluators. These include almost all splines used in computer graphics, including B-splines, Bezier curves, Hermite splines, and so on.

Evaluators define curves based on Bernstein polynomials. Define $\mathbf{p}(\hat{u})$ as

$$\mathbf{p}(\hat{u}) = \sum_{i=0}^{n} B_i^n(\hat{u}) \mathbf{R}_i$$

where $\mathbf{R}_i$ is a control point and $B_i^n(\hat{u})$ is the ith Bernstein polynomial of degree n ($order = n+1$):

$$B_i^n(\hat{u}) = \binom{n}{i} \hat{u}^i (1-\hat{u})^{n-i}$$

Recall that

$$0^0 \equiv 1 \text{ and } \binom{n}{0} \equiv 1$$

glMap1 is used to define the basis and to specify what kind of values are produced. Once defined, a map can be enabled and disabled by calling glEnable and glDisable with the map name, one of the nine predefined values for *target* described below. glEvalCoord1 evaluates the one-dimensional maps that are enabled. When glEvalCoord1 presents a value u, the Bernstein functions are evaluated using $\hat{u}$, where

$$\hat{u} = \frac{u - u1}{u2 - u1}$$

target is a symbolic constant that indicates what kind of control points are provided in *points*, and what output is generated when the map is evaluated. It can assume one of nine predefined values:

GL_MAP1_VERTEX_3   Each control point is three floating-point values representing x, y, and z. Internal **glVertex3** commands are generated when the map is evaluated.

GL_MAP1_VERTEX_4   Each control point is four floating-point values representing x, y, z, and w. Internal **glVertex4** commands are generated when the map is evaluated.

GL_MAP1_INDEX   Each control point is a single floating-point value representing a color index. Internal **glIndex** commands are generated when the map is evaluated. The current index is not updated with the value of these **glIndex** commands, however.

GL_MAP1_COLOR_4   Each control point is four floating-point values representing red, green, blue, and alpha. Internal **glColor4** commands are generated when the map is evaluated. The current color is not updated with the value of these **glColor4** commands, however.

GL_MAP1_NORMAL   Each control point is three floating-point values representing the x, y, and z components of a normal vector. Internal **glNormal** commands are generated when the map is evaluated. The current normal is not updated with the value of these **glNormal** commands, however.

GL_MAP1_TEXTURE_COORD_1

Each control point is a single floating-point value representing the s texture coordinate. Internal **glTexCoord1** commands are generated when the map is evaluated. The current texture coordinates are not updated with the value of these **glTexCoord** commands, however.

GL_MAP1_TEXTURE_COORD_2

Each control point is two floating-point values representing the s and t texture coordinates. Internal **glTexCoord2** commands are generated when the map is evaluated. The current texture coordinates are not updated with the value of these **glTexCoord** commands, however.

GL_MAP1_TEXTURE_COORD_3

Each control point is three floating-point values representing the s, t, and r texture coordinates. Internal **glTexCoord3** commands are generated when the map is evaluated. The current texture coordinates are not updated with the value of these **glTexCoord** commands, however.

GL_MAP1_TEXTURE_COORD_4

Each control point is four floating-point values representing the s, t, r, and q texture coordinates. Internal **glTexCoord4** commands are generated when the map is evaluated. The current texture coordinates are not updated with the value of these **glTexCoord** commands, however.

stride, *order*, and *points* define the array addressing for accessing the control points. *points* is the location of the first control point, which occupies one, two, three, or four contiguous memory locations, depending on which map is being defined. *order* is the number of control points in the array. *stride* tells how many float or double locations to advance the internal memory pointer to reach the next control point.

NOTES

As is the case with all GL commands that accept pointers to data, it is as if the contents of *points* were copied by **glMap1** before it returned. Changes to the contents of *points* have no effect after **glMap1** is called.

ERRORS

GL_INVALID_ENUM is generated if *target* is not an accepted value.

GL_INVALID_VALUE is generated if *u1* is equal to *u2*.

GL_INVALID_VALUE is generated if *stride* is less than the number of values in a control point.

GL_INVALID_VALUE is generated if *order* is less than one or greater than GL_MAX_EVAL_ORDER.

GL_INVALID_OPERATION is generated if **glMap1** is called between a call to **glBegin** and the corresponding call to **glEnd**.

ASSOCIATED GETS

glGetMap
glGet with argument GL_MAX_EVAL_ORDER
glIsEnabled with argument GL_MAP1_VERTEX_3
glIsEnabled with argument GL_MAP1_VERTEX_4
glIsEnabled with argument GL_MAP1_INDEX
glIsEnabled with argument GL_MAP1_COLOR_4
glIsEnabled with argument GL_MAP1_NORMAL
glIsEnabled with argument GL_MAP1_TEXTURE_COORD_1
glIsEnabled with argument GL_MAP1_TEXTURE_COORD_2
glIsEnabled with argument GL_MAP1_TEXTURE_COORD_3
glIsEnabled with argument GL_MAP1_TEXTURE_COORD_4

SEE ALSO

glBegin, glColor, glEnable, glEvalCoord, glEvalMesh, glEvalPoint, glMap2, glMapGrid, glNormal, glTexCoord, glVertex

NAME

glMap2d, **glMap2f** – define a two-dimensional evaluator

C SPECIFICATION

```
void glMap2d( GLenum target,
              GLdouble u1,
              GLdouble u2,
              GLint ustride,
              GLint uorder,
              GLdouble v1,
              GLdouble v2,
              GLint vstride,
              GLint vorder,
              const GLdouble *points )
void glMap2f( GLenum target,
              GLfloat u1,
              GLfloat u2,
              GLint ustride,
              GLint uorder,
              GLfloat v1,
              GLfloat v2,
              GLint vstride,
              GLint vorder,
              const GLfloat *points )
```

PARAMETERS

target Specifies the kind of values that are generated by the evaluator. Symbolic constants GL_MAP2_VERTEX_3, GL_MAP2_VERTEX_4, GL_MAP2_INDEX, GL_MAP2_COLOR_4, GL_MAP2_NORMAL, GL_MAP2_TEXTURE_COORD_1, GL_MAP2_TEXTURE_COORD_2, GL_MAP2_TEXTURE_COORD_3, and GL_MAP2_TEXTURE_COORD_4 are accepted.

u1, u2 Specify a linear mapping of u, as presented to **glEvalCoord2**, to $\hat{u}$, one of the two variables that is evaluated by the equations specified by this command.

ustride Specifies the number of floats or doubles between the beginning of control point $\mathbf{R}_{ij}$ and the beginning of control point $\mathbf{R}_{(i+1)j}$, where i and j are the u and v control point indices, respectively. This allows control points to be embedded in arbitrary data structures. The only constraint is that the values for a particular control point must occupy contiguous memory locations.

uorder Specifies the dimension of the control point array in the *u* axis. Must be positive.

v1, v2 Specify a linear mapping of *v*, as presented to **glEvalCoord2**, to $\hat{v}$, one of the two variables that is evaluated by the equations specified by this command.

vstride Specifies the number of floats or doubles between the beginning of control point R_{ij} and the beginning of control point $R_{i(j+1)}$, where *i* and *j* are the *u* and *v* control point indices, respectively. This allows control points to be embedded in arbitrary data structures. The only constraint is that the values for a particular control point must occupy contiguous memory locations.

vorder Specifies the dimension of the control point array in the *v* axis. Must be positive.

points Specifies a pointer to the array of control points.

DESCRIPTION

Evaluators provide a way to use polynomial or rational polynomial mapping to produce vertices, normals, texture coordinates, and colors. The values produced by an evaluator are sent on to further stages of GL processing just as if they had been presented using **glVertex**, **glNormal**, **glTexCoord**, and **glColor** commands, except that the generated values do not update the current normal, texture coordinates, or color.

All polynomial or rational polynomial splines of any degree (up to the maximum degree supported by the GL implementation) can be described using evaluators. These include almost all surfaces used in computer graphics, including B-spline surfaces, NURBS surfaces, Bezier surfaces, and so on.

Evaluators define surfaces based on bivariate Bernstein polynomials. Define $\mathbf{p}(\hat{u},\hat{v})$ as

$$\mathbf{p}(\hat{u},\hat{v}) = \sum_{i=0}^{n}\sum_{j=0}^{m} B_i^n(\hat{u})B_j^m(\hat{v})\mathbf{R}_{ij}$$

where $\mathbf{R}_{ij}$ is a control point, $B_i^n(\hat{u})$ is the *i*th Bernstein polynomial of degree *n* (*uorder* = *n*+1)

$$B_i^n(\hat{u}) = \begin{bmatrix} n \\ i \end{bmatrix} \hat{u}^i(1-\hat{u})^{n-i}$$

and $B_j^m(\hat{v})$ is the jth Bernstein polynomial of degree m (*vorder* = $m+1$)

$$B_j^m(\hat{v}) = \begin{bmatrix} m \\ j \end{bmatrix} \hat{v}^j (1-\hat{v})^{m-j}$$

Recall that

$$0^0 \equiv 1 \text{ and } \begin{bmatrix} n \\ 0 \end{bmatrix} \equiv 1$$

glMap2 is used to define the basis and to specify what kind of values are produced. Once defined, a map can be enabled and disabled by calling **glEnable** and **glDisable** with the map name, one of the nine predefined values for *target*, described below. When **glEvalCoord2** presents values u and v, the bivariate Bernstein polynomials are evaluated using $\hat{u}$ and $\hat{v}$, where

$$\hat{u} = \frac{u - u1}{u2 - u1}$$

$$\hat{v} = \frac{v - v1}{v2 - v1}$$

target is a symbolic constant that indicates what kind of control points are provided in *points*, and what output is generated when the map is evaluated. It can assume one of nine predefined values:

GL_MAP2_VERTEX_3   Each control point is three floating-point values representing x, y, and z. Internal **glVertex3** commands are generated when the map is evaluated.

GL_MAP2_VERTEX_4   Each control point is four floating-point values representing x, y, z, and w. Internal **glVertex4** commands are generated when the map is evaluated.

GL_MAP2_INDEX   Each control point is a single floating-point value representing a color index. Internal **glIndex** commands are generated when the map is evaluated. The current index is not updated with the value of these **glIndex** commands, however.

GL_MAP2_COLOR_4   Each control point is four floating-point values representing red, green, blue, and alpha. Internal **glColor4** commands are generated when the map is evaluated. The current color is not updated with the value of these **glColor4** commands, however.

GL_MAP2_NORMAL   Each control point is three floating-point values representing the x, y, and z components of a normal vector. Internal **glNormal** commands are generated when the map is evaluated. The current normal is not updated with the value of these **glNormal** commands, however.

GL_MAP2_TEXTURE_COORD_1

Each control point is a single floating-point value representing the s texture coordinate. Internal **glTexCoord1** commands are generated when the map is evaluated. The current texture coordinates are not updated with the value of these **glTexCoord** commands, however.

GL_MAP2_TEXTURE_COORD_2

Each control point is two floating-point values representing the s and t texture coordinates. Internal **glTexCoord2** commands are generated when the map is evaluated. The current texture coordinates are not updated with the value of these **glTexCoord** commands, however.

GL_MAP2_TEXTURE_COORD_3

Each control point is three floating-point values representing the s, t, and r texture coordinates. Internal **glTexCoord3** commands are generated when the map is evaluated. The current texture coordinates are not updated with the value of these **glTexCoord** commands, however.

GL_MAP2_TEXTURE_COORD_4

Each control point is four floating-point values representing the s, t, r, and q texture coordinates. Internal **glTexCoord4** commands are generated when the map is evaluated. The current texture coordinates are not updated with the value of these **glTexCoord** commands, however.

ustride, *uorder*, *vstride*, *vorder*, and *points* define the array addressing for accessing the control points. *v1* is the location of the first control point, which occupies one, two, three, or four contiguous memory locations, depending on which map is being defined. There are *uorder×vorder* control points in the array. *ustride* tells how many float or double locations are skipped to advance the internal memory pointer from control point R_{ij} to control point $R_{(i+1)j}$. *vstride* tells how many float or double locations are skipped to advance the internal memory pointer from control point R_{ij} to control point $R_{i(j+1)}$.

NOTES

As is the case with all GL commands that accept pointers to data, it is as if the contents of *points* were copied by **glMap2** before it returned. Changes to the contents of *points* have no effect after **glMap2** is called.

ERRORS

GL_INVALID_ENUM is generated if *target* is not an accepted value.

GL_INVALID_VALUE is generated if *u1* is equal to *u2*, or if *v1* is equal to *v2*.

GL_INVALID_VALUE is generated if either *ustride* or *vstride* is less than the number of values in a control point.

GL_INVALID_VALUE is generated if either *uorder* or *vorder* is less than one or greater than GL_MAX_EVAL_ORDER.

GL_INVALID_OPERATION is generated if **glMap2** is called between a call to **glBegin** and the corresponding call to **glEnd**.

ASSOCIATED GETS

glGetMap
glGet with argument GL_MAX_EVAL_ORDER
glIsEnabled with argument GL_MAP2_VERTEX_3
glIsEnabled with argument GL_MAP2_VERTEX_4
glIsEnabled with argument GL_MAP2_INDEX
glIsEnabled with argument GL_MAP2_COLOR_4
glIsEnabled with argument GL_MAP2_NORMAL
glIsEnabled with argument GL_MAP2_TEXTURE_COORD_1
glIsEnabled with argument GL_MAP2_TEXTURE_COORD_2
glIsEnabled with argument GL_MAP2_TEXTURE_COORD_3
glIsEnabled with argument GL_MAP2_TEXTURE_COORD_4

SEE ALSO

glBegin, glColor, glEnable, glEvalCoord, glEvalMesh, glEvalPoint, glMap1, glMapGrid, glNormal, glTexCoord, glVertex

NAME

glMapGrid1d, glMapGrid1f, glMapGrid2d, glMapGrid2f – define a one- or two-dimensional mesh

C SPECIFICATION

```
void glMapGrid1d( GLint un,
                  GLdouble u1,
                  GLdouble u2 )
void glMapGrid1f( GLint un,
                  GLfloat u1,
                  GLfloat u2 )
void glMapGrid2d( GLint un,
                  GLdouble u1,
                  GLdouble u2,
                  GLint vn,
                  GLdouble v1,
                  GLdouble v2 )
void glMapGrid2f( GLint un,
                  GLfloat u1,
                  GLfloat u2,
                  GLint vn,
                  GLfloat v1,
                  GLfloat v2 )
```

PARAMETERS

un Specifies the number of partitions in the grid range interval [*u1, u2*]. Must be positive.

u1, u2
Specify the mappings for integer grid domain values $i=0$ and $i=un$.

vn Specifies the number of partitions in the grid range interval [*v1, v2*] (**glMap-Grid2** only).

v1, v2
Specify the mappings for integer grid domain values $j=0$ and $j=vn$ (**glMapGrid2** only).

DESCRIPTION

glMapGrid and **glEvalMesh** are used in tandem to efficiently generate and evaluate a series of evenly spaced map domain values. **glEvalMesh** steps through the integer domain of a one- or two-dimensional grid, whose range is the domain of the evaluation maps specified by **glMap1** and **glMap2**.

glMapGrid1 and **glMapGrid2** specify the linear grid mappings between the i (or i and j) integer grid coordinates, to the u (or u and v) floating-point evaluation map coordinates. See **glMap1** and **glMap2** for details of how u and v coordinates are evaluated.

glMapGrid1 specifies a single linear mapping such that integer grid coordinate 0 maps exactly to $u1$, and integer grid coordinate un maps exactly to $u2$. All other integer grid coordinates i are mapped such that

$$u = i(u2-u1)/un + u1$$

glMapGrid2 specifies two such linear mappings. One maps integer grid coordinate $i=0$ exactly to $u1$, and integer grid coordinate $i=un$ exactly to $u2$. The other maps integer grid coordinate $j=0$ exactly to $v1$, and integer grid coordinate $j=vn$ exactly to $v2$. Other integer grid coordinates i and j are mapped such that

$$u = i(u2-u1)/un + u1$$

$$v = j(v2-v1)/vn + v1$$

The mappings specified by **glMapGrid** are used identically by **glEvalMesh** and **glEvalPoint**.

ERRORS

GL_INVALID_VALUE is generated if either un or vn is not positive.

GL_INVALID_OPERATION is generated if **glMapGrid** is called between a call to **glBegin** and the corresponding call to **glEnd**.

ASSOCIATED GETS

glGet with argument GL_MAP1_GRID_DOMAIN
glGet with argument GL_MAP2_GRID_DOMAIN
glGet with argument GL_MAP1_GRID_SEGMENTS
glGet with argument GL_MAP2_GRID_SEGMENTS

SEE ALSO

glEvalCoord, glEvalMesh, glEvalPoint, glMap1, glMap2

NAME

glMaterialf, glMateriali, glMaterialfv, glMaterialiv – specify material parameters for the lighting model

C SPECIFICATION

```
void glMaterialf( GLenum face,
                  GLenum pname,
                  GLfloat param )
void glMateriali( GLenum face,
                  GLenum pname,
                  GLint param )
```

PARAMETERS

face   Specifies which face or faces are being updated. Must be one of **GL_FRONT**, **GL_BACK**, or **GL_FRONT_AND_BACK**.

pname   Specifies the single-valued material parameter of the face or faces that is being updated. Must be **GL_SHININESS**.

param   Specifies the value that parameter **GL_SHININESS** will be set to.

C SPECIFICATION

```
void glMaterialfv( GLenum face,
                   GLenum pname,
                   const GLfloat *params )
void glMaterialiv( GLenum face,
                   GLenum pname,
                   const GLint *params )
```

PARAMETERS

face   Specifies which face or faces are being updated. Must be one of **GL_FRONT**, **GL_BACK**, or **GL_FRONT_AND_BACK**.

pname   Specifies the material parameter of the face or faces that is being updated. Must be one of **GL_AMBIENT**, **GL_DIFFUSE**, **GL_SPECULAR**, **GL_EMISSION**, **GL_SHININESS**, **GL_AMBIENT_AND_DIFFUSE**, or **GL_COLOR_INDEXES**.

params   Specifies a pointer to the value or values that *pname* will be set to.

DESCRIPTION

glMaterial assigns values to material parameters. There are two matched sets of material parameters. One, the *front-facing* set, is used to shade points, lines, bitmaps, and all polygons (when two-sided lighting is disabled), or just front-facing polygons (when two-sided lighting is enabled). The other set, *back-facing*, is used to shade back-facing polygons only when two-sided lighting is enabled. Refer to the **glLightModel** reference page for details concerning one- and two-sided lighting calculations.

glMaterial takes three arguments. The first, *face*, specifies whether the **GL_FRONT** materials, the **GL_BACK** materials, or both **GL_FRONT_AND_BACK** materials will be modified. The second, *pname*, specifies which of several parameters in one or both sets will be modified. The third, *params*, specifies what value or values will be assigned to the specified parameter.

Material parameters are used in the lighting equation that is optionally applied to each vertex. The equation is discussed in the **glLightModel** reference page. The parameters that can be specified using **glMaterial**, and their interpretations by the lighting equation, are as follows:

GL_AMBIENT *params* contains four integer or floating-point values that specify the ambient RGBA reflectance of the material. Integer values are mapped linearly such that the most positive representable value maps to 1.0, and the most negative representable value maps to −1.0. Floating-point values are mapped directly. Neither integer nor floating-point values are clamped. The default ambient reflectance for both front- and back-facing materials is (0.2, 0.2, 0.2, 1.0).

GL_DIFFUSE *params* contains four integer or floating-point values that specify the diffuse RGBA reflectance of the material. Integer values are mapped linearly such that the most positive representable value maps to 1.0, and the most negative representable value maps to −1.0. Floating-point values are mapped directly. Neither integer nor floating-point values are clamped. The default diffuse reflectance for both front- and back-facing materials is (0.8, 0.8, 0.8, 1.0).

GL_SPECULAR *params* contains four integer or floating-point values that specify the specular RGBA reflectance of the material. Integer values are mapped linearly such that the most positive representable value maps to 1.0, and the most negative representable value maps to −1.0. Floating-point values are mapped directly. Neither integer nor floating-point values are clamped. The default specular reflectance for both front- and back-facing materials is (0.0, 0.0, 0.0, 1.0).

GL_EMISSION *params* contains four integer or floating-point values that specify the RGBA emitted light intensity of the material. Integer values are mapped linearly such that the most positive representable value maps to 1.0, and the most negative representable value maps to –1.0. Floating-point values are mapped directly. Neither integer nor floating-point values are clamped. The default emission intensity for both front- and back-facing materials is (0.0, 0.0, 0.0, 1.0).

GL_SHININESS   *params* is a single integer or floating-point value that specifies the RGBA specular exponent of the material. Integer and floating-point values are mapped directly. Only values in the range [0,128] are accepted. The default specular exponent for both front- and back-facing materials is 0.

GL_AMBIENT_AND_DIFFUSE
Equivalent to calling **glMaterial** twice with the same parameter values, once with **GL_AMBIENT** and once with **GL_DIFFUSE**.

GL_COLOR_INDEXES
params contains three integer or floating-point values specifying the color indices for ambient, diffuse, and specular lighting. These values are the only material values used by the color index mode lighting equation. (Likewise, all other material parameters are used only by the RGBA-mode lighting equation.) Refer to the **glLightModel** reference page for a discussion of color index lighting.

NOTES

The material parameters can be updated at any time. In particular, **glMaterial** can be called between a call to **glBegin** and the corresponding call to **glEnd**. If only a single material parameter is to be changed per vertex, however, **glColorMaterial** is preferred over **glMaterial** (see **glColorMaterial**).

ERRORS

GL_INVALID_ENUM is generated if either *face* or *pname* is not an accepted value.

GL_INVALID_VALUE is generated if a specular exponent outside the range [0,128] is specified.

ASSOCIATED GETS
glGetMaterial

SEE ALSO
glColorMaterial, glLight, glLightModel

NAME

glMatrixMode – specify which matrix is the current matrix

C SPECIFICATION

void **glMatrixMode**(GLenum *mode*)

PARAMETERS

mode Specifies which matrix stack is the target for subsequent matrix operations. Three values are accepted: **GL_MODELVIEW**, **GL_PROJECTION**, and **GL_TEXTURE**.

DESCRIPTION

glMatrixMode sets the current matrix mode. *mode* can assume one of three values:

GL_MODELVIEW Applies subsequent matrix operations to the modelview matrix stack.

GL_PROJECTION Applies subsequent matrix operations to the projection matrix stack.

GL_TEXTURE Applies subsequent matrix operations to the texture matrix stack.

ERRORS

GL_INVALID_ENUM is generated if *mode* is not an accepted value.

GL_INVALID_OPERATION is generated if **glMatrixMode** is called between a call to **glBegin** and the corresponding call to **glEnd**.

ASSOCIATED GETS

glGet with argument **GL_MATRIX_MODE**

SEE ALSO

glLoadMatrix, **glMatrixMode**, **glPushMatrix**

NAME

glMultMatrixf, glMultMatrixd – multiply the current matrix by an arbitrary matrix

C SPECIFICATION

void **glMultMatrixf**(const GLfloat *m)
void **glMultMatrixd**(const GLdouble *m)

PARAMETERS

m   Specifies a pointer a to 4×4 matrix stored in column-major order as sixteen consecutive values.

DESCRIPTION

glMultMatrix multiplies the current matrix with the one specified in m. That is, if M is the current matrix and T is the matrix passed to **glMultMatrix**, then M is replaced with M • T.

The current matrix is the projection matrix, modelview matrix, or texture matrix, determined by the current matrix mode (see **glMatrixMode**).

m points to a 4×4 matrix of single- or double-precision floating-point values stored in column-major order. That is, the matrix is stored as

$$\begin{bmatrix} a_0 & a_4 & a_8 & a_{12} \\ a_1 & a_5 & a_9 & a_{13} \\ a_2 & a_6 & a_{10} & a_{14} \\ a_3 & a_7 & a_{11} & a_{15} \end{bmatrix}$$

ERRORS

GL_INVALID_OPERATION is generated if **glMultMatrix** is called between a call to **glBegin** and the corresponding call to **glEnd**.

ASSOCIATED GETS

glGet with argument GL_MATRIX_MODE
glGet with argument GL_MODELVIEW_MATRIX
glGet with argument GL_PROJECTION_MATRIX
glGet with argument GL_TEXTURE_MATRIX

SEE ALSO

glMatrixMode, glLoadIdentity, glLoadMatrix, glPushMatrix

NAME

    glNewList, **glEndList** – create or replace a display list

C SPECIFICATION

    void **glNewList**(GLuint *list*,
                   GLenum *mode*)

PARAMETERS

    list Specifies the display list name.

    mode

        Specifies the compilation mode, which can be **GL_COMPILE** or
        GL_COMPILE_AND_EXECUTE.

C SPECIFICATION

    void **glEndList**(void *void*)

DESCRIPTION

    Display lists are groups of GL commands that have been stored for subsequent exe-
cution. The display lists are created with **glNewList**. All subsequent commands are
placed in the display list, in the order issued, until **glEndList** is called.

    glNewList has two arguments. The first argument, *list*, is a positive integer that
becomes the unique name for the display list. Names can be created and reserved
with **glGenLists** and tested for uniqueness with **glIsList**. The second argument,
mode, is a symbolic constant that can assume one of two values:

GL_COMPILE   Commands are merely compiled.

GL_COMPILE_AND_EXECUTE

        Commands are executed as they are compiled into the display
        list.

    Certain commands are not compiled into the display list, but are executed immedi-
ately, regardless of the display-list mode. These commands are **glIsList**, **glGenLists**,
glDeleteLists, **glFeedbackBuffer**, **glSelectBuffer**, **glRenderMode**, **glReadPixels**,
glPixelStore, **glFlush**, **glFinish**, **glIsEnabled**, and all of the **glGet** routines.

    When **glEndList** is encountered, the display-list definition is completed by associat-
ing the list with the unique name *list* (specified in the **glNewList** command). If a
display list with name *list* already exists, it is replaced only when **glEndList** is called.

NOTES

    glCallList and **glCallLists** can be entered into display lists. The commands in the
display list or lists executed by **glCallList** or **glCallLists** are not included in the
display list being created, even if the list creation mode is
GL_COMPILE_AND_EXECUTE.

ERRORS

GL_INVALID_VALUE is generated if *list* is zero.

GL_INVALID_ENUM is generated if *mode* is not an accepted value.

GL_INVALID_OPERATION is generated if **glEndList** is called without a preceding **glNewList**, or if **glNewList** is called while a display list is being defined.

GL_INVALID_OPERATION is generated if **glNewList** is called between a call to **glBegin** and the corresponding call to **glEnd**.

ASSOCIATED GETS

glIsList

SEE ALSO

glCallList, glCallLists, glDeleteLists, glGenLists

NAME

glNormal3b, glNormal3d, glNormal3f, glNormal3i, glNormal3s, glNormal3bv, glNormal3dv, glNormal3fv, glNormal3iv, glNormal3sv
– set the current normal vector

C SPECIFICATION

void **glNormal3b**(GLbyte *nx*,
                    GLbyte *ny*,
                    GLbyte *nz*)
void **glNormal3d**(GLdouble *nx*,
                    GLdouble *ny*,
                    GLdouble *nz*)
void **glNormal3f**(GLfloat *nx*,
                    GLfloat *ny*,
                    GLfloat *nz*)
void **glNormal3i**(GLint *nx*,
                    GLint *ny*,
                    GLint *nz*)
void **glNormal3s**(GLshort *nx*,
                    GLshort *ny*,
                    GLshort *nz*)

PARAMETERS

nx, *ny*, *nz*
         Specify the *x*, *y*, and *z* coordinates of the new current normal. The initial
         value of the current normal is (0,0,1).

C SPECIFICATION

void **glNormal3bv**(const GLbyte **v*)
void **glNormal3dv**(const GLdouble **v*)
void **glNormal3fv**(const GLfloat **v*)
void **glNormal3iv**(const GLint **v*)
void **glNormal3sv**(const GLshort **v*)

PARAMETERS

v   Specifies a pointer to an array of three elements: the *x*, *y*, and *z* coordinates
         of the new current normal.

DESCRIPTION

The current normal is set to the given coordinates whenever **glNormal** is issued. Byte, short, or integer arguments are converted to floating-point format with a linear mapping that maps the most positive representable integer value to 1.0, and the most negative representable integer value to –1.0.

Normals specified with **glNormal** need not have unit length. If normalization is enabled, then normals specified with **glNormal** are normalized after transformation. Normalization is controlled using **glEnable** and **glDisable** with the argument **GL_NORMALIZE**. By default, normalization is disabled.

NOTES

The current normal can be updated at any time. In particular, **glNormal** can be called between a call to **glBegin** and the corresponding call to **glEnd**.

ASSOCIATED GETS

glGet with argument **GL_CURRENT_NORMAL**
glIsEnable with argument **GL_NORMALIZE**

SEE ALSO

glBegin, **glColor**, **glIndex**, **glTexCoord**, **glVertex**

NAME

glOrtho – multiply the current matrix by an orthographic matrix

C SPECIFICATION

void **glOrtho**(GLdouble *left,*
                 GLdouble *right,*
                 GLdouble *bottom,*
                 GLdouble *top,*
                 GLdouble *near,*
                 GLdouble *far*)

PARAMETERS

left, right

Specify the coordinates for the left and right vertical clipping planes.

bottom, top

Specify the coordinates for the bottom and top horizontal clipping planes.

near, far Specify the distances to the nearer and farther depth clipping planes.
These distances are negative if the plane is to be behind the viewer.

DESCRIPTION

glOrtho describes a perspective matrix that produces a parallel projection. (*left, bottom, −near*) and (*right, top, −near*) specify the points on the near clipping plane that are mapped to the lower left and upper right corners of the window, respectively, assuming that the eye is located at (0, 0, 0). *−far* specifies the location of the far clipping plane. Both *near* and *far* can be either positive or negative. The corresponding matrix is

$$\begin{bmatrix} \dfrac{2}{right-left} & 0 & 0 & t_x \\ 0 & \dfrac{2}{top-bottom} & 0 & t_y \\ 0 & 0 & \dfrac{-2}{far-near} & t_z \\ 0 & 0 & 0 & 1 \end{bmatrix}$$

where

$$t_x = -\frac{right+left}{right-left}$$

$$t_y = -\frac{top+bottom}{top-bottom}$$

$$t_z = -\frac{far+near}{far-near}$$

The current matrix is multiplied by this matrix with the result replacing the current matrix. That is, if M is the current matrix and O is the ortho matrix, then M is replaced with M ● O.

Use **glPushMatrix** and **glPopMatrix** to save and restore the current matrix stack.

ERRORS

GL_INVALID_OPERATION is generated if **glOrtho** is called between a call to **glBegin** and the corresponding call to **glEnd**.

ASSOCIATED GETS

glGet with argument GL_MATRIX_MODE
glGet with argument GL_MODELVIEW_MATRIX
glGet with argument GL_PROJECTION_MATRIX
glGet with argument GL_TEXTURE_MATRIX

SEE ALSO

glFrustum, glMatrixMode, glMultMatrix, glPushMatrix, glViewport

NAME

glPassThrough – place a marker in the feedback buffer

C SPECIFICATION

void **glPassThrough**(GLfloat *token*)

PARAMETERS

token Specifies a marker value to be placed in the feedback buffer following a **GL_PASS_THROUGH_TOKEN**.

DESCRIPTION

Feedback is a GL render mode. The mode is selected by calling **glRenderMode** with **GL_FEEDBACK**. When the GL is in feedback mode, no pixels are produced by rasterization. Instead, information about primitives that would have been rasterized is fed back to the application using the GL. See **glFeedbackBuffer** for a description of the feedback buffer and the values in it.

glPassThrough inserts a user-defined marker in the feedback buffer when it is executed in feedback mode. *token* is returned as if it were a primitive; it is indicated with its own unique identifying value: **GL_PASS_THROUGH_TOKEN**. The order of **glPassThrough** commands with respect to the specification of graphics primitives is maintained.

NOTES

glPassThrough is ignored if the GL is not in feedback mode.

ERRORS

GL_INVALID_OPERATION is generated if **glPassThrough** is called between a call to **glBegin** and the corresponding call to **glEnd**.

ASSOCIATED GETS

glGet with argument **GL_RENDER_MODE**

SEE ALSO

glFeedbackBuffer, **glRenderMode**

NAME

glPixelMapfv, glPixelMapuiv, glPixelMapusv – set up pixel transfer maps

C SPECIFICATION

void **glPixelMapfv**(GLenum *map*,
                    GLint *mapsize*,
                    const GLfloat **values*)
void **glPixelMapuiv**(GLenum *map*,
                    GLint *mapsize*,
                    const GLuint **values*)
void **glPixelMapusv**(GLenum *map*,
                    GLint *mapsize*,
                    const GLushort **values*)

PARAMETERS

map   Specifies a symbolic map name. Must be one of the following:
            GL_PIXEL_MAP_I_TO_I, GL_PIXEL_MAP_S_TO_S,
            GL_PIXEL_MAP_I_TO_R, GL_PIXEL_MAP_I_TO_G,
            GL_PIXEL_MAP_I_TO_B, GL_PIXEL_MAP_I_TO_A,
            GL_PIXEL_MAP_R_TO_R, GL_PIXEL_MAP_G_TO_G,
            GL_PIXEL_MAP_B_TO_B, or GL_PIXEL_MAP_A_TO_A.

mapsize
            Specifies the size of the map being defined.

values   Specifies an array of *mapsize* values.

DESCRIPTION

glPixelMap sets up translation tables, or *maps*, used by **glDrawPixels**, **glReadPixels**, **glCopyPixels**, **glTexImage1D**, and **glTexImage2D**. Use of these maps is described completely in the **glPixelTransfer** reference page, and partly in the reference pages for the pixel and texture image commands. Only the specification of the maps is described in this reference page.

map is a symbolic map name, indicating one of ten maps to set. *mapsize* specifies the number of entries in the map, and *values* is a pointer to an array of *mapsize* map values.

The ten maps are as follows:

GL_PIXEL_MAP_I_TO_I	Maps color indices to color indices.
GL_PIXEL_MAP_S_TO_S	Maps stencil indices to stencil indices.
GL_PIXEL_MAP_I_TO_R	Maps color indices to red components.
GL_PIXEL_MAP_I_TO_G	Maps color indices to green components.
GL_PIXEL_MAP_I_TO_B	Maps color indices to blue components.
GL_PIXEL_MAP_I_TO_A	Maps color indices to alpha components.
GL_PIXEL_MAP_R_TO_R	Maps red components to red components.
GL_PIXEL_MAP_G_TO_G	Maps green components to green components.
GL_PIXEL_MAP_B_TO_B	Maps blue components to blue components.
GL_PIXEL_MAP_A_TO_A	Maps alpha components to alpha components.

The entries in a map can be specified as single-precision floating-point numbers, unsigned short integers, or unsigned long integers. Maps that store color component values (all but **GL_PIXEL_MAP_I_TO_I** and **GL_PIXEL_MAP_S_TO_S**) retain their values in floating-point format, with unspecified mantissa and exponent sizes. Floating-point values specified by **glPixelMapfv** are converted directly to the internal floating-point format of these maps, then clamped to the range [0,1]. Unsigned integer values specified by **glPixelMapusv** and **glPixelMapuiv** are converted linearly such that the largest representable integer maps to 1.0, and zero maps to 0.0.

Maps that store indices, **GL_PIXEL_MAP_I_TO_I** and **GL_PIXEL_MAP_S_TO_S**, retain their values in fixed-point format, with an unspecified number of bits to the right of the binary point. Floating-point values specified by **glPixelMapfv** are converted directly to the internal fixed-point format of these maps. Unsigned integer values specified by **glPixelMapusv** and **glPixelMapuiv** specify integer values, with all zeros to the right of the binary point.

The table below shows the initial sizes and values for each of the maps. Maps that are indexed by either color or stencil indices must have *mapsize* = 2^n for some n or results are undefined. The maximum allowable size for each map depends on the implementation and can be determined by calling **glGet** with argument **GL_MAX_PIXEL_MAP_TABLE**. The single maximum applies to all maps, and it is at least 32.

map	lookup index	lookup value	initial size	initial value
GL_PIXEL_MAP_I_TO_I	color index	color index	1	0.0
GL_PIXEL_MAP_S_TO_S	stencil index	stencil index	1	0
GL_PIXEL_MAP_I_TO_R	color index	R	1	0.0
GL_PIXEL_MAP_I_TO_G	color index	G	1	0.0
GL_PIXEL_MAP_I_TO_B	color index	B	1	0.0
GL_PIXEL_MAP_I_TO_A	color index	A	1	0.0
GL_PIXEL_MAP_R_TO_R	R	R	1	0.0
GL_PIXEL_MAP_G_TO_G	G	G	1	0.0
GL_PIXEL_MAP_B_TO_B	B	B	1	0.0
GL_PIXEL_MAP_A_TO_A	A	A	1	0.0

ERRORS

GL_INVALID_ENUM is generated if *map* is not an accepted value.

GL_INVALID_VALUE is generated if *mapsize* is negative or larger than GL_MAX_PIXEL_MAP_TABLE.

GL_INVALID_VALUE is generated if *map* is GL_PIXEL_MAP_I_TO_I, GL_PIXEL_MAP_S_TO_S, GL_PIXEL_MAP_I_TO_R, GL_PIXEL_MAP_I_TO_G, GL_PIXEL_MAP_I_TO_B, or GL_PIXEL_MAP_I_TO_A, and *mapsize* is not a power of two.

GL_INVALID_OPERATION is generated if **glPixelMap** is called between a call to **glBegin** and the corresponding call to **glEnd**.

ASSOCIATED GETS

glGetPixelMap
glGet with argument GL_PIXEL_MAP_I_TO_I_SIZE
glGet with argument GL_PIXEL_MAP_S_TO_S_SIZE
glGet with argument GL_PIXEL_MAP_I_TO_R_SIZE
glGet with argument GL_PIXEL_MAP_I_TO_G_SIZE
glGet with argument GL_PIXEL_MAP_I_TO_B_SIZE
glGet with argument GL_PIXEL_MAP_I_TO_A_SIZE
glGet with argument GL_PIXEL_MAP_R_TO_R_SIZE
glGet with argument GL_PIXEL_MAP_G_TO_G_SIZE
glGet with argument GL_PIXEL_MAP_B_TO_B_SIZE
glGet with argument GL_PIXEL_MAP_A_TO_A_SIZE
glGet with argument GL_MAX_PIXEL_MAP_TABLE

SEE ALSO

glCopyPixels, glDrawPixels, glPixelStore, glPixelTransfer, glReadPixels, glTexImage1D, glTexImage2D

NAME

glPixelStoref, **glPixelStorei** – set pixel storage modes

C SPECIFICATION

void **glPixelStoref**(GLenum *pname*,
                    GLfloat *param*)
void **glPixelStorei**(GLenum *pname*,
                    GLint *param*)

PARAMETERS

pname Specifies the symbolic name of the parameter to be set. Six values affect the packing of pixel data into memory: **GL_PACK_SWAP_BYTES**, **GL_PACK_LSB_FIRST**, **GL_PACK_ROW_LENGTH**, **GL_PACK_SKIP_PIXELS**, **GL_PACK_SKIP_ROWS**, and **GL_PACK_ALIGNMENT**. Six more affect the unpacking of pixel data *from* memory: **GL_UNPACK_SWAP_BYTES**, **GL_UNPACK_LSB_FIRST**, **GL_UNPACK_ROW_LENGTH**, **GL_UNPACK_SKIP_PIXELS**, **GL_UNPACK_SKIP_ROWS**, and **GL_UNPACK_ALIGNMENT**.

param Specifies the value that *pname* is set to.

DESCRIPTION

glPixelStore sets pixel storage modes that affect the operation of subsequent **glDrawPixels** and **glReadPixels** as well as the unpacking of polygon stipple patterns (see **glPolygonStipple**), bitmaps (see **glBitmap**), and texture patterns (see **glTexImage1D** and **glTexImage2D**).

pname is a symbolic constant indicating the parameter to be set, and *param* is the new value. Six of the twelve storage parameters affect how pixel data is returned to client memory, and are therefore significant only for **glReadPixels** commands. They are as follows:

GL_PACK_SWAP_BYTES

If true, byte ordering for multibyte color components, depth components, color indices, or stencil indices is reversed. That is, if a four-byte component is made up of bytes b_0, b_1, b_2, b_3, it is stored in memory as b_3, b_2, b_1, b_0 if **GL_PACK_SWAP_BYTES** is true. **GL_PACK_SWAP_BYTES** has no effect on the memory order of components within a pixel, only on the order of bytes within components or indices. For example, the three components of a **GL_RGB** format pixel are always stored with red first, green second, and blue third, regardless of the value of **GL_PACK_SWAP_BYTES**.

GL_PACK_LSB_FIRST

> If true, bits are ordered within a byte from least significant to most significant; otherwise, the first bit in each byte is the most significant one. This parameter is significant for bitmap data only.

GL_PACK_ROW_LENGTH

> If greater than zero, **GL_PACK_ROW_LENGTH** defines the number of pixels in a row. If the first pixel of a row is placed at location p in memory, then the location of the first pixel of the next row is obtained by skipping

$$k = \begin{cases} nl & s \geq a \\ \dfrac{a}{s} \left\lceil \dfrac{snl}{a} \right\rceil & s < a \end{cases}$$

components or indices, where n is the number of components or indices in a pixel, l is the number of pixels in a row (**GL_PACK_ROW_LENGTH** if it is greater than zero), a is the value of **GL_PACK_ALIGNMENT**, and s is the size, in bytes, of a single component (if $a < s$, then it is as if $a = s$). In the case of 1-bit values, the location of the next row is obtained by skipping

$$k = 8a \left\lceil \frac{nl}{8a} \right\rceil$$

components or indices.

The word *component* in this description refers to the nonindex values red, green, blue, alpha, and depth. Storage format **GL_RGB**, for example, has three components per pixel: first red, then green, and finally blue.

GL_PACK_SKIP_PIXELS and **GL_PACK_SKIP_ROWS**

> These values are provided as a convenience to the programmer; they provide no functionality that cannot be duplicated simply by incrementing the pointer passed to **glReadPixels**. Setting **GL_PACK_SKIP_PIXELS** to i is equivalent to incrementing the pointer by in components or indices, where n is the number of components or indices in each pixel. Setting **GL_PACK_SKIP_ROWS** to j is equivalent to incrementing the pointer by jk components or indices, where k is the number of components or indices per row, as computed above in the **GL_PACK_ROW_LENGTH** section.

GL_PACK_ALIGNMENT

Specifies the alignment requirements for the start of each pixel row in memory. The allowable values are 1 (byte-alignment), 2 (rows aligned to even-numbered bytes), 4 (word alignment), and 8 (rows start on double-word boundaries).

The other six of the twelve storage parameters affect how pixel data is read from client memory. These values are significant for **glDrawPixels**, **glTexImage1D**, **glTexImage2D**, **glBitmap**, and **glPolygonStipple**. They are as follows:

GL_UNPACK_SWAP_BYTES

If true, byte ordering for multibyte color components, depth components, color indices, or stencil indices is reversed. That is, if a four-byte component is made up of bytes b_0, b_1, b_2, b_3, it is taken from memory as b_3, b_2, b_1, b_0 if **GL_UNPACK_SWAP_BYTES** is true. **GL_UNPACK_SWAP_BYTES** has no effect on the memory order of components within a pixel, only on the order of bytes within components or indices. For example, the three components of a **GL_RGB** format pixel are always stored with red first, green second, and blue third, regardless of the value of **GL_UNPACK_SWAP_BYTES**.

GL_UNPACK_LSB_FIRST

If true, bits are ordered within a byte from least significant to most significant; otherwise, the first bit in each byte is the most significant one. This is significant for bitmap data only.

GL_UNPACK_ROW_LENGTH

If greater than zero, **GL_UNPACK_ROW_LENGTH** defines the number of pixels in a row. If the first pixel of a row is placed at location p in memory, then the location of the first pixel of the next row is obtained by skipping

$$k = \begin{cases} nl & s \geq a \\ \dfrac{a}{s} \left\lceil \dfrac{snl}{a} \right\rceil & s < a \end{cases}$$

components or indices, where n is the number of components or indices in a pixel, l is the number of pixels in a row (**GL_UNPACK_ROW_LENGTH** if it is greater than zero), a is the value of **GL_UNPACK_ALIGNMENT**, and s is the size, in bytes, of a single component (if $a<s$, then it is as if $a=s$). In the case of 1-bit values, the location of the next row is obtained by skipping

$$k = 8a \left\lceil \frac{nl}{8a} \right\rceil$$

components or indices.

The word *component* in this description refers to the nonindex values red, green, blue, alpha, and depth. Storage format **GL_RGB**, for example, has three components per pixel: first red, then green, and finally blue.

GL_UNPACK_SKIP_PIXELS and GL_UNPACK_SKIP_ROWS

These values are provided as a convenience to the programmer; they provide no functionality that cannot be duplicated simply by incrementing the pointer passed to **glDrawPixels**, **glTexImage1D**, **glTexImage2D**, **glBitmap**, or **glPolygonStipple**. Setting **GL_UNPACK_SKIP_PIXELS** to *i* is equivalent to incrementing the pointer by *in* components or indices, where *n* is the number of components or indices in each pixel. Setting **GL_UNPACK_SKIP_ROWS** to *j* is equivalent to incrementing the pointer by *jk* components or indices, where *k* is the number of components or indices per row, as computed above in the **GL_UNPACK_ROW_LENGTH** section.

GL_UNPACK_ALIGNMENT

Specifies the alignment requirements for the start of each pixel row in memory. The allowable values are 1 (byte-alignment), 2 (rows aligned to even-numbered bytes), 4 (word alignment), and 8 (rows start on double-word boundaries).

The following table gives the type, initial value, and range of valid values for each of the storage parameters that can be set with **glPixelStore**.

pname	type	initial value	valid range
GL_PACK_SWAP_BYTES	Boolean	false	true or false
GL_PACK_LSB_FIRST	Boolean	false	true or false
GL_PACK_ROW_LENGTH	integer	0	$[0,\infty)$
GL_PACK_SKIP_ROWS	integer	0	$[0,\infty)$
GL_PACK_SKIP_PIXELS	integer	0	$[0,\infty)$
GL_PACK_ALIGNMENT	integer	4	1, 2, 4, or 8
GL_UNPACK_SWAP_BYTES	Boolean	false	true or false
GL_UNPACK_LSB_FIRST	Boolean	false	true or false
GL_UNPACK_ROW_LENGTH	integer	0	$[0,\infty)$
GL_UNPACK_SKIP_ROWS	integer	0	$[0,\infty)$
GL_UNPACK_SKIP_PIXELS	integer	0	$[0,\infty)$
GL_UNPACK_ALIGNMENT	integer	4	1, 2, 4, or 8

glPixelStoref can be used to set any pixel store parameter. If the parameter type is Boolean, then if *param* is 0.0, the parameter is false; otherwise it is set to true. If *pname* is a integer type parameter, *param* is rounded to the nearest integer.

Likewise, **glPixelStorei** can also be used to set any of the pixel store parameters. Boolean parameters are set to false if *param* is 0 and true otherwise. *param* is converted to floating point before being assigned to real-valued parameters.

NOTES

The pixel storage modes in effect when **glDrawPixels, glReadPixels, glTexImage1D, glTexImage2D, glBitmap,** or **glPolygonStipple** is placed in a display list control the interpretation of memory data. The pixel storage modes in effect when a display list is executed are not significant.

ERRORS

GL_INVALID_ENUM is generated if *pname* is not an accepted value.

GL_INVALID_VALUE is generated if a negative row length, pixel skip, or row skip value is specified, or if alignment is specified as other than 1, 2, 4, or 8.

GL_INVALID_OPERATION is generated if **glPixelStore** is called between a call to **glBegin** and the corresponding call to **glEnd**.

ASSOCIATED GETS

glGet with argument GL_PACK_SWAP_BYTES
glGet with argument GL_PACK_LSB_FIRST
glGet with argument GL_PACK_ROW_LENGTH
glGet with argument GL_PACK_SKIP_ROWS
glGet with argument GL_PACK_SKIP_PIXELS
glGet with argument GL_PACK_ALIGNMENT
glGet with argument GL_UNPACK_SWAP_BYTES
glGet with argument GL_UNPACK_LSB_FIRST
glGet with argument GL_UNPACK_ROW_LENGTH
glGet with argument GL_UNPACK_SKIP_ROWS
glGet with argument GL_UNPACK_SKIP_PIXELS
glGet with argument GL_UNPACK_ALIGNMENT

SEE ALSO

glBitmap, glDrawPixels, glPixelMap, glPixelTransfer, glPixelZoom, glPolygonStipple, glReadPixels, glTexImage1D, glTexImage2D

NAME

glPixelTransferf, glPixelTransferi – set pixel transfer modes

C SPECIFICATION

void **glPixelTransferf**(GLenum *pname*,
                GLfloat *param*)
void **glPixelTransferi**(GLenum *pname*,
                GLint *param*)

PARAMETERS

pname Specifies the symbolic name of the pixel transfer parameter to be set. Must
be one of the following: GL_MAP_COLOR, GL_MAP_STENCIL,
GL_INDEX_SHIFT, GL_INDEX_OFFSET, GL_RED_SCALE, GL_RED_BIAS,
GL_GREEN_SCALE, GL_GREEN_BIAS, GL_BLUE_SCALE, GL_BLUE_BIAS,
GL_ALPHA_SCALE, GL_ALPHA_BIAS, GL_DEPTH_SCALE, or
GL_DEPTH_BIAS.

param Specifies the value that *pname* is set to.

DESCRIPTION

glPixelTransfer sets pixel transfer modes that affect the operation of subsequent
glDrawPixels, **glReadPixels**, **glCopyPixels**, **glTexImage1D**, and **glTexImage2D**
commands. The algorithms that are specified by pixel transfer modes operate on
pixels after they are read from the frame buffer (**glReadPixels** and **glCopyPixels**) or
unpacked from client memory (**glDrawPixels**, **glTexImage1D**, and **glTexImage2D**).
Pixel transfer operations happen in the same order, and in the same manner, regardless of the command that resulted in the pixel operation. Pixel storage modes (see
glPixelStore) control the unpacking of pixels being read from client memory, and
the packing of pixels being written back into client memory.

Pixel transfer operations handle four fundamental pixel types: *color*, *color index*,
depth, and *stencil*. *Color* pixels are made up of four floating-point values with
unspecified mantissa and exponent sizes, scaled such that 0.0 represents zero intensity and 1.0 represents full intensity. *Color indices* comprise a single fixed-point
value, with unspecified precision to the right of the binary point. *Depth* pixels
comprise a single floating-point value, with unspecified mantissa and exponent
sizes, scaled such that 0.0 represents the minimum depth buffer value, and 1.0
represents the maximum depth buffer value. Finally, *stencil* pixels comprise a single
fixed-point value, with unspecified precision to the right of the binary point.

The pixel transfer operations performed on the four basic pixel types are as follows:

Color   Each of the four color components is multiplied by a scale factor, then added to a bias factor. That is, the red component is multiplied by **GL_RED_SCALE**, then added to **GL_RED_BIAS**; the green component is multiplied by **GL_GREEN_SCALE**, then added to **GL_GREEN_BIAS**; the blue component is multiplied by **GL_BLUE_SCALE**, then added to **GL_BLUE_BIAS**; and the alpha component is multiplied by **GL_ALPHA_SCALE**, then added to **GL_ALPHA_BIAS**. After all four color components are scaled and biased, each is clamped to the range [0,1]. All color scale and bias values are specified with **glPixelTransfer**.

If **GL_MAP_COLOR** is true, each color component is scaled by the size of the corresponding color-to-color map, then replaced by the contents of that map indexed by the scaled component. That is, the red component is scaled by **GL_PIXEL_MAP_R_TO_R_SIZE**, then replaced by the contents of **GL_PIXEL_MAP_R_TO_R** indexed by itself. The green component is scaled by **GL_PIXEL_MAP_G_TO_G_SIZE**, then replaced by the contents of **GL_PIXEL_MAP_G_TO_G** indexed by itself. The blue component is scaled by **GL_PIXEL_MAP_B_TO_B_SIZE**, then replaced by the contents of **GL_PIXEL_MAP_B_TO_B** indexed by itself. And the alpha component is scaled by **GL_PIXEL_MAP_A_TO_A_SIZE**, then replaced by the contents of **GL_PIXEL_MAP_A_TO_A** indexed by itself. All components taken from the maps are then clamped to the range [0,1]. **GL_MAP_COLOR** is specified with **glPixelTransfer**. The contents of the various maps are specified with **glPixelMap**.

Color index   Each color index is shifted left by **GL_INDEX_SHIFT** bits, filling with zeros any bits beyond the number of fraction bits carried by the fixed-point index. If **GL_INDEX_SHIFT** is negative, the shift is to the right, again zero filled. Then **GL_INDEX_OFFSET** is added to the index. **GL_INDEX_SHIFT** and **GL_INDEX_OFFSET** are specified with **glPixelTransfer**.

From this point, operation diverges depending on the required format of the resulting pixels. If the resulting pixels are to be written to a color index buffer, or if they are being read back to client memory in **GL_COLOR_INDEX** format, the pixels continue to be treated as indices. If **GL_MAP_COLOR** is true, each index is masked by $2^n - 1$, where n is **GL_PIXEL_MAP_I_TO_I_SIZE**, then replaced by the contents of **GL_PIXEL_MAP_I_TO_I** indexed by the masked value. **GL_MAP_COLOR** is specified with **glPixelTransfer**. The contents of the index map are specified with **glPixelMap**.

If the resulting pixels are to be written to an RGBA color buffer, or if they are being read back to client memory in a format other than GL_COLOR_INDEX, the pixels are converted from indices to colors by referencing the four maps GL_PIXEL_MAP_I_TO_R, GL_PIXEL_MAP_I_TO_G, GL_PIXEL_MAP_I_TO_B, and GL_PIXEL_MAP_I_TO_A. Before being dereferenced, the index is masked by $2^n - 1$, where n is GL_PIXEL_MAP_I_TO_R_SIZE for the red map, GL_PIXEL_MAP_I_TO_G_SIZE for the green map, GL_PIXEL_MAP_I_TO_B_SIZE for the blue map, and GL_PIXEL_MAP_I_TO_A_SIZE for the alpha map. All components taken from the maps are then clamped to the range [0,1]. The contents of the four maps are specified with **glPixelMap**.

Depth   Each depth value is multiplied by GL_DEPTH_SCALE, added to GL_DEPTH_BIAS, then clamped to the range [0,1].

Stencil   Each index is shifted GL_INDEX_SHIFT bits just as a color index is, then added to GL_INDEX_OFFSET. If GL_MAP_STENCIL is true, each index is masked by $2^n - 1$, where n is GL_PIXEL_MAP_S_TO_S_SIZE, then replaced by the contents of GL_PIXEL_MAP_S_TO_S indexed by the masked value.

The following table gives the type, initial value, and range of valid values for each of the pixel transfer parameters that are set with **glPixelTransfer**.

pname	type	initial value	valid range
GL_MAP_COLOR	Boolean	false	true/false
GL_MAP_STENCIL	Boolean	false	true/false
GL_INDEX_SHIFT	integer	0	$(-\infty, \infty)$
GL_INDEX_OFFSET	integer	0	$(-\infty, \infty)$
GL_RED_SCALE	float	1.0	$(-\infty, \infty)$
GL_GREEN_SCALE	float	1.0	$(-\infty, \infty)$
GL_BLUE_SCALE	float	1.0	$(-\infty, \infty)$
GL_ALPHA_SCALE	float	1.0	$(-\infty, \infty)$
GL_DEPTH_SCALE	float	1.0	$(-\infty, \infty)$
GL_RED_BIAS	float	0.0	$(-\infty, \infty)$
GL_GREEN_BIAS	float	0.0	$(-\infty, \infty)$
GL_BLUE_BIAS	float	0.0	$(-\infty, \infty)$
GL_ALPHA_BIAS	float	0.0	$(-\infty, \infty)$
GL_DEPTH_BIAS	float	0.0	$(-\infty, \infty)$

glPixelTransferf can be used to set any pixel transfer parameter. If the parameter type is Boolean, 0.0 implies false and any other value implies true. If *pname* is an integer parameter, *param* is rounded to the nearest integer.

Likewise, **glPixelTransferi** can also be used to set any of the pixel transfer parameters. Boolean parameters are set to false if *param* is 0 and true otherwise. *param* is converted to floating point before being assigned to real-valued parameters.

NOTES

If a **glDrawPixels**, **glReadPixels**, **glCopyPixels**, **glTexImage1D**, or **glTexImage2D** command is placed in a display list (see **glNewList** and **glCallList**), the pixel transfer mode settings in effect when the display list is *executed* are the ones that are used. They may be different from the settings when the command was compiled into the display list.

ERRORS

GL_INVALID_ENUM is generated if *pname* is not an accepted value.

GL_INVALID_OPERATION is generated if **glPixelTransfer** is called between a call to **glBegin** and the corresponding call to **glEnd**.

ASSOCIATED GETS

glGet with argument GL_MAP_COLOR
glGet with argument GL_MAP_STENCIL
glGet with argument GL_INDEX_SHIFT
glGet with argument GL_INDEX_OFFSET
glGet with argument GL_RED_SCALE
glGet with argument GL_RED_BIAS
glGet with argument GL_GREEN_SCALE
glGet with argument GL_GREEN_BIAS
glGet with argument GL_BLUE_SCALE
glGet with argument GL_BLUE_BIAS
glGet with argument GL_ALPHA_SCALE
glGet with argument GL_ALPHA_BIAS
glGet with argument GL_DEPTH_SCALE
glGet with argument GL_DEPTH_BIAS

SEE ALSO

glCallList, glCopyPixels, glDrawPixels, glNewList, glPixelMap, glPixelStore, glPixelZoom, glReadPixels, glTexImage1D, glTexImage2D

NAME

glPixelZoom – specify the pixel zoom factors

C SPECIFICATION

void **glPixelZoom**(GLfloat *xfactor,*
GLfloat *yfactor*)

PARAMETERS

xfactor, yfactor

Specify the *x* and *y* zoom factors for pixel write operations.

DESCRIPTION

glPixelZoom specifies values for the *x* and *y* zoom factors. During the execution of **glDrawPixels** or **glCopyPixels**, if (x_r, y_r) is the current raster position, and a given element is in the *n*th row and *m*th column of the pixel rectangle, then pixels whose centers are in the rectangle with corners at

$$(x_r + n \cdot xfactor, \ y_r + m \cdot yfactor)$$

$$(x_r + (n+1) \cdot xfactor, \ y_r + (m+1) \cdot yfactor)$$

are candidates for replacement. Any pixel whose center lies on the bottom or left edge of this rectangular region is also modified.

Pixel zoom factors are not limited to positive values. Negative zoom factors reflect the resulting image about the current raster position.

ERRORS

GL_INVALID_OPERATION is generated if **glPixelZoom** is called between a call to **glBegin** and the corresponding call to **glEnd**.

ASSOCIATED GETS

glGet with argument GL_ZOOM_X
glGet with argument GL_ZOOM_Y

SEE ALSO

glCopyPixels, **glDrawPixels**

NAME

glPointSize – specify the diameter of rasterized points

C SPECIFICATION

void **glPointSize**(GLfloat *size*)

PARAMETERS

size Specifies the diameter of rasterized points. The default is 1.0.

DESCRIPTION

glPointSize specifies the rasterized diameter of both aliased and antialiased points. Using a point size other than 1.0 has different effects, depending on whether point antialiasing is enabled. Point antialiasing is controlled by calling **glEnable** and **glDisable** with argument GL_POINT_SMOOTH.

If point antialiasing is disabled, the actual size is determined by rounding the supplied size to the nearest integer. (If the rounding results in the value 0, it is as if the point size were 1.) If the rounded size is odd, then the center point (x, y) of the pixel fragment that represents the point is computed as

$$(\lfloor x_w \rfloor + .5, \lfloor y_w \rfloor + .5)$$

where w subscripts indicate window coordinates. All pixels that lie within the square grid of the rounded size centered at (x, y) make up the fragment. If the size is even, the center point is

$$(\lfloor x_w + .5 \rfloor, \lfloor y_w + .5 \rfloor)$$

and the rasterized fragment's centers are the half-integer window coordinates within the square of the rounded size centered at (x, y). All pixel fragments produced in rasterizing a nonantialiased point are assigned the same associated data, that of the vertex corresponding to the point.

If antialiasing is enabled, then point rasterization produces a fragment for each pixel square that intersects the region lying within the circle having diameter equal to the current point size and centered at the point's (x_w, y_w). The coverage value for each fragment is the window coordinate area of the intersection of the circular region with the corresponding pixel square. This value is saved and used in the final rasterization step. The data associated with each fragment is the data associated with the point being rasterized.

Not all sizes are supported when point antialiasing is enabled. If an unsupported size is requested, the nearest supported size is used. Only size 1.0 is guaranteed to be supported; others depend on the implementation. The range of supported sizes and the size difference between supported sizes within the range can be queried by calling **glGet** with arguments GL_POINT_SIZE_RANGE and GL_POINT_SIZE_GRANULARITY.

NOTES

The point size specified by **glPointSize** is always returned when GL_POINT_SIZE is queried. Clamping and rounding for aliased and antialiased points have no effect on the specified value.

ERRORS

GL_INVALID_VALUE is generated if *size* is less than or equal to zero.

GL_INVALID_OPERATION is generated if **glPointSize** is called between a call to **glBegin** and the corresponding call to **glEnd**.

ASSOCIATED GETS

glGet with argument GL_POINT_SIZE
glGet with argument GL_POINT_SIZE_RANGE
glGet with argument GL_POINT_SIZE_GRANULARITY
glIsEnabled with argument GL_POINT_SMOOTH

SEE ALSO

glEnable, glPointSmooth

NAME

glPolygonMode – select a polygon rasterization mode

C SPECIFICATION

void **glPolygonMode**(GLenum *face*,
                       GLenum *mode*)

PARAMETERS

face   Specifies the polygons that *mode* applies to. Must be **GL_FRONT** for front-facing polygons, **GL_BACK** for back-facing polygons, or **GL_FRONT_AND_BACK** for front- and back-facing polygons.

mode
Specifies the way polygons will be rasterized. Accepted values are **GL_POINT**, **GL_LINE**, and **GL_FILL**. The default is **GL_FILL** for both front- and back-facing polygons.

DESCRIPTION

glPolygonMode controls the interpretation of polygons for rasterization. *face* describes which polygons *mode* applies to: front-facing polygons (**GL_FRONT**), back-facing polygons (**GL_BACK**), or both (**GL_FRONT_AND_BACK**). The polygon mode affects only the final rasterization of polygons. In particular, a polygon's vertices are lit and the polygon is clipped and possibly culled before these modes are applied.

Three modes are defined and can be specified in *mode*:

GL_POINT   Polygon vertices that are marked as the start of a boundary edge are drawn as points. Point attributes such as **GL_POINT_SIZE** and **GL_POINT_SMOOTH** control the rasterization of the points. Polygon rasterization attributes other than **GL_POLYGON_MODE** have no effect.

GL_LINE   Boundary edges of the polygon are drawn as line segments. They are treated as connected line segments for line stippling; the line stipple counter and pattern are not reset between segments (see **glLineStipple**). Line attributes such as **GL_LINE_WIDTH** and **GL_LINE_SMOOTH** control the rasterization of the lines. Polygon rasterization attributes other than **GL_POLYGON_MODE** have no effect.

GL_FILL   The interior of the polygon is filled. Polygon attributes such as **GL_POLYGON_STIPPLE** and **GL_POLYGON_SMOOTH** control the rasterization of the polygon.

EXAMPLES

To draw a surface with filled back-facing polygons and outlined front-facing polygons, call

> **glPolygonMode**(GL_FRONT, GL_LINE);

NOTES

Vertices are marked as boundary or nonboundary with an edge flag. Edge flags are generated internally by the GL when it decomposes polygons, and they can be set explicitly using **glEdgeFlag**.

ERRORS

GL_INVALID_ENUM is generated if either *face* or *mode* is not an accepted value.

GL_INVALID_OPERATION is generated if **glPolygonMode** is called between a call to **glBegin** and the corresponding call to **glEnd**.

ASSOCIATED GETS

glGet with argument GL_POLYGON_MODE

SEE ALSO

glBegin, glEdgeFlag, glLineStipple, glLineWidth, glPointSize, glPolygonStipple

NAME

glPolygonStipple – set the polygon stippling pattern

C SPECIFICATION

void **glPolygonStipple**(const GLubyte *mask*)

PARAMETERS

mask Specifies a pointer to a 32×32 stipple pattern that will be unpacked from memory in the same way that **glDrawPixels** unpacks pixels.

DESCRIPTION

Polygon stippling, like line stippling (see **glLineStipple**), masks out certain fragments produced by rasterization, creating a pattern. Stippling is independent of polygon antialiasing.

mask is a pointer to a 32×32 stipple pattern that is stored in memory just like the pixel data supplied to a **glDrawPixels** with *height* and *width* both equal to 32, a pixel *format* of GL_COLOR_INDEX, and data *type* of GL_BITMAP. That is, the stipple pattern is represented as a 32×32 array of 1-bit color indices packed in unsigned bytes. **glPixelStore** parameters like **GL_UNPACK_SWAP_BYTES** and **GL_UNPACK_LSB_FIRST** affect the assembling of the bits into a stipple pattern. Pixel transfer operations (shift, offset, pixel map) are not applied to the stipple image, however.

Polygon stippling is enabled and disabled with **glEnable** and **glDisable**, using argument GL_POLYGON_STIPPLE. If enabled, a rasterized polygon fragment with window coordinates x_w and y_w is sent to the next stage of the GL if and only if the (x_w mod 32)th bit in the (y_w mod 32)th row of the stipple pattern is one. When polygon stippling is disabled, it is as if the stipple pattern were all ones.

ERRORS

GL_INVALID_OPERATION is generated if **glPolygonStipple** is called between a call to **glBegin** and the corresponding call to **glEnd**.

ASSOCIATED GETS

glGetPolygonStipple
glIsEnabled with argument GL_POLYGON_STIPPLE

SEE ALSO

glDrawPixels, **glLineStipple**, **glPixelStore**, **glPixelTransfer**

NAME

> **glPushAttrib, glPopAttrib** – push and pop the attribute stack

C SPECIFICATION

> void **glPushAttrib**(GLbitfield *mask*)

PARAMETERS

> *mask* Specifies a mask that indicates which attributes to save. Values for *mask* are listed in the table below.

C SPECIFICATION

> void **glPopAttrib**(void *void*)

DESCRIPTION

> **glPushAttrib** takes one argument, a mask that indicates which groups of state variables to save on the attribute stack. Symbolic constants are used to set bits in the mask. *mask* is typically constructed by ORing several of these constants together. The special mask **GL_ALL_ATTRIB_BITS** can be used to save all stackable states.
>
> The symbolic mask constants and their associated GL state are as follows (the second column lists which attributes are saved):

GL_ACCUM_BUFFER_BIT	Accumulation buffer clear value
GL_COLOR_BUFFER_BIT	**GL_ALPHA_TEST** enable bit Alpha test function and reference value **GL_BLEND** enable bit Blending source and destination functions **GL_DITHER** enable bit **GL_DRAW_BUFFER** setting **GL_LOGIC_OP** enable bit Logic op function Color mode and index mode clear values Color mode and index mode writemasks
GL_CURRENT_BIT	Current RGBA color Current color index Current normal vector Current texture coordinates Current raster position **GL_CURRENT_RASTER_POSITION_VALID** flag RGBA color associated with current raster position

	Color index associated with current raster position
	Texture coordinates associated with current raster position
	GL_EDGE_FLAG flag
GL_DEPTH_BUFFER_BIT	**GL_DEPTH_TEST** enable bit
	Depth buffer test function
	Depth buffer clear value
	GL_DEPTH_WRITEMASK enable bit
GL_ENABLE_BIT	**GL_ALPHA_TEST** flag
	GL_AUTO_NORMAL flag
	GL_BLEND flag
	Enable bits for the user-definable clipping planes
	GL_COLOR_MATERIAL
	GL_CULL_FACE flag
	GL_DEPTH_TEST flag
	GL_DITHER flag
	GL_FOG flag
	GL_LIGHTi where $0 <= i <$**GL_MAX_LIGHTS**
	GL_LIGHTING flag
	GL_LINE_SMOOTH flag
	GL_LINE_STIPPLE flag
	GL_LOGIC_OP flag
	GL_MAP1_x where x is a map type
	GL_MAP2_x where x is a map type
	GL_NORMALIZE flag
	GL_POINT_SMOOTH flag
	GL_POLYGON_SMOOTH flag
	GL_POLYGON_STIPPLE flag
	GL_SCISSOR_TEST flag
	GL_STENCIL_TEST flag
	GL_TEXTURE_1D flag
	GL_TEXTURE_2D flag
	Flags **GL_TEXTURE_GEN_**x where x is **S**, **T**, **R**, or **Q**
GL_EVAL_BIT	**GL_MAP1_**x enable bits, where x is a map type
	GL_MAP2_x enable bits, where x is a map type
	1-D grid endpoints and divisions
	2-D grid endpoints and divisions
	GL_AUTO_NORMAL enable bit

GL_FOG_BIT	**GL_FOG** enable flag
	Fog color
	Fog density
	Linear fog start
	Linear fog end
	Fog index
	GL_FOG_MODE value
GL_HINT_BIT	**GL_PERSPECTIVE_CORRECTION_HINT** setting
	GL_POINT_SMOOTH_HINT setting
	GL_LINE_SMOOTH_HINT setting
	GL_POLYGON_SMOOTH_HINT setting
	GL_FOG_HINT setting
GL_LIGHTING_BIT	**GL_COLOR_MATERIAL** enable bit
	GL_COLOR_MATERIAL_FACE value
	Color material parameters that are tracking the current color
	Ambient scene color
	GL_LIGHT_MODEL_LOCAL_VIEWER value
	GL_LIGHT_MODEL_TWO_SIDE setting
	GL_LIGHTING enable bit
	Enable bit for each light
	Ambient, diffuse, and specular intensity for each light
	Direction, position, exponent, and cutoff angle for each light
	Constant, linear, and quadratic attenuation factors for each light
	Ambient, diffuse, specular, and emissive color for each material
	Ambient, diffuse, and specular color indices for each material
	Specular exponent for each material
	GL_SHADE_MODEL setting
GL_LINE_BIT	**GL_LINE_SMOOTH** flag
	GL_LINE_STIPPLE enable bit
	Line stipple pattern and repeat counter
	Line width

GL_LIST_BIT	**GL_LIST_BASE** setting
GL_PIXEL_MODE_BIT	**GL_RED_BIAS** and **GL_RED_SCALE** settings **GL_GREEN_BIAS** and **GL_GREEN_SCALE** values **GL_BLUE_BIAS** and **GL_BLUE_SCALE** **GL_ALPHA_BIAS** and **GL_ALPHA_SCALE** **GL_DEPTH_BIAS** and **GL_DEPTH_SCALE** **GL_INDEX_OFFSET** and **GL_INDEX_SHIFT** values **GL_MAP_COLOR** and **GL_MAP_STENCIL** flags **GL_ZOOM_X** and **GL_ZOOM_Y** factors **GL_READ_BUFFER** setting GL_x where x is a pixel map table name GL_x_SIZE where x is a pixel map table name
GL_POINT_BIT	**GL_POINT_SMOOTH** flag Point size
GL_POLYGON_BIT	**GL_CULL_FACE** enable bit **GL_CULL_FACE_MODE** value **GL_FRONT_FACE** indicator **GL_POLYGON_MODE** setting **GL_POLYGON_SMOOTH** flag **GL_POLYGON_STIPPLE** enable bit
GL_POLYGON_STIPPLE_BIT	Polygon stipple image
GL_SCISSOR_BIT	**GL_SCISSOR_TEST** flag Scissor box
GL_STENCIL_BUFFER_BIT	**GL_STENCIL_TEST** enable bit Stencil function and reference value Stencil value mask Stencil fail, pass, and depth buffer pass actions Stencil buffer clear value Stencil buffer writemask
GL_TEXTURE_BIT	Enable bits for the four texture coordinates Border color for each texture image Minification function for each texture image Magnification function for each texture image

Texture coordinates and wrap mode for each texture image

Color and mode for each texture environment

Enable bits **GL_TEXTURE_GEN_**_x_, _x_ is **S**, **T**, **R**, and **Q**

GL_TEXTURE_GEN_MODE setting for **S**, **T**, **R**, and **Q**

glTexGen plane equations for **S**, **T**, **R**, and **Q**

GL_TRANSFORM_BIT

Coefficients of the six clipping planes

Enable bits for the user-definable clipping planes

GL_MATRIX_MODE value

GL_NORMALIZE flag

GL_VIEWPORT_BIT

Depth range (near and far)

Viewport origin and extent

glPopAttrib restores the values of the state variables saved with the last **glPushAttrib** command. Those not saved are left unchanged. Note that it's an error to push attributes onto a full stack, or to pop attributes off an empty stack. In either case, the error flag is set and no other change is made to GL state. Initially, the attribute stack is empty.

NOTES

Not all values for GL state can be saved on the attribute stack. For example, pixel pack and unpack state, render mode state, and select and feedback state cannot be saved.

The depth of the attribute stack depends on the implementation, but it must be at least 16.

ERRORS

GL_STACK_OVERFLOW is generated if **glPushAttrib** is called while the attribute stack is full.

GL_STACK_UNDERFLOW is generated if **glPopAttrib** is called while the attribute stack is empty.

GL_INVALID_OPERATION is generated if **glPushAttrib** is called between a call to **glBegin** and the corresponding call to **glEnd**.

ASSOCIATED GETS

glGet with argument GL_ATTRIB_STACK_DEPTH.

glGet with argument GL_MAX_ATTRIB_STACK_DEPTH.

SEE ALSO

glGet, glGetClipPlane, glGetError, glGetLight, glGetMap, glGetMaterial, glGet-PixelMap, glGetPolygonStipple, glGetString, glGetTexEnv, glGetTexGen, glGetTexImage1D, glGetTexImage2D, glGetTexLevelParameter, glGetTexParam-eter, glIsEnabled

NAME

glPushMatrix, glPopMatrix – push and pop the current matrix stack

C SPECIFICATION

void **glPushMatrix**(void *void*)
void **glPopMatrix**(void *void*)

DESCRIPTION

There is a stack of matrices for each of the matrix modes. In **GL_MODELVIEW** mode, the stack depth is at least 32. In the other two modes, **GL_PROJECTION** and **GL_TEXTURE**, the depth is at least 2. The current matrix in any mode is the matrix on the top of the stack for that mode.

glPushMatrix pushes the current matrix stack down by one, duplicating the current matrix. That is, after a **glPushMatrix** call, the matrix on the top of the stack is identical to the one below it. **glPopMatrix** pops the current matrix stack, replacing the current matrix with the one below it on the stack. Initially, each of the stacks contains one matrix, an identity matrix.

It is an error to push a full matrix stack, or to pop a matrix stack that contains only a single matrix. In either case, the error flag is set and no other change is made to GL state.

ERRORS

GL_STACK_OVERFLOW is generated if **glPushMatrix** is called while the current matrix stack is full.

GL_STACK_UNDERFLOW is generated if **glPopMatrix** is called while the current matrix stack contains only a single matrix.

GL_INVALID_OPERATION is generated if **glPushMatrix** is called between a call to **glBegin** and the corresponding call to **glEnd**.

ASSOCIATED GETS

glGet with argument GL_MATRIX_MODE
glGet with argument GL_MODELVIEW_MATRIX
glGet with argument GL_PROJECTION_MATRIX
glGet with argument GL_TEXTURE_MATRIX
glGet with argument GL_MODELVIEW_STACK_DEPTH
glGet with argument GL_PROJECTION_STACK_DEPTH
glGet with argument GL_TEXTURE_STACK_DEPTH
glGet with argument GL_MAX_MODELVIEW_STACK_DEPTH
glGet with argument GL_MAX_PROJECTION_STACK_DEPTH
glGet with argument GL_MAX_TEXTURE_STACK_DEPTH

SEE ALSO

glFrustum, glLoadIdentity, glLoadMatrix, glMatrixMode, glMultMatrix, glOrtho, glRotate, glScale, glTranslate, glViewport

NAME

glPushName, glPopName – push and pop the name stack

C SPECIFICATION

void **glPushName**(GLuint *name*)
void **glPopName**(void *void*)

PARAMETERS

name   Specifies a name that will be pushed onto the name stack.

DESCRIPTION

The name stack is used during selection mode to allow sets of rendering commands to be uniquely identified. It consists of an ordered set of unsigned integers. **glPush-Name** causes *name* to be pushed onto the name stack, which is initially empty. **glPopName** pops one name off the top of the stack.

It is an error to push a name onto a full stack, or to pop a name off an empty stack. It is also an error to manipulate the name stack between a call to **glBegin** and the corresponding call to **glEnd**. In any of these cases, the error flag is set and no other change is made to GL state.

The name stack is always empty while the render mode is not **GL_SELECT**. Calls to **glPushName** or **glPopName** while the render mode is not **GL_SELECT** are ignored.

ERRORS

GL_STACK_OVERFLOW is generated if **glPushName** is called while the name stack is full.

GL_STACK_UNDERFLOW is generated if **glPopName** is called while the name stack is empty.

GL_INVALID_OPERATION is generated if **glPushName** or **glPopName** is called between a call to **glBegin** and the corresponding call to **glEnd**.

ASSOCIATED GETS

glGet with argument GL_NAME_STACK_DEPTH
glGet with argument GL_MAX_NAME_STACK_DEPTH

SEE ALSO

glInitNames, glLoadName, glRenderMode, glSelectBuffer

NAME

glRasterPos2d, glRasterPos2f, glRasterPos2i, glRasterPos2s, glRasterPos3d, glRasterPos3f, glRasterPos3i, glRasterPos3s, glRasterPos4d, glRasterPos4f, glRasterPos4i, glRasterPos4s, glRasterPos2dv, glRasterPos2fv, glRasterPos2iv, glRasterPos2sv, glRasterPos3dv, glRasterPos3fv, glRasterPos3iv, glRasterPos3sv, glRasterPos4dv, glRasterPos4fv, glRasterPos4iv, glRasterPos4sv
– specify the raster position for pixel operations

C SPECIFICATION

void **glRasterPos2d**(GLdouble x,
                        GLdouble y)
void **glRasterPos2f**(GLfloat x,
                        GLfloat y)
void **glRasterPos2i**(GLint x,
                        GLint y)
void **glRasterPos2s**(GLshort x,
                        GLshort y)
void **glRasterPos3d**(GLdouble x,
                        GLdouble y,
                        GLdouble z)
void **glRasterPos3f**(GLfloat x,
                        GLfloat y,
                        GLfloat z)
void **glRasterPos3i**(GLint x,
                        GLint y,
                        GLint z)
void **glRasterPos3s**(GLshort x,
                        GLshort y,
                        GLshort z)
void **glRasterPos4d**(GLdouble x,
                        GLdouble y,
                        GLdouble z,
                        GLdouble w)
void **glRasterPos4f**(GLfloat x,
                        GLfloat y,
                        GLfloat z,
                        GLfloat w)
void **glRasterPos4i**(GLint x,
                        GLint y,
                        GLint z,
                        GLint w)

```
void glRasterPos4s( GLshort x,
                    GLshort y,
                    GLshort z,
                    GLshort w )
```

PARAMETERS

x, y, z, w

Specify the *x*, *y*, *z*, and *w* object coordinates (if present) for the raster position.

C SPECIFICATION

```
void glRasterPos2dv( const GLdouble *v )
void glRasterPos2fv( const GLfloat *v )
void glRasterPos2iv( const GLint *v )
void glRasterPos2sv( const GLshort *v )
void glRasterPos3dv( const GLdouble *v )
void glRasterPos3fv( const GLfloat *v )
void glRasterPos3iv( const GLint *v )
void glRasterPos3sv( const GLshort *v )
void glRasterPos4dv( const GLdouble *v )
void glRasterPos4fv( const GLfloat *v )
void glRasterPos4iv( const GLint *v )
void glRasterPos4sv( const GLshort *v )
```

v   Specifies a pointer to an array of two, three, or four elements, specifying *x*, *y*, *z*, and *w* coordinates, respectively.

DESCRIPTION

The GL maintains a 3-D position in window coordinates. This position, called the raster position, is maintained with subpixel accuracy. It is used to position pixel and bitmap write operations. See **glBitmap**, **glDrawPixels**, and **glCopyPixels**.

The current raster position consists of four window coordinates (*x*, *y*, *z*, *w*), a valid bit, and associated color data and texture coordinates. The *w* coordinate is actually a clip coordinate, because *w* is not projected to window coordinates. **glRasterPos4** specifies object coordinates *x*, *y*, *z*, and *w* explicitly. **glRasterPos3** specifies object coordinate *x*, *y*, and *z* explicitly, while *w* is implicitly set to one. **glRasterPos2** uses the argument values for *x* and *y* while implicitly setting *z* and *w* to zero and one.

The object coordinates presented by **glRasterPos** are treated just like those of a **glVertex** command: They are transformed by the current modelview and projection matrices and passed to the clipping stage. If the vertex is not culled, then it is projected and scaled to window coordinates, which become the new current raster position, and the **GL_CURRENT_RASTER_POSITION_VALID** flag is set. If the vertex *is* culled, then the valid bit is cleared and the current raster position and associated color and texture coordinates are undefined.

The current raster position also includes some associated color data and texture coordinates. If lighting is enabled, then GL_CURRENT_RASTER_COLOR, in RGBA mode, or the GL_CURRENT_RASTER_INDEX, in color index mode, is set to the color produced by the lighting calculation (see **glLight**, **glLightModel**, and **glShadeModel**). If lighting is disabled, current color (in RGBA mode, state variable GL_CURRENT_COLOR) or color index (in color index mode, state variable GL_CURRENT_INDEX) is used to update the current raster color.

Likewise, GL_CURRENT_RASTER_TEXTURE_COORDS is updated as a function of GL_CURRENT_TEXTURE_COORDS, based on the texture matrix and the texture generation functions (see **glTexGen**).

Initially, the current raster position is (0,0,0,1), the valid bit is set, the associated RGBA color is (1,1,1,1), the associated color index is 1, and the associated texture coordinates are (0, 0, 0, 1). In RGBA mode, GL_CURRENT_RASTER_INDEX is always 1; in color index mode, the current raster RGBA color always maintains its initial value.

NOTES

The raster position is modified both by **glRasterPos** and by **glBitmap**.

When the raster position coordinates are invalid, drawing commands that are based on the raster position are ignored (that is, they do not result in changes to GL state).

ERRORS

GL_INVALID_OPERATION is generated if **glRasterPos** is called between a call to **glBegin** and the corresponding call to **glEnd**.

ASSOCIATED GETS

glGet with argument GL_CURRENT_RASTER_POSITION
glGet with argument GL_CURRENT_RASTER_POSITION_VALID
glGet with argument GL_CURRENT_RASTER_COLOR
glGet with argument GL_CURRENT_RASTER_INDEX
glGet with argument GL_CURRENT_RASTER_TEXTURE_COORDS

SEE ALSO

glBitmap, glCopyPixels, glDrawPixels, glLight, glLightModel, glShadeModel, glTexCoord, glTexGen, glVertex

NAME

glReadBuffer – select a color buffer source for pixels

C SPECIFICATION

void **glReadBuffer**(GLenum *mode*)

PARAMETERS

mode   Specifies a color buffer. Accepted values are **GL_FRONT_LEFT**, **GL_FRONT_RIGHT**, **GL_BACK_LEFT**, **GL_BACK_RIGHT**, **GL_FRONT**, **GL_BACK**, **GL_LEFT**, **GL_RIGHT**, and **GL_AUX***i*, where *i* is between 0 and **GL_AUX_BUFFERS** −1.

DESCRIPTION

glReadBuffer specifies a color buffer as the source for subsequent **glReadPixels** and **glCopyPixels** commands. *mode* accepts one of twelve or more predefined values. (**GL_AUX0** through **GL_AUX3** are always defined.) In a fully configured system, **GL_FRONT**, **GL_LEFT**, and **GL_FRONT_LEFT** all name the front left buffer, **GL_FRONT_RIGHT** and **GL_RIGHT** name the front right buffer, and **GL_BACK_LEFT** and **GL_BACK** name the back left buffer. Nonstereo configurations have only a left buffer, or a front left and a back left buffer if double-buffered. Single-buffered configurations have only a front buffer, or a front left and a front right buffer if stereo. It is an error to specify a nonexistent buffer to **glReadBuffer**.

By default, *mode* is **GL_FRONT** in single-buffered configurations, and **GL_BACK** in double-buffered configurations.

ERRORS

GL_INVALID_ENUM is generated if *mode* is not one of the twelve (or more) accepted values.

GL_INVALID_OPERATION is generated if *mode* specifies a buffer that does not exist.

GL_INVALID_OPERATION is generated if **glReadBuffer** is called between a call to **glBegin** and the corresponding call to **glEnd**.

ASSOCIATED GETS

glGet with argument **GL_READ_BUFFER**

SEE ALSO

glCopyPixels, **glDrawBuffer**, **glReadPixels**

NAME

glReadPixels – read a block of pixels from the frame buffer

C SPECIFICATION

void **glReadPixels**(GLint *x*,
GLint *y*,
GLsizei *width*,
GLsizei *height*,
GLenum *format*,
GLenum *type*,
GLvoid **pixels*)

PARAMETERS

x, y

Specify the window coordinates of the first pixel that is read from the frame buffer. This location is the lower left corner of a rectangular block of pixels.

width, height

Specify the dimensions of the pixel rectangle. *width* and *height* of one correspond to a single pixel.

format

Specifies the format of the pixel data. The following symbolic values are accepted: **GL_COLOR_INDEX**, **GL_STENCIL_INDEX**, **GL_DEPTH_COMPONENT**, **GL_RED**, **GL_GREEN**, **GL_BLUE**, **GL_ALPHA**, **GL_RGB**, **GL_RGBA**, **GL_LUMINANCE**, and **GL_LUMINANCE_ALPHA**.

type

Specifies the data type of the pixel data. Must be one of **GL_UNSIGNED_BYTE**, **GL_BYTE**, **GL_BITMAP**, **GL_UNSIGNED_SHORT**, **GL_SHORT**, **GL_UNSIGNED_INT**, **GL_INT**, or **GL_FLOAT**.

pixels

Returns the pixel data.

DESCRIPTION

glReadPixels returns pixel data from the frame buffer, starting with the pixel whose lower left corner is at location (*x, y*), into client memory starting at location *pixels*. Several parameters control the processing of the pixel data before it is placed into client memory. These parameters are set with three commands: **glPixelStore**, **glPixelTransfer**, and **glPixelMap**. This reference page describes the effects on **glReadPixels** of most, but not all of the parameters specified by these three commands.

glReadPixels returns values from each pixel with lower left-hand corner at $(x + i, y + j)$ for $0{\leq}i{<}width$ and $0{\leq}j{<}height$. This pixel is said to be the ith pixel in the jth row. Pixels are returned in row order from the lowest to the highest row, left to right in each row.

format specifies the format for the returned pixel values. Accepted values for *format* are as follows:

GL_COLOR_INDEX
> Color indices are read from the color buffer selected by **glReadBuffer**. Each index is converted to fixed point, shifted left or right depending on the value and sign of **GL_INDEX_SHIFT**, and added to **GL_INDEX_OFFSET**. If **GL_MAP_COLOR** is **GL_TRUE**, indices are replaced by their mappings in the table **GL_PIXEL_MAP_I_TO_I**.

GL_STENCIL_INDEX
> Stencil values are read from the stencil buffer. Each index is converted to fixed point, shifted left or right depending on the value and sign of **GL_INDEX_SHIFT**, and added to **GL_INDEX_OFFSET**. If **GL_MAP_STENCIL** is **GL_TRUE**, indices are replaced by their mappings in the table **GL_PIXEL_MAP_S_TO_S**.

GL_DEPTH_COMPONENT
> Depth values are read from the depth buffer. Each component is converted to floating point such that the minimum depth value maps to 0.0 and the maximum value maps to 1.0. Each component is then multiplied by **GL_DEPTH_SCALE**, added to **GL_DEPTH_BIAS**, and finally clamped to the range [0,1].

GL_RED

GL_GREEN

GL_BLUE

GL_ALPHA

GL_RGB

GL_RGBA

GL_LUMINANCE

GL_LUMINANCE_ALPHA
> Processing differs depending on whether color buffers store color indices or RGBA color components. If color indices are stored, they are read from the color buffer selected by **glReadBuffer**. Each index is converted to fixed point, shifted left or right depending on the value and sign of **GL_INDEX_SHIFT**, and added to **GL_INDEX_OFFSET**. Indices are then replaced by the red, green, blue, and alpha values obtained by indexing

the **GL_PIXEL_MAP_I_TO_R**, **GL_PIXEL_MAP_I_TO_G**, **GL_PIXEL_MAP_I_TO_B**, and **GL_PIXEL_MAP_I_TO_A** tables.

If RGBA color components are stored in the color buffers, they are read from the color buffer selected by **glReadBuffer**. Each color component is converted to floating point such that zero intensity maps to 0.0 and full intensity maps to 1.0. Each component is then multiplied by **GL_c_SCALE** and added to **GL_c_BIAS**, where c is **GL_RED**, **GL_GREEN**, **GL_BLUE**, and **GL_ALPHA**. Each component is clamped to the range [0,1]. Finally, if **GL_MAP_COLOR** is **GL_TRUE**, each color component c is replaced by its mapping in the table **GL_PIXEL_MAP_c_TO_c**, where c again is **GL_RED**, **GL_GREEN**, **GL_BLUE**, and **GL_ALPHA**. Each component is scaled to the size its corresponding table before the lookup is performed.

Finally, unneeded data is discarded. For example, **GL_RED** discards the green, blue, and alpha components, while **GL_RGB** discards only the alpha component. **GL_LUMINANCE** computes a single component value as the sum of the red, green, and blue components, and **GL_LUMINANCE_ALPHA** does the same, while keeping alpha as a second value.

The shift, scale, bias, and lookup factors described above are all specified by **glPixelTransfer**. The lookup table contents themselves are specified by **glPixelMap**.

The final step involves converting the indices or components to the proper format, as specified by *type*. If *format* is **GL_COLOR_INDEX** or **GL_STENCIL_INDEX** and *type* is not **GL_FLOAT**, each index is masked with the mask value given in the following table. If *type* is **GL_FLOAT**, then each integer index is converted to single-precision floating-point format.

If *format* is **GL_RED**, **GL_GREEN**, **GL_BLUE**, **GL_ALPHA**, **GL_RGB**, **GL_RGBA**, **GL_LUMINANCE**, or **GL_LUMINANCE_ALPHA** and *type* is not **GL_FLOAT**, each component is multiplied by the multiplier shown in the following table. If type is **GL_FLOAT**, then each component is passed as is (or converted to the client's single-precision floating-point format if it is different from the one used by the GL).

type	index mask	component conversion
GL_UNSIGNED_BYTE	2^8-1	$(2^8-1)c$
GL_BYTE	2^7-1	$[(2^7-1)c-1]/2$
GL_BITMAP	1	1
GL_UNSIGNED_SHORT	$2^{16}-1$	$(2^{16}-1)c$
GL_SHORT	$2^{15}-1$	$[(2^{15}-1)c-1]/2$
GL_UNSIGNED_INT	$2^{32}-1$	$(2^{32}-1)c$
GL_INT	$2^{31}-1$	$[(2^{31}-1)c-1]/2$
GL_FLOAT	none	c

Return values are placed in memory as follows. If *format* is **GL_COLOR_INDEX**, GL_STENCIL_INDEX, GL_DEPTH_COMPONENT, GL_RED, GL_GREEN, GL_BLUE, GL_ALPHA, or **GL_LUMINANCE**, a single value is returned and the data for the ith pixel in the jth row is placed in location (j) *width* $+ i$. **GL_RGB** returns three values, **GL_RGBA** returns four values, and **GL_LUMINANCE_ALPHA** returns two values for each pixel, with all values corresponding to a single pixel occupying contiguous space in *pixels*. Storage parameters set by **glPixelStore**, such as **GL_PACK_SWAP_BYTES** and **GL_PACK_LSB_FIRST**, affect the way that data is written into memory. See **glPixelStore** for a description.

NOTES

Values for pixels that lie outside the window connected to the current GL context are undefined.

If an error is generated, no change is made to the contents of *pixels*.

ERRORS

GL_INVALID_ENUM is generated if *format* or *type* is not an accepted value.

GL_INVALID_VALUE is generated if either *width* or *height* is negative.

GL_INVALID_OPERATION is generated if *format* is **GL_COLOR_INDEX** and the color buffers store RGBA color components.

GL_INVALID_OPERATION is generated if *format* is **GL_STENCIL_INDEX** and there is no stencil buffer.

GL_INVALID_OPERATION is generated if *format* is **GL_DEPTH_COMPONENT** and there is no depth buffer.

GL_INVALID_OPERATION is generated if **glReadPixels** is called between a call to **glBegin** and the corresponding call to **glEnd**.

ASSOCIATED GETS

glGet with argument GL_INDEX_MODE

SEE ALSO

glCopyPixels, glDrawPixels, glPixelMap, glPixelStore, glPixelTransfer, glRead-Buffer

NAME

glRectd, glRectf, glRecti, glRects, glRectdv, glRectfv, glRectiv, glRectsv
– draw a rectangle

C SPECIFICATION

```
void glRectd( GLdouble x1,
              GLdouble y1,
              GLdouble x2,
              GLdouble y2 )
void glRectf( GLfloat x1,
              GLfloat y1,
              GLfloat x2,
              GLfloat y2 )
void glRecti( GLint x1,
              GLint y1,
              GLint x2,
              GLint y2 )
void glRects( GLshort x1,
              GLshort y1,
              GLshort x2,
              GLshort y2 )
```

PARAMETERS

x1, y1

Specify one vertex of a rectangle.

x2, y2

Specify the opposite vertex of the rectangle.

C SPECIFICATION

```
void glRectdv( const GLdouble *v1,
               const GLdouble *v2 )
void glRectfv( const GLfloat *v1,
               const GLfloat *v2 )
void glRectiv( const GLint *v1,
               const GLint *v2 )
void glRectsv( const GLshort *v1,
               const GLshort *v2 )
```

PARAMETERS

v1   Specifies a pointer to one vertex of a rectangle.

v2   Specifies a pointer to the opposite vertex of the rectangle.

DESCRIPTION

glRect supports efficient specification of rectangles as two corner points. Each rectangle command takes four arguments, organized either as two consecutive pairs of (x,y) coordinates, or as two pointers to arrays, each containing an (x,y) pair. The resulting rectangle is defined in the $z=0$ plane.

glRect2($x1$, $y1$, $x2$, $y2$) is exactly equivalent to the following sequence:

```
glBegin (GL_POLYGON) ;
glVertex2 (x1, y1) ;
glVertex2 (x2, y1) ;
glVertex2 (x2, y2) ;
glVertex2 (x1, y2) ;
glEnd () ;
```

Note that if the second vertex is above and to the right of the first vertex, the rectangle is constructed with a counterclockwise winding.

ERRORS

GL_INVALID_OPERATION is generated if **glRect** is called between a call to **glBegin** and the corresponding call to **glEnd**.

SEE ALSO

glBegin, glVertex

NAME

glRenderMode – set rasterization mode

C SPECIFICATION

GLint **glRenderMode**(GLenum *mode*)

PARAMETERS

mode Specifies the rasterization mode. Three values are accepted: **GL_RENDER**, **GL_SELECT**, and **GL_FEEDBACK**. The default value is **GL_RENDER**.

DESCRIPTION

glRenderMode sets the rasterization mode. It takes one argument, *mode*, which can assume one of three predefined values:

GL_RENDER Render mode. Primitives are rasterized, producing pixel fragments, which are written into the frame buffer. This is the normal mode and also the default mode.

GL_SELECT Selection mode. No pixel fragments are produced, and no change to the frame buffer contents is made. Instead, a record of the names of primitives that would have been drawn if the render mode was **GL_RENDER** is returned in a select buffer, which must be created (see **glSelectBuffer**) before selection mode is entered.

GL_FEEDBACK Feedback mode. No pixel fragments are produced, and no change to the frame buffer contents is made. Instead, the coordinates and attributes of vertices that would have been drawn had the render mode been **GL_RENDER** is returned in a feedback buffer, which must be created (see **glFeedbackBuffer**) before feedback mode is entered.

The return value of **glRenderMode** is determined by the render mode at the time **glRenderMode** is called, rather than by *mode*. The values returned for the three render modes are as follows:

GL_RENDER Zero.

GL_SELECT The number of hit records transferred to the select buffer.

GL_FEEDBACK The number of values (not vertices) transferred to the feedback buffer.

Refer to the **glSelectBuffer** and **glFeedbackBuffer** reference pages for more details concerning selection and feedback operation.

NOTES

If an error is generated, **glRenderMode** returns zero regardless of the current render mode.

ERRORS

GL_INVALID_ENUM is generated if *mode* is not one of the three accepted values.

GL_INVALID_OPERATION is generated if **glSelectBuffer** is called while the render mode is GL_SELECT, or if **glRenderMode** is called with argument GL_SELECT before **glSelectBuffer** is called at least once.

GL_INVALID_OPERATION is generated if **glFeedbackBuffer** is called while the render mode is GL_FEEDBACK, or if **glRenderMode** is called with argument GL_FEEDBACK before **glFeedbackBuffer** is called at least once.

GL_INVALID_OPERATION is generated if **glRenderMode** is called between a call to **glBegin** and the corresponding call to **glEnd**.

ASSOCIATED GETS

glGet with argument GL_RENDER_MODE

SEE ALSO

glFeedbackBuffer, glInitNames, glLoadName, glPassThrough, glPushName, glSelectBuffer

NAME

glRotated, glRotatef – multiply the current matrix by a rotation matrix

C SPECIFICATION

```
void glRotated( GLdouble angle,
                GLdouble x,
                GLdouble y,
                GLdouble z )
void glRotatef( GLfloat angle,
                GLfloat x,
                GLfloat y,
                GLfloat z )
```

PARAMETERS

angle   Specifies the angle of rotation, in degrees.

x, y, z

Specify the *x*, *y*, and *z* coordinates of a vector, respectively.

DESCRIPTION

glRotate computes a matrix that performs a counterclockwise rotation of *angle* degrees about the vector from the origin through the point (*x*, *y*, *z*).

The current matrix (see **glMatrixMode**) is multiplied by this rotation matrix, with the product replacing the current matrix. That is, if M is the current matrix and R is the translation matrix, then M is replaced with M ● R.

If the matrix mode is either **GL_MODELVIEW** or **GL_PROJECTION**, all objects drawn after **glRotate** is called are rotated. Use **glPushMatrix** and **glPopMatrix** to save and restore the unrotated coordinate system.

ERRORS

GL_INVALID_OPERATION is generated if **glRotate** is called between a call to **glBegin** and the corresponding call to **glEnd**.

ASSOCIATED GETS

glGet with argument GL_MATRIX_MODE
glGet with argument GL_MODELVIEW_MATRIX
glGet with argument GL_PROJECTION_MATRIX
glGet with argument GL_TEXTURE_MATRIX

SEE ALSO

glMatrixMode, **glMultMatrix**, **glPushMatrix**, **glScale**, **glTranslate**

NAME

glScaled, glScalef – multiply the current matrix by a general scaling matrix

C SPECIFICATION

void **glScaled**(GLdouble *x,*
                   GLdouble *y,*
                   GLdouble *z*)
void **glScalef**(GLfloat *x,*
                   GLfloat *y,*
                   GLfloat *z*)

PARAMETERS

x, y, z

Specify scale factors along the *x*, *y*, and *z* axes, respectively.

DESCRIPTION

glScale produces a general scaling along the *x*, *y*, and *z* axes. The three arguments indicate the desired scale factors along each of the three axes. The resulting matrix is

$$
\begin{bmatrix}
x & 0 & 0 & 0 \\
0 & y & 0 & 0 \\
0 & 0 & z & 0 \\
0 & 0 & 0 & 1
\end{bmatrix}
$$

The current matrix (see **glMatrixMode**) is multiplied by this scale matrix, with the product replacing the current matrix. That is, if M is the current matrix and S is the scale matrix, then M is replaced with M • S.

If the matrix mode is either **GL_MODELVIEW** or **GL_PROJECTION**, all objects drawn after **glScale** is called are scaled. Use **glPushMatrix** and **glPopMatrix** to save and restore the unscaled coordinate system.

NOTES

If scale factors other than 1.0 are applied to the modelview matrix and lighting is enabled, automatic normalization of normals should probably also be enabled (**glEnable** and **glDisable** with argument **GL_NORMALIZE**).

ERRORS

GL_INVALID_OPERATION is generated if **glScale** is called between a call to **glBegin** and the corresponding call to **glEnd**.

ASSOCIATED GETS

glGet with argument GL_MATRIX_MODE
glGet with argument GL_MODELVIEW_MATRIX
glGet with argument GL_PROJECTION_MATRIX
glGet with argument GL_TEXTURE_MATRIX

SEE ALSO

glMatrixMode, glMultMatrix, glPushMatrix, glRotate, glTranslate

NAME

glScissor – define the scissor box

C SPECIFICATION

void **glScissor**(GLint *x*,
                    GLint *y*,
                    GLsizei *width*,
                    GLsizei *height*)

PARAMETERS

x, y

Specify the lower left corner of the scissor box. Initially (0,0).

width, height

Specify the width and height of the scissor box. When a GL context is *first* attached to a window, *width* and *height* are set to the dimensions of that window.

DESCRIPTION

The **glScissor** routine defines a rectangle, called the scissor box, in window coordinates. The first two arguments, *x* and *y*, specify the lower left corner of the box. *width* and *height* specify the width and height of the box.

The scissor test is enabled and disabled using **glEnable** and **glDisable** with argument GL_SCISSOR_TEST. While the scissor test is enabled, only pixels that lie within the scissor box can be modified by drawing commands. Window coordinates have integer values at the shared corners of frame buffer pixels, so **glScissor**(0,0,1,1) allows only the lower left pixel in the window to be modified, and **glScissor**(0,0,0,0) disallows modification to all pixels in the window.

When the scissor test is disabled, it is as though the scissor box includes the entire window.

ERRORS

GL_INVALID_VALUE is generated if either *width* or *height* is negative.

GL_INVALID_OPERATION is generated if **glScissor** is called between a call to **glBegin** and the corresponding call to **glEnd**.

ASSOCIATED GETS

glGet with argument GL_SCISSOR_BOX
glIsEnabled with argument GL_SCISSOR_TEST

SEE ALSO

glEnable, glViewport

NAME

glSelectBuffer – establish a buffer for selection mode values

C SPECIFICATION

void **glSelectBuffer**(GLsizei *size*,
                                      GLuint **buffer*)

PARAMETERS

size   Specifies the size of *buffer*.

buffer Returns the selection data.

DESCRIPTION

glSelectBuffer has two arguments: *buffer* is a pointer to an array of unsigned integers, and *size* indicates the size of the array. *buffer* returns values from the name stack (see **glInitNames**, **glLoadName**, **glPushName**) when the rendering mode is GL_SELECT (see **glRenderMode**). **glSelectBuffer** must be issued before selection mode is enabled, and it must not be issued while the rendering mode is GL_SELECT.

Selection is used by a programmer to determine which primitives are drawn into some region of a window. The region is defined by the current modelview and perspective matrices.

In selection mode, no pixel fragments are produced from rasterization. Instead, if a primitive intersects the clipping volume defined by the viewing frustum and the user-defined clipping planes, this primitive causes a selection hit. (With polygons, no hit occurs if the polygon is culled.) When a change is made to the name stack, or when **glRenderMode** is called, a hit record is copied to *buffer* if any hits have occurred since the last such event (name stack change or **glRenderMode** call). The hit record consists of the number of names in the name stack at the time of the event, followed by the minimum and maximum depth values of all vertices that hit since the previous event, followed by the name stack contents, bottom name first.

An internal index into *buffer* is reset to zero whenever selection mode is entered. Each time a hit record is copied into *buffer*, the index is incremented to point to the cell just past the end of the block of names – that is, to the next available cell. If the hit record is larger than the number of remaining locations in *buffer*, as much data as can fit is copied, and the overflow flag is set. If the name stack is empty when a hit record is copied, that record consists of zero followed by the minimum and maximum depth values.

Selection mode is exited by calling **glRenderMode** with an argument other than **GL_SELECT**. Whenever **glRenderMode** is called while the render mode is **GL_SELECT**, it returns the number of hit records copied to *buffer*, resets the overflow flag and the selection buffer pointer, and initializes the name stack to be empty. If the overflow bit was set when **glRenderMode** was called, a negative hit record count is returned.

NOTES

The contents of *buffer* are undefined until **glRenderMode** is called with an argument other than **GL_SELECT**.

Returned depth values are mapped such that the largest unsigned integer value corresponds to window coordinate depth 1.0, and zero corresponds to window coordinate depth 0.0.

glBegin/glEnd primitives and calls to **glRasterPos** can result in hits.

ERRORS

GL_INVALID_VALUE is generated if *size* is negative.

GL_INVALID_OPERATION is generated if **glSelectBuffer** is called while the render mode is **GL_SELECT**, or if **glRenderMode** is called with argument **GL_SELECT** before **glSelectBuffer** is called at least once.

GL_INVALID_OPERATION is generated if **glSelectBuffer** is called between a call to **glBegin** and the corresponding call to **glEnd**.

ASSOCIATED GETS

glGet with argument GL_NAME_STACK_DEPTH

SEE ALSO

glFeedbackBuffer, glInitNames, glLoadName, glPushName, glRenderMode

NAME

glShadeModel – select flat or smooth shading

C SPECIFICATION

void **glShadeModel**(GLenum *mode*)

PARAMETERS

mode Specifies a symbolic value representing a shading technique. Accepted values are **GL_FLAT** and **GL_SMOOTH**. The default is **GL_SMOOTH**.

DESCRIPTION

GL primitives can have either flat or smooth shading. Smooth shading, the default, causes the computed colors of vertices to be interpolated as the primitive is rasterized, typically assigning different colors to each resulting pixel fragment. Flat shading selects the computed color of just one vertex and assigns it to all the pixel fragments generated by rasterizing a single primitive. In either case, the computed color of a vertex is the result of lighting, if lighting is enabled, or it is the current color at the time the vertex was specified, if lighting is disabled.

Flat and smooth shading are indistinguishable for points. Counting vertices and primitives from one starting when **glBegin** is issued, each flat-shaded line segment i is given the computed color of vertex $i+1$, its second vertex. Counting similarly from one, each flat-shaded polygon is given the computed color of the vertex listed in the following table. This is the last vertex to specify the polygon in all cases except single polygons, where the first vertex specifies the flat-shaded color.

primitive type of polygon i	vertex
Single polygon ($i \equiv 1$)	1
Triangle strip	$i+2$
Triangle fan	$i+2$
Independent triangle	$3i$
Quad strip	$2i+2$
Independent quad	$4i$

Flat and smooth shading are specified by **glShadeModel** with *mode* set to **GL_FLAT** and **GL_SMOOTH**, respectively.

ERRORS

GL_INVALID_ENUM is generated if *mode* is any value other than **GL_FLAT** or **GL_SMOOTH**.

GL_INVALID_OPERATION is generated if **glShadeModel** is called between a call to **glBegin** and the corresponding call to **glEnd**.

ASSOCIATED GETS

glGet with argument GL_SHADE_MODEL

SEE ALSO

glBegin, **glColor**, **glLight**, **glLightModel**

NAME

glStencilFunc – set function and reference value for stencil testing

C SPECIFICATION

void **glStencilFunc**(GLenum *func,*
GLint *ref,*
GLuint *mask*)

PARAMETERS

func Specifies the test function. Eight tokens are valid: **GL_NEVER, GL_LESS, GL_LEQUAL, GL_GREATER, GL_GEQUAL, GL_EQUAL, GL_NOTEQUAL,** and **GL_ALWAYS.**

ref Specifies the reference value for the stencil test. *ref* is clamped to the range $[0, 2^n-1]$, where n is the number of bitplanes in the stencil buffer.

mask
Specifies a mask that is ANDed with both the reference value and the stored stencil value when the test is done.

DESCRIPTION

Stenciling, like z-buffering, enables and disables drawing on a per-pixel basis. You draw into the stencil planes using GL drawing primitives, then render geometry and images, using the stencil planes to mask out portions of the screen. Stenciling is typically used in multipass rendering algorithms to achieve special effects, such as decals, outlining, and constructive solid geometry rendering.

The stencil test conditionally eliminates a pixel based on the outcome of a comparison between the reference value and the value in the stencil buffer. The test is enabled by **glEnable** and **glDisable** with argument GL_STENCIL. Actions taken based on the outcome of the stencil test are specified with **glStencilOp.**

func is a symbolic constant that determines the stencil comparison function. It accepts one of eight values, shown below. *ref* is an integer reference value that is used in the stencil comparison. It is clamped to the range $[0, 2^n-1]$, where n is the number of bitplanes in the stencil buffer. *mask* is bitwise ANDed with both the reference value and the stored stencil value, with the ANDed values participating in the comparison.

If *stencil* represents the value stored in the corresponding stencil buffer location, the following list shows the effect of each comparison function that can be specified by *ref*. Only if the comparison succeeds is the pixel passed through to the next stage in the rasterization process (see **glStencilOp**). All tests treat *stencil* values as unsigned integers in the range $[0, 2^n-1]$, where n is the number of bitplanes in the stencil buffer.

Here are the values accepted by *func*:

GL_NEVER	Always fails.
GL_LESS	Passes if (*ref* & *mask*) < (*stencil* & *mask*).
GL_LEQUAL	Passes if (*ref* & *mask*) ≤ (*stencil* & *mask*).
GL_GREATER	Passes if (*ref* & *mask*) > (*stencil* & *mask*).
GL_GEQUAL	Passes if (*ref* & *mask*) ≥ (*stencil* & *mask*).
GL_EQUAL	Passes if (*ref* & *mask*) = (*stencil* & *mask*).
GL_NOTEQUAL	Passes if (*ref* & *mask*) ≠ (*stencil* & *mask*).
GL_ALWAYS	Always passes.

NOTES

Initially, the stencil test is disabled. If there is no stencil buffer, no stencil modification can occur and it is as if the stencil test always passes.

ERRORS

GL_INVALID_ENUM is generated if *func* is not one of the eight accepted values.

GL_INVALID_OPERATION is generated if **glStencilFunc** is called between a call to **glBegin** and the corresponding call to **glEnd**.

ASSOCIATED GETS

glGet with argument GL_STENCIL_FUNC
glGet with argument GL_STENCIL_VALUE_MASK
glGet with argument GL_STENCIL_REF
glGet with argument GL_STENCIL_BITS
glIsEnabled with argument GL_STENCIL_TEST

SEE ALSO

glAlphaFunc, glBlendFunc, glDepthFunc, glEnable, glIsEnabled, glLogicOp, glStencilOp

NAME

glStencilMask – control the writing of individual bits in the stencil planes

C SPECIFICATION

void **glStencilMask**(GLuint *mask*)

PARAMETERS

mask Specifies a bit mask to enable and disable writing of individual bits in the stencil planes. Initially, the mask is all ones.

DESCRIPTION

glStencilMask controls the writing of individual bits in the stencil planes. The least significant *n* bits of *mask*, where *n* is the number of bits in the stencil buffer, specify a mask. Wherever a one appears in the mask, the corresponding bit in the stencil buffer is made writable. Where a zero appears, the bit is write-protected. Initially, all bits are enabled for writing.

ERRORS

GL_INVALID_OPERATION is generated if **glStencilMask** is called between a call to **glBegin** and the corresponding call to **glEnd**.

ASSOCIATED GETS

glGet with argument GL_STENCIL_WRITEMASK
glGet with argument GL_STENCIL_BITS

SEE ALSO

glColorMask, glDepthMask, glIndexMask, glStencilFunc, glStencilOp

NAME

glStencilOp – set stencil test actions

C SPECIFICATION

void **glStencilOp**(GLenum *fail*,
                    GLenum *zfail*,
                    GLenum *zpass*)

PARAMETERS

fail   Specifies the action to take when the stencil test fails. Six symbolic constants are accepted: **GL_KEEP**, **GL_ZERO**, **GL_REPLACE**, **GL_INCR**, **GL_DECR**, and **GL_INVERT**.

zfail Specifies stencil action when the stencil test passes, but the depth test fails. *zfail* accepts the same symbolic constants as *fail*.

zpass

     Specifies stencil action when both the stencil test and the depth test pass, or when the stencil test passes and either there is no depth buffer or depth testing is not enabled. *zpass* accepts the same symbolic constants as *fail*.

DESCRIPTION

Stenciling, like z-buffering, enables and disables drawing on a per-pixel basis. You draw into the stencil planes using GL drawing primitives, then render geometry and images, using the stencil planes to mask out portions of the screen. Stenciling is typically used in multipass rendering algorithms to achieve special effects, such as decals, outlining, and constructive solid geometry rendering.

The stencil test conditionally eliminates a pixel based on the outcome of a comparison between the value in the stencil buffer and a reference value. The test is enabled with **glEnable** and **glDisable** calls with argument **GL_STENCIL**, and controlled with **glStencilFunc**.

glStencilOp takes three arguments that indicate what happens to the stored stencil value while stenciling is enabled. If the stencil test fails, no change is made to the pixel's color or depth buffers, and *fail* specifies what happens to the stencil buffer contents. The six possible actions are as follows:

GL_KEEP   Keeps the current value.

GL_ZERO   Sets the stencil buffer value to zero.

GL_REPLACE   Sets the stencil buffer value to *ref*, as specified by **glStencilFunc**.

GL_INCR	Increments the current stencil buffer value. Clamps to the maximum representable unsigned value.
GL_DECR	Decrements the current stencil buffer value. Clamps to zero.
GL_INVERT	Bitwise inverts the current stencil buffer value.

Stencil buffer values are treated as unsigned integers. When incremented and decremented, values are clamped to 0 and 2^n-1, where n is the value returned by querying **GL_STENCIL_BITS**.

The other two arguments to **glStencilOp** specify stencil buffer actions should subsequent depth buffer tests succeed (*zpass*) or fail (*zfail*). (See **glDepthFunc**.) They are specified using the same six symbolic constants as *fail*. Note that *zfail* is ignored when there is no depth buffer, or when the depth buffer is not enabled. In these cases, *fail* and *zpass* specify stencil action when the stencil test fails and passes, respectively.

NOTES

Initially the stencil test is disabled. If there is no stencil buffer, no stencil modification can occur and it is as if the stencil tests always pass, regardless of any call to **glStencilOp**.

ERRORS

GL_INVALID_ENUM is generated if *fail*, *zfail*, or *zpass* is any value other than the six defined constant values.

GL_INVALID_OPERATION is generated if **glStencilOp** is called between a call to **glBegin** and the corresponding call to **glEnd**.

ASSOCIATED GETS

glGet with argument GL_STENCIL_FAIL
glGet with argument GL_STENCIL_PASS_DEPTH_PASS
glGet with argument GL_STENCIL_PASS_DEPTH_FAIL
glGet with argument GL_STENCIL_BITS
glIsEnabled with argument GL_STENCIL_TEST

SEE ALSO

glAlphaFunc, glBlendFunc, glDepthFunc, glEnable, glLogicOp, glStencilFunc

NAME

glTexCoord1d, glTexCoord1f, glTexCoord1i, glTexCoord1s, glTexCoord2d, glTexCoord2f, glTexCoord2i, glTexCoord2s, glTexCoord3d, glTexCoord3f, glTexCoord3i, glTexCoord3s, glTexCoord4d, glTexCoord4f, glTexCoord4i, glTexCoord4s, glTexCoord1dv, glTexCoord1fv, glTexCoord1iv, glTexCoord1sv, glTexCoord2dv, glTexCoord2fv, glTexCoord2iv, glTexCoord2sv, glTexCoord3dv, glTexCoord3fv, glTexCoord3iv, glTexCoord3sv, glTexCoord4dv, glTexCoord4fv, glTexCoord4iv, glTexCoord4sv
– set the current texture coordinates

C SPECIFICATION

```
void glTexCoord1d( GLdouble s )
void glTexCoord1f( GLfloat s )
void glTexCoord1i( GLint s )
void glTexCoord1s( GLshort s )
void glTexCoord2d( GLdouble s,
                   GLdouble t )
void glTexCoord2f( GLfloat s,
                   GLfloat t )
void glTexCoord2i( GLint s,
                   GLint t )
void glTexCoord2s( GLshort s,
                   GLshort t )
void glTexCoord3d( GLdouble s,
                   GLdouble t,
                   GLdouble r )
void glTexCoord3f( GLfloat s,
                   GLfloat t,
                   GLfloat r )
void glTexCoord3i( GLint s,
                   GLint t,
                   GLint r )
void glTexCoord3s( GLshort s,
                   GLshort t,
                   GLshort r )
void glTexCoord4d( GLdouble s,
                   GLdouble t,
                   GLdouble r,
                   GLdouble q )
void glTexCoord4f( GLfloat s,
                   GLfloat t,
                   GLfloat r,
                   GLfloat q )
```

```
        void glTexCoord4i( GLint s,
                           GLint t,
                           GLint r,
                           GLint q )
        void glTexCoord4s( GLshort s,
                           GLshort t,
                           GLshort r,
                           GLshort q )
```

PARAMETERS

    s, t, r, q

        Specify s, t, r, and q texture coordinates. Not all parameters are present in all forms of the command.

C SPECIFICATION

```
        void glTexCoord1dv( const GLdouble *v )
        void glTexCoord1fv( const GLfloat *v )
        void glTexCoord1iv( const GLint *v )
        void glTexCoord1sv( const GLshort *v )
        void glTexCoord2dv( const GLdouble *v )
        void glTexCoord2fv( const GLfloat *v )
        void glTexCoord2iv( const GLint *v )
        void glTexCoord2sv( const GLshort *v )
        void glTexCoord3dv( const GLdouble *v )
        void glTexCoord3fv( const GLfloat *v )
        void glTexCoord3iv( const GLint *v )
        void glTexCoord3sv( const GLshort *v )
        void glTexCoord4dv( const GLdouble *v )
        void glTexCoord4fv( const GLfloat *v )
        void glTexCoord4iv( const GLint *v )
        void glTexCoord4sv( const GLshort *v )
```

PARAMETERS

    v Specifies a pointer to an array of one, two, three, or four elements, which in turn specify the s, t, r, and q texture coordinates.

DESCRIPTION

The current texture coordinates are part of the data that is associated with polygon vertices. They are set with **glTexCoord**.

glTexCoord specifies texture coordinates in one, two, three, or four dimensions. **glTexCoord1** sets the current texture coordinates to $(s, 0, 0, 1)$; a call to **glTexCoord2** sets them to $(s, t, 0, 1)$.

Similarly, **glTexCoord3** specifies the texture coordinates as $(s, t, r, 1)$, and **glTexCoord4** defines all four components explicitly as (s, t, r, q).

NOTES

The current texture coordinates can be updated at any time. In particular, **glTexCoord** can be called between a call to **glBegin** and the corresponding call to **glEnd**.

ASSOCIATED GETS

glGet with argument GL_CURRENT_TEXTURE_COORDS

SEE ALSO

glVertex

NAME

glTexEnvf, glTexEnvi, glTexEnvfv, glTexEnviv – set texture environment parameters

C SPECIFICATION

void **glTexEnvf**(GLenum *target*,
                        GLenum *pname*,
                        GLfloat *param*)
void **glTexEnvi**(GLenum *target*,
                        GLenum *pname*,
                        GLint *param*)

PARAMETERS

target   Specifies a texture environment. Must be **GL_TEXTURE_ENV**.

pname

> Specifies the symbolic name of a single-valued texture environment parameter. Must be **GL_TEXTURE_ENV_MODE**.

param

> Specifies a single symbolic constant, one of **GL_MODULATE**, **GL_DECAL**, or **GL_BLEND**.

C SPECIFICATION

void **glTexEnvfv**(GLenum *target*,
                        GLenum *pname*,
                        const GLfloat **params*)
void **glTexEnviv**(GLenum *target*,
                        GLenum *pname*,
                        const GLint **params*)

PARAMETERS

target   Specifies a texture environment. Must be **GL_TEXTURE_ENV**.

pname   Specifies the symbolic name of a texture environment parameter. Accepted values are **GL_TEXTURE_ENV_MODE** and **GL_TEXTURE_ENV_COLOR**.

params   Specifies a pointer to an array of parameters: either a single symbolic constant or an RGBA color.

DESCRIPTION

A texture environment specifies how texture values are interpreted when a fragment is textured. *target* must be **GL_TEXTURE_ENV**. *pname* can be either **GL_TEXTURE_ENV_MODE** or **GL_TEXTURE_ENV_COLOR**.

If *pname* is **GL_TEXTURE_ENV_MODE**, then *params* is (or points to) the symbolic name of a texture function. Three texture functions are defined: **GL_MODULATE**, **GL_DECAL**, and **GL_BLEND**

A texture function acts on the fragment to be textured using the texture image value that applies to the fragment (see **glTexParameter**) and produces an RGBA color for that fragment. The following table shows how the RGBA color is produced for each of the three texture functions that can be chosen. *C* is a triple of color values (RGB) and *A* is the associated alpha value. RGBA values extracted from a texture image are in the range [0,1]. The subscript *f* refers to the incoming fragment, the subscript *t* to the texture image, the subscript *c* to the texture environment color, and subscript *v* indicates a value produced by the texture function.

A texture image can have up to four components per texture element (see **glTexImage1D** and **glTexImage2D**). In a one-component image, L_t indicates that single component. A two-component image uses L_t and A_t. A three-component image has only a color value, C_t. A four-component image has both a color value C_t and an alpha value A_t.

number of components	texture functions		
	GL_MODULATE	GL_DECAL	GL_BLEND
1	$C_v = L_t C_f$ $A_v = A_f$	undefined	$C_v = (1 - L_t)C_f + L_t C_c$ $A_v = A_f$
2	$C_v = L_t C_f$ $A_v = A_t A_f$	undefined	$C_v = (1 - L_t)C_f + L_t C_c$ $A_v = A_t A_f$
3	$C_v = C_t C_f$ $A_v = A_f$	$C_v = C_t$ $A_v = A_f$	undefined
4	$C_v = C_t C_f$ $A_v = A_t A_f$	$C_v = (1 - A_t)C_f + A_t C_t$ $A_v = A_f$	undefined

If *pname* is **GL_TEXTURE_ENV_COLOR**, *params* is a pointer to an array that holds an RGBA color consisting of four values. Integer color components are interpreted linearly such that the most positive integer maps to 1.0, and the most negative integer maps to -1.0. The values are clamped to the range [0,1] when they are specified. C_c takes these four values.

GL_TEXTURE_ENV_MODE defaults to **GL_MODULATE** and **GL_TEXTURE_ENV_COLOR** defaults to (0,0,0,0).

ERRORS

GL_INVALID_ENUM is generated when *target* or *pname* is not one of the accepted defined values, or when *params* should have a defined constant value (based on the value of *pname*) and does not.

GL_INVALID_OPERATION is generated if **glTexEnv** is called between a call to **glBegin** and the corresponding call to **glEnd**.

ASSOCIATED GETS

glGetTexEnv

SEE ALSO

glTexImage1D, **glTexImage2D**, **glTexParameter**

NAME

glTexGend, glTexGenf, glTexGeni, glTexGendv, glTexGenfv, glTexGeniv
– control the generation of texture coordinates

C SPECIFICATION

```
void glTexGend( GLenum coord,
                GLenum pname,
                GLdouble param )
void glTexGenf( GLenum coord,
                GLenum pname,
                GLfloat param )
void glTexGeni( GLenum coord,
                GLenum pname,
                GLint param )
```

PARAMETERS

coord   Specifies a texture coordinate. Must be one of the following: **GL_S, GL_T, GL_R**, or **GL_Q**.

pname Specifies the symbolic name of the texture-coordinate generation function. Must be **GL_TEXTURE_GEN_MODE**.

param Specifies a single-valued texture generation parameter, one of **GL_OBJECT_LINEAR, GL_EYE_LINEAR**, or **GL_SPHERE_MAP**.

C SPECIFICATION

```
void glTexGendv( GLenum coord,
                 GLenum pname,
                 const GLdouble *params )
void glTexGenfv( GLenum coord,
                 GLenum pname,
                 const GLfloat *params )
void glTexGeniv( GLenum coord,
                 GLenum pname,
                 const GLint *params )
```

PARAMETERS

coord   Specifies a texture coordinate. Must be one of the following: **GL_S, GL_T, GL_R**, or **GL_Q**.

pname Specifies the symbolic name of the texture-coordinate generation function or function parameters. Must be **GL_TEXTURE_GEN_MODE, GL_OBJECT_PLANE**, or **GL_EYE_PLANE**.

params Specifies a pointer to an array of texture generation parameters. If *pname* is **GL_TEXTURE_GEN_MODE**, then the array must contain a single symbolic constant, one of **GL_OBJECT_LINEAR, GL_EYE_LINEAR,** or **GL_SPHERE_MAP**. Otherwise, *params* holds the coefficients for the texture-coordinate generation function specified by *pname*.

DESCRIPTION

glTexGen selects a texture-coordinate generation function or supplies coefficients for one of the functions. *coord* names one of the (s,t,r,q) texture coordinates, and it must be one of these symbols: **GL_S, GL_T, GL_R,** or **GL_Q.** *pname* must be one of three symbolic constants: **GL_TEXTURE_GEN_MODE, GL_OBJECT_PLANE,** or **GL_EYE_PLANE.** If *pname* is **GL_TEXTURE_GEN_MODE,** then *params* chooses a mode, one of **GL_OBJECT_LINEAR, GL_EYE_LINEAR,** or **GL_SPHERE_MAP.** If *pname* is either **GL_OBJECT_PLANE** or **GL_EYE_PLANE,** *params* contains coefficients for the corresponding texture generation function.

If the texture generation function is **GL_OBJECT_LINEAR,** the function

$$g = p_1 x_o + p_2 y_o + p_3 z_o + p_4 w_o$$

is used, where g is the value computed for the coordinate named in *coord*, $p_1, p_2, p_3,$ and p_4 are the four values supplied in *params*, and $x_o, y_o, z_o,$ and w_o are the object coordinates of the vertex. This function can be used to texture-map terrain using sea level as a reference plane (defined by $p_1, p_2, p_3,$ and p_4). The altitude of a terrain vertex is computed by the **GL_OBJECT_LINEAR** coordinate generation function as its distance from sea level; that altitude is used to index the texture image to map white snow onto peaks and green grass onto foothills, for example.

If the texture generation function is **GL_EYE_LINEAR,** the function

$$g = p_1' x_e + p_2' y_e + p_3' z_e + p_4' w_e$$

is used, where

$$(p_1' \ \ p_2' \ \ p_3' \ \ p_4') = (p_1 \ \ p_2 \ \ p_3 \ \ p_4) \, M^{-1}$$

and $x_e, y_e, z_e,$ and w_e are the eye coordinates of the vertex, $p_1, p_2, p_3,$ and p_4 are the values supplied in *params*, and M is the modelview matrix when **glTexGen** is invoked. If M is poorly conditioned or singular, texture coordinates generated by the resulting function may be inaccurate or undefined.

Note that the values in *params* define a reference plane in eye coordinates. The modelview matrix that is applied to them may not be the same one in effect when the polygon vertices are transformed. This function establishes a field of texture coordinates that can produce dynamic contour lines on moving objects.

If *pname* is **GL_SPHERE_MAP** and *coord* is either **GL_TEXTURE_GEN_S** or **GL_TEXTURE_GEN_T**, *s* and *t* texture coordinates are generated as follows. Let **u** be the unit vector pointing from the origin to the polygon vertex (in eye coordinates). Let **n′** be the current normal, after transformation to eye coordinates. Let $\mathbf{f} = (f_x\ f_y\ f_z)^T$ be the reflection vector such that

$$\mathbf{f} = \mathbf{u} - 2\mathbf{n}'\mathbf{n}'^T\mathbf{u}$$

Finally, let $m = 2\sqrt{f_x^2 + f_y^2 + (f_z + 1)^2}$. Then the values assigned to the *s* and *t* texture coordinates are

$$s = \frac{f_x}{m} + \frac{1}{2}$$

$$t = \frac{f_y}{m} + \frac{1}{2}$$

A texture-coordinate generation function is enabled or disabled using **glEnable** or **glDisable** with one of the symbolic texture-coordinate names (**GL_TEXTURE_GEN_S**, **GL_TEXTURE_GEN_T**, **GL_TEXTURE_GEN_R**, or **GL_TEXTURE_GEN_Q**) as the argument. When enabled, the specified texture coordinate is computed according to the generating function associated with that coordinate. When disabled, subsequent vertices take the specified texture coordinate from the current set of texture coordinates. Initially, all texture generation functions are set to **GL_EYE_LINEAR** and are disabled. Both *s* plane equations are (1,0,0,0), both *t* plane equations are (0,1,0,0), and all *r* and *q* plane equations are (0,0,0,0).

ERRORS

GL_INVALID_ENUM is generated when *coord* or *pname* is not an accepted defined value, or when *pname* is **GL_TEXTURE_GEN_MODE** and *params* is not an accepted defined value.

GL_INVALID_ENUM is generated when *pname* is **GL_TEXTURE_GEN_MODE**, *params* is **GL_SPHERE_MAP**, and *coord* is either **GL_TEXTURE_GEN_R** or **GL_TEXTURE_GEN_Q**.

GL_INVALID_OPERATION is generated if **glTexGen** is called between a call to **glBegin** and the corresponding call to **glEnd**.

ASSOCIATED GETS

glGetTexGen

glIsEnabled with argument GL_TEXTURE_GEN_S

glIsEnabled with argument GL_TEXTURE_GEN_T

glIsEnabled with argument GL_TEXTURE_GEN_R

glIsEnabled with argument GL_TEXTURE_GEN_Q

SEE ALSO

glTexEnv, **glTexImage1D**, **glTexImage2D**, **glTexParameter**

NAME

glTexImage1D – specify a one-dimensional texture image

C SPECIFICATION

```
void glTexImage1D( GLenum target,
                   GLint level,
                   GLint components,
                   GLsizei width,
                   GLint border,
                   GLenum format,
                   GLenum type,
                   const GLvoid *pixels )
```

PARAMETERS

target   Specifies the target texture. Must be **GL_TEXTURE_1D**.

level   Specifies the level-of-detail number. Level 0 is the base image level.
              Level n is the nth mipmap reduction image.

components
              Specifies the number of color components in the texture. Must be 1, 2,
              3, or 4.

width   Specifies the width of the texture image. Must be $2^n+2(border)$ for some
              integer n. The height of the texture image is 1.

border   Specifies the width of the border. Must be either 0 or 1.

format   Specifies the format of the pixel data. The following symbolic values are
              accepted: **GL_COLOR_INDEX, GL_RED, GL_GREEN, GL_BLUE,
              GL_ALPHA, GL_RGB, GL_RGBA, GL_LUMINANCE,** and
              GL_LUMINANCE_ALPHA.

type   Specifies the data type of the pixel data. The following symbolic values
              are accepted: **GL_UNSIGNED_BYTE, GL_BYTE, GL_BITMAP,
              GL_UNSIGNED_SHORT, GL_SHORT, GL_UNSIGNED_INT, GL_INT,**
              and **GL_FLOAT.**

pixels   Specifies a pointer to the image data in memory.

DESCRIPTION

Texturing maps a portion of a specified *texture image* onto each graphical primitive
for which texturing is enabled. One-dimensional texturing is enabled and disabled
using **glEnable** and **glDisable** with argument **GL_TEXTURE_1D.**

Texture images are defined with **glTexImage1D**. The arguments describe the parameters of the texture image, such as width, width of the border, level-of-detail number (see **glTexParameter**), and number of color components provided. The last three arguments describe the way the image is represented in memory, and they are identical to the pixel formats used for **glDrawPixels**.

Data is read from *pixels* as a sequence of signed or unsigned bytes, shorts, or longs, or single-precision floating-point values, depending on *type*. These values are grouped into sets of one, two, three, or four values, depending on *format*, to form an element. If *type* is GL_BITMAP, the data is considered as a string of unsigned bytes. *components* must be GL_COLOR_INDEX. Each data byte is treated as eight 1-bit elements, with bit ordering determined by **GL_UNPACK_LSB_FIRST** (see **glPixelStore**).

format determines the composition of each element in *pixels* and selects the target frame buffer. It can assume one of nine symbolic values:

GL_COLOR_INDEX

Each element is a single value, a color index. It is converted to fixed point (with an unspecified number of zero bits to the right of the binary point), shifted left or right depending on the value and sign of **GL_INDEX_SHIFT**, and added to **GL_INDEX_OFFSET** (see **glPixelTransfer**). The resulting index is converted to a set of color components using the **GL_PIXEL_MAP_I_TO_R**, **GL_PIXEL_MAP_I_TO_G**, **GL_PIXEL_MAP_I_TO_B**, and **GL_PIXEL_MAP_I_TO_A** tables, and clamped to the range [0,1].

GL_RED Each element is a single red component. It is converted to floating point and assembled into an RGBA element by attaching 0.0 for green and blue, and 1.0 for alpha. Each component is then multiplied by the signed scale factor **GL_c_SCALE**, added to the signed bias **GL_c_BIAS**, and clamped to the range [0,1] (see **glPixelTransfer**).

GL_GREEN

Each element is a single green component. It is converted to floating point and assembled into an RGBA element by attaching 0.0 for red and blue, and 1.0 for alpha. Each component is then multiplied by the signed scale factor **GL_c_SCALE**, added to the signed bias **GL_c_BIAS**, and clamped to the range [0,1] (see **glPixelTransfer**).

GL_BLUE Each element is a single blue component. It is converted to floating point and assembled into an RGBA element by attaching 0.0 for red and green, and 1.0 for alpha. Each component is then multiplied by the signed scale factor **GL_c_SCALE**, added to the signed bias **GL_c_BIAS**, and clamped to the range [0,1] (see **glPixelTransfer**).

GL_ALPHA

Each element is a single red component. It is converted to floating point and assembled into an RGBA element by attaching 0.0 for red, green, and blue. Each component is then multiplied by the signed scale factor **GL_c_SCALE**, added to the signed bias **GL_c_BIAS**, and clamped to the range [0,1] (see **glPixelTransfer**).

GL_RGB Each element is an RGB triple. It is converted to floating point and assembled into an RGBA element by attaching 1.0 for alpha. Each component is then multiplied by the signed scale factor **GL_c_SCALE**, added to the signed bias **GL_c_BIAS**, and clamped to the range [0,1] (see **glPixelTransfer**).

GL_RGBA

Each element is a complete RGBA element. It is converted to floating point. Each component is then multiplied by the signed scale factor **GL_c_SCALE**, added to the signed bias **GL_c_BIAS**, and clamped to the range [0,1] (see **glPixelTransfer**).

GL_LUMINANCE

Each element is a single luminance value. It is converted to floating point, then assembled into an RGBA element by replicating the luminance value three times for red, green, and blue and attaching 1.0 for alpha. Each component is then multiplied by the signed scale factor **GL_c_SCALE**, added to the signed bias **GL_c_BIAS**, and clamped to the range [0,1] (see **glPixelTransfer**).

GL_LUMINANCE_ALPHA

Each element is a luminance/alpha pair. It is converted to floating point, then assembled into an RGBA element by replicating the luminance value three times for red, green, and blue. Each component is then multiplied by the signed scale factor **GL_c_SCALE**, added to the signed bias **GL_c_BIAS**, and clamped to the range [0,1] (see **glPixelTransfer**).

A texture image can have up to four components per texture element, depending on *components*. A one-component texture image uses only the red component of the RGBA color extracted from *pixels*. A two-component image uses the R and A values. A three-component image uses the R, G, and B values. A four-component image uses all of the RGBA components.

NOTES

Texturing has no effect in color index mode.

The texture image can be represented by the same data formats as the pixels in a **glDrawPixels** command, except that **GL_STENCIL_INDEX** and **GL_DEPTH_COMPONENT** cannot be used. **glPixelStore** and **glPixelTransfer** modes affect texture images in exactly the way they affect **glDrawPixels**.

A texture image with zero width indicates the null texture. If the null texture is specified for level-of-detail 0, it is as if texturing were disabled.

ERRORS

GL_INVALID_ENUM is generated when *target* is not **GL_TEXTURE_1D**.

GL_INVALID_ENUM is generated when *format* is not an accepted *format* constant. Format constants other than **GL_STENCIL_INDEX** and **GL_DEPTH_COMPONENT** are accepted.

GL_INVALID_ENUM is generated when *type* is not a *type* constant.

GL_INVALID_VALUE is generated if *level* is less than zero or greater than $\log_2 max$, where *max* is the returned value of **GL_MAX_TEXTURE_SIZE**.

GL_INVALID_VALUE is generated if *components* is not 1, 2, 3, or 4.

GL_INVALID_VALUE is generated if *width* is less than zero or greater than 2 + **GL_MAX_TEXTURE_SIZE**, or if it cannot be represented as $2^n + 2(border)$ for some integer value of *n*.

GL_INVALID_VALUE is generated if *border* is not 0 or 1.

GL_INVALID_OPERATION is generated if **glTexImage1D** is called between a call to **glBegin** and the corresponding call to **glEnd**.

ASSOCIATED GETS

glGetTexImage
glIsEnabled with argument **GL_TEXTURE_1D**

SEE ALSO

glDrawPixels, **glFog**, **glPixelStore**, **glPixelTransfer**, **glTexEnv**, **glTexGen**, **glTexImage2D**, **glTexParameter**

NAME

glTexImage2D – specify a two-dimensional texture image

C SPECIFICATION

void **glTexImage2D**(GLenum *target*,
                GLint *level*,
                GLint *components*,
                GLsizei *width*,
                GLsizei *height*,
                GLint *border*,
                GLenum *format*,
                GLenum *type*,
                const GLvoid **pixels*)

PARAMETERS

target   Specifies the target texture. Must be **GL_TEXTURE_2D**.

level   Specifies the level-of-detail number. Level 0 is the base image level.
             Level *n* is the *n*th mipmap reduction image.

components
             Specifies the number of color components in the texture. Must be 1, 2,
             3, or 4.

width   Specifies the width of the texture image. Must be $2^n+2(border)$ for some
             integer *n*.

height   Specifies the height of the texture image. Must be $2^m+2(border)$ for some
             integer *m*.

border   Specifies the width of the border. Must be either 0 or 1.

format   Specifies the format of the pixel data. The following symbolic values are
             accepted: **GL_COLOR_INDEX**, **GL_RED**, **GL_GREEN**, **GL_BLUE**,
             GL_ALPHA, **GL_RGB**, **GL_RGBA**, **GL_LUMINANCE**, and
             GL_LUMINANCE_ALPHA.

type   Specifies the data type of the pixel data. The following symbolic values
             are accepted: **GL_UNSIGNED_BYTE**, **GL_BYTE**, **GL_BITMAP**,
             GL_UNSIGNED_SHORT, **GL_SHORT**, **GL_UNSIGNED_INT**, **GL_INT**,
             and **GL_FLOAT**.

pixels   Specifies a pointer to the image data in memory.

DESCRIPTION

Texturing maps a portion of a specified *texture image* onto each graphical primitive for which texturing is enabled. Two-dimensional texturing is enabled and disabled using **glEnable** and **glDisable** with argument **GL_TEXTURE_2D**.

Texture images are defined with **glTexImage2D**. The arguments describe the parameters of the texture image, such as height, width, width of the border, level-of-detail number (see **glTexParameter**), and number of color components provided. The last three arguments describe the way the image is represented in memory, and they are identical to the pixel formats used for **glDrawPixels**.

Data is read from *pixels* as a sequence of signed or unsigned bytes, shorts, or longs, or single-precision floating-point values, depending on *type*. These values are grouped into sets of one, two, three, or four values, depending on *components*, to form an element. If *type* is **GL_BITMAP**, the data is considered as a string of unsigned bytes (and *components* must be **GL_COLOR_INDEX**). Each data byte is treated as eight 1-bit elements, with bit ordering determined by **GL_UNPACK_LSB_FIRST** (see **glPixelStore**).

format determines the composition of each element in *pixels* and selects the target frame buffer. It can assume one of nine symbolic values:

GL_COLOR_INDEX

> Each element is a single value, a color index. It is converted to fixed point (with an unspecified number of zero bits to the right of the binary point), shifted left or right depending on the value and sign of **GL_INDEX_SHIFT**, and added to **GL_INDEX_OFFSET** (see **glPixel-Transfer**). The resulting index is converted to a set of color components using the **GL_PIXEL_MAP_I_TO_R**, **GL_PIXEL_MAP_I_TO_G**, **GL_PIXEL_MAP_I_TO_B**, and **GL_PIXEL_MAP_I_TO_A** tables, and clamped to the range [0,1].

GL_RED Each element is a single red component. It is converted to floating point and assembled into an RGBA element by attaching 0.0 for green and blue, and 1.0 for alpha. Each component is then multiplied by the signed scale factor **GL_c_SCALE**, added to the signed bias **GL_c_BIAS**, and clamped to the range [0,1] (see **glPixelTransfer**).

GL_GREEN

> Each element is a single green component. It is converted to floating point and assembled into an RGBA element by attaching 0.0 for red and blue, and 1.0 for alpha. Each component is then multiplied by the signed scale factor **GL_c_SCALE**, added to the signed bias **GL_c_BIAS**, and clamped to the range [0,1] (see **glPixelTransfer**).

GL_BLUE Each element is a single blue component. It is converted to floating point and assembled into an RGBA element by attaching 0.0 for red and green, and 1.0 for alpha. Each component is then multiplied by the signed scale factor **GL_c_SCALE**, added to the signed bias **GL_c_BIAS**, and clamped to the range [0,1] (see **glPixelTransfer**).

GL_ALPHA

Each element is a single red component. It is converted to floating point and assembled into an RGBA element by attaching 0.0 for red, green, and blue. Each component is then multiplied by the signed scale factor **GL_c_SCALE**, added to the signed bias **GL_c_BIAS**, and clamped to the range [0,1] (see **glPixelTransfer**).

GL_RGB Each element is an RGB triple. It is converted to floating point and assembled into an RGBA element by attaching 1.0 for alpha. Each component is then multiplied by the signed scale factor **GL_c_SCALE**, added to the signed bias **GL_c_BIAS**, and clamped to the range [0,1] (see **glPixelTransfer**).

GL_RGBA

Each element is a complete RGBA element. It is converted to floating point. Each component is then multiplied by the signed scale factor **GL_c_SCALE**, added to the signed bias **GL_c_BIAS**, and clamped to the range [0,1] (see **glPixelTransfer**).

GL_LUMINANCE

Each element is a single luminance value. It is converted to floating point, then assembled into an RGBA element by replicating the luminance value three times for red, green, and blue and attaching 1.0 for alpha. Each component is then multiplied by the signed scale factor **GL_c_SCALE**, added to the signed bias **GL_c_BIAS**, and clamped to the range [0,1] (see **glPixelTransfer**).

GL_LUMINANCE_ALPHA

Each element is a luminance/alpha pair. It is converted to floating point, then assembled into an RGBA element by replicating the luminance value three times for red, green, and blue. Each component is then multiplied by the signed scale factor **GL_c_SCALE**, added to the signed bias **GL_c_BIAS**, and clamped to the range [0,1] (see **glPixelTransfer**).

Please refer to the **glDrawPixels** reference page for a description of the acceptable values for the *type* parameter.

A texture image can have up to four components per texture element, depending on *components*. A one-component texture image uses only the red component of the RGBA color extracted from *pixels*. A two-component image uses the R and A values. A three-component image uses the R, G, and B values. A four-component image uses all of the RGBA components.

NOTES

Texturing has no effect in color index mode.

The texture image can be represented by the same data formats as the pixels in a **glDrawPixels** command, except that **GL_STENCIL_INDEX** and **GL_DEPTH_COMPONENT** cannot be used. **glPixelStore** and **glPixelTransfer** modes affect texture images in exactly the way they affect **glDrawPixels**.

A texture image with zero height or width indicates the null texture. If the null texture is specified for level-of-detail 0, it is as if texturing were disabled.

ERRORS

GL_INVALID_ENUM is generated when *target* is not **GL_TEXTURE_2D**.

GL_INVALID_ENUM is generated when *format* is not an accepted *format* constant. Format constants other than **GL_STENCIL_INDEX** and **GL_DEPTH_COMPONENT** are accepted.

GL_INVALID_ENUM is generated when *type* is not a *type* constant.

GL_INVALID_VALUE is generated if *level* is less than zero or greater than $\log_2 max$, where *max* is the returned value of **GL_MAX_TEXTURE_SIZE**.

GL_INVALID_VALUE is generated if *components* is not 1, 2, 3, or 4.

GL_INVALID_VALUE is generated if *width* or *height* is less than zero or greater than 2 + **GL_MAX_TEXTURE_SIZE**, or if either cannot be represented as $2^k + 2(border)$ for some integer value of *k*.

GL_INVALID_VALUE is generated if *border* is not 0 or 1.

GL_INVALID_OPERATION is generated if **glTexImage2D** is called between a call to **glBegin** and the corresponding call to **glEnd**.

ASSOCIATED GETS

glGetTexImage
glIsEnabled with argument GL_TEXTURE_2D

SEE ALSO

glDrawPixels, **glFog**, **glPixelStore**, **glPixelTransfer**, **glTexEnv**, **glTexGen**, **glTexImage1D**, **glTexParameter**

NAME

glTexParameterf, glTexParameteri, glTexParameterfv, glTexParameteriv
– set texture parameters

C SPECIFICATION

void **glTexParameterf**(GLenum *target*,
                         GLenum *pname*,
                         GLfloat *param*)

void **glTexParameteri**(GLenum *target*,
                         GLenum *pname*,
                         GLint *param*)

PARAMETERS

target   Specifies the target texture, which must be either **GL_TEXTURE_1D** or **GL_TEXTURE_2D**.

pname

Specifies the symbolic name of a single-valued texture parameter. *pname* can be one of the following: **GL_TEXTURE_MIN_FILTER**, **GL_TEXTURE_MAG_FILTER**, **GL_TEXTURE_WRAP_S**, or **GL_TEXTURE_WRAP_T**.

param

Specifies the value of *pname*.

C SPECIFICATION

```
void glTexParameterfv( GLenum target,
                       GLenum pname,
                       const GLfloat *params )
void glTexParameteriv( GLenum target,
                       GLenum pname,
                       const GLint *params )
```

PARAMETERS

target   Specifies the target texture, which must be either **GL_TEXTURE_1D** or **GL_TEXTURE_2D**.

pname   Specifies the symbolic name of a texture parameter. *pname* can be one of the following: **GL_TEXTURE_MIN_FILTER**, **GL_TEXTURE_MAG_FILTER**, **GL_TEXTURE_WRAP_S**, **GL_TEXTURE_WRAP_T**, or **GL_TEXTURE_BORDER_COLOR**.

params Specifies a pointer to an array where the value or values of *pname* are stored.

DESCRIPTION

Texture mapping is a technique that applies an image onto an object's surface as if the image were a decal or cellophane shrink-wrap. The image is created in texture space, with an (*s*, *t*) coordinate system. A texture is a one- or two-dimensional image and a set of parameters that determine how samples are derived from the image.

glTexParameter assigns the value or values in *params* to the texture parameter specified as *pname*. *target* defines the target texture, either **GL_TEXTURE_1D** or **GL_TEXTURE_2D**. The following symbols are accepted in *pname*:

GL_TEXTURE_MIN_FILTER

The texture minifying function is used whenever the pixel being textured maps to an area greater than one texture element. There are six defined minifying functions. Two of them use the nearest one or nearest four texture elements to compute the texture value. The other four use mipmaps.

A mipmap is an ordered set of arrays representing the same image at progressively lower resolutions. If the texture has dimensions $2^n \times 2^m$ there are $\max(n,m)+1$ mipmaps. The first mipmap is the original texture, with dimensions $2^n \times 2^m$. Each subsequent mipmap has dimensions $2^{k-1} \times 2^{l-1}$ where $2^k \times 2^l$ are the dimensions of the previous mipmap, until either $k=0$ or $l=0$. At that point, subsequent mipmaps have dimension $1 \times 2^{l-1}$ or $2^{k-1} \times 1$ until the final mipmap, which has dimension 1×1. Mipmaps are defined using **glTexImage1D** or **glTexImage2D** with the level-of-detail argument indicating the order of the mipmaps. Level 0 is the original texture; level $\max(n,m)$ is the final 1×1 mipmap.

params supplies a function for minifying the texture as one of the following:

GL_NEAREST
> Returns the value of the texture element that is nearest (in Manhattan distance) to the center of the pixel being textured.

GL_LINEAR
> Returns the weighted average of the four texture elements that are closest to the center of the pixel being textured. These can include border texture elements, depending on the values of **GL_TEXTURE_WRAP_S** and **GL_TEXTURE_WRAP_T**, and on the exact mapping.

GL_NEAREST_MIPMAP_NEAREST
> Chooses the mipmap that most closely matches the size of the pixel being textured and uses the **GL_NEAREST** criterion (the texture element nearest to the center of the pixel) to produce a texture value.

GL_LINEAR_MIPMAP_NEAREST
> Chooses the mipmap that most closely matches the size of the pixel being textured and uses the **GL_LINEAR** criterion (a weighted average of the four texture elements that are closest to the center of the pixel) to produce a texture value.

GL_NEAREST_MIPMAP_LINEAR
> Chooses the two mipmaps that most closely match the size of the pixel being textured and uses the **GL_NEAREST** criterion (the texture element nearest to the center of the pixel) to produce a texture value from each mipmap. The final texture value is a weighted average of those two values.

GL_LINEAR_MIPMAP_LINEAR

Chooses the two mipmaps that most closely match the size of the pixel being textured and uses the **GL_LINEAR** criterion (a weighted average of the four texture elements that are closest to the center of the pixel) to produce a texture value from each mipmap. The final texture value is a weighted average of those two values.

As more texture elements are sampled in the minification process, fewer aliasing artifacts will be apparent. While the **GL_NEAREST** and **GL_LINEAR** minification functions can be faster than the other four, they sample only one or four texture elements to determine the texture value of the pixel being rendered and can produce moire patterns or ragged transitions. The default value of **GL_TEXTURE_MIN_FILTER** is **GL_NEAREST_MIPMAP_LINEAR**.

GL_TEXTURE_MAG_FILTER

The texture magnification function is used when the pixel being textured maps to an area less than or equal to one texture element. It sets the texture magnification function to either of the following:

GL_NEAREST

Returns the value of the texture element that is nearest (in Manhattan distance) to the center of the pixel being textured.

GL_LINEAR Returns the weighted average of the four texture elements that are closest to the center of the pixel being textured. These can include border texture elements, depending on the values of **GL_TEXTURE_WRAP_S** and **GL_TEXTURE_WRAP_T**, and on the exact mapping.

GL_NEAREST is generally faster than **GL_LINEAR**, but it can produce textured images with sharper edges because the transition between texture elements is not as smooth. The default value of **GL_TEXTURE_MAG_FILTER** is **GL_LINEAR**.

GL_TEXTURE_WRAP_S

Sets the wrap parameter for texture coordinate s to either **GL_CLAMP** or **GL_REPEAT**. **GL_CLAMP** causes s coordinates to be clamped to the range [0,1] and is useful for preventing wrapping artifacts when mapping a single image onto an object. **GL_REPEAT** causes the integer part of the s coordinate to be ignored; the GL uses only the fractional part, thereby creating a repeating pattern. Border texture elements are accessed only if wrapping is set to **GL_CLAMP**. Initially, **GL_TEXTURE_WRAP_S** is set to **GL_REPEAT**.

GL_TEXTURE_WRAP_T

Sets the wrap parameter for texture coordinate *t* to either **GL_CLAMP** or **GL_REPEAT**. See the discussion under **GL_TEXTURE_WRAP_S**. Initially, **GL_TEXTURE_WRAP_T** is set to **GL_REPEAT**.

GL_TEXTURE_BORDER_COLOR

Sets a border color. *params* contains four values that comprise the RGBA color of the texture border. Integer color components are interpreted linearly such that the most positive integer maps to 1.0, and the most negative integer maps to -1.0. The values are clamped to the range [0,1] when they are specified. Initially, the border color is (0, 0, 0, 0).

NOTES

Suppose texturing is enabled (by calling **glEnable** with argument GL_TEXTURE_1D or GL_TEXTURE_2D) and **GL_TEXTURE_MIN_FILTER** is set to one of the functions that requires a mipmap. If either the dimensions of the texture images currently defined (with previous calls to **glTexImage**) do not follow the proper sequence for mipmaps (described above), or there are fewer texture images defined than are needed, or the set of texture images have differing numbers of texture components, then it is as if texture mapping were disabled.

Linear filtering accesses the four nearest texture elements only in 2-D textures. In 1-D textures, linear filtering accesses the two nearest texture elements.

ERRORS

GL_INVALID_ENUM is generated when *target* or *pname* is not one of the accepted defined values, or when *params* should have a defined constant value (based on the value of *pname*) and does not.

GL_INVALID_OPERATION is generated if **glTexParameter** is called between a call to **glBegin** and the corresponding call to **glEnd**.

ASSOCIATED GETS

glGetTexParameter
glGetTexLevelParameter

SEE ALSO

glTexEnv, glTexImage1D, glTexImage2D, glTexGen

NAME

glTranslated, glTranslatef – multiply the current matrix by a translation matrix

C SPECIFICATION

```
void glTranslated( GLdouble x,
                   GLdouble y,
                   GLdouble z )
void glTranslatef( GLfloat x,
                   GLfloat y,
                   GLfloat z )
```

PARAMETERS

x, y, z

Specify the *x*, *y*, and *z* coordinates of a translation vector.

DESCRIPTION

glTranslate moves the coordinate system origin to the point specified by (x,y,z). The translation vector is used to compute a 4×4 translation matrix:

$$\begin{bmatrix} 1 & 0 & 0 & x \\ 0 & 1 & 0 & y \\ 0 & 0 & 1 & z \\ 0 & 0 & 0 & 1 \end{bmatrix}$$

The current matrix (see **glMatrixMode**) is multiplied by this translation matrix, with the product replacing the current matrix. That is, if M is the current matrix and T is the translation matrix, then M is replaced with M • T.

If the matrix mode is either **GL_MODELVIEW** or **GL_PROJECTION**, all objects drawn after **glTranslate** is called are translated. Use **glPushMatrix** and **glPopMatrix** to save and restore the untranslated coordinate system.

ERRORS

GL_INVALID_OPERATION is generated if **glTranslate** is called between a call to **glBegin** and the corresponding call to **glEnd**.

ASSOCIATED GETS

      glGet with argument GL_MATRIX_MODE
      glGet with argument GL_MODELVIEW_MATRIX
      glGet with argument GL_PROJECTION_MATRIX
      glGet with argument GL_TEXTURE_MATRIX

SEE ALSO

      glMatrixMode, glMultMatrix, glPushMatrix, glRotate, glScale

NAME

glVertex2d, glVertex2f, glVertex2i, glVertex2s, glVertex3d, glVertex3f, glVertex3i, glVertex3s, glVertex4d, glVertex4f, glVertex4i, glVertex4s, glVertex2dv, glVertex2fv, glVertex2iv, glVertex2sv, glVertex3dv, glVertex3fv, glVertex3iv, glVertex3sv, glVertex4dv, glVertex4fv, glVertex4iv, glVertex4sv – specify a vertex

C SPECIFICATION

```
void glVertex2d( GLdouble x,
                 GLdouble y )
void glVertex2f( GLfloat x,
                 GLfloat y )
void glVertex2i( GLint x,
                 GLint y )
void glVertex2s( GLshort x,
                 GLshort y )
void glVertex3d( GLdouble x,
                 GLdouble y,
                 GLdouble z )
void glVertex3f( GLfloat x,
                 GLfloat y,
                 GLfloat z )
void glVertex3i( GLint x,
                 GLint y,
                 GLint z )
void glVertex3s( GLshort x,
                 GLshort y,
                 GLshort z )
void glVertex4d( GLdouble x,
                 GLdouble y,
                 GLdouble z,
                 GLdouble w )
void glVertex4f( GLfloat x,
                 GLfloat y,
                 GLfloat z,
                 GLfloat w )
void glVertex4i( GLint x,
                 GLint y,
                 GLint z,
                 GLint w )
```

```
void glVertex4s( GLshort x,
                 GLshort y,
                 GLshort z,
                 GLshort w )
```

PARAMETERS

x, y, z, w

Specify x, y, z, and w coordinates of a vertex. Not all parameters are present in all forms of the command.

C SPECIFICATION

```
void glVertex2dv( const GLdouble *v )
void glVertex2fv( const GLfloat *v )
void glVertex2iv( const GLint *v )
void glVertex2sv( const GLshort *v )
void glVertex3dv( const GLdouble *v )
void glVertex3fv( const GLfloat *v )
void glVertex3iv( const GLint *v )
void glVertex3sv( const GLshort *v )
void glVertex4dv( const GLdouble *v )
void glVertex4fv( const GLfloat *v )
void glVertex4iv( const GLint *v )
void glVertex4sv( const GLshort *v )
```

PARAMETERS

v

Specifies a pointer to an array of two, three, or four elements. The elements of a two-element array are x and y; of a three-element array, x, y, and z; and of a four-element array, x, y, z, and w.

DESCRIPTION

glVertex commands are used within **glBegin/glEnd** pairs to specify point, line, and polygon vertices. The current color, normal, and texture coordinates are associated with the vertex when **glVertex** is called.

When only x and y are specified, z defaults to 0.0 and w defaults to 1.0. When x, y, and z are specified, w defaults to 1.0.

NOTES

Invoking **glVertex** outside of a **glBegin/glEnd** pair results in undefined behavior.

SEE ALSO

glBegin, glCallList, glColor, glEdgeFlag, glEvalCoord, glIndex, glMaterial, glNormal, glRect, glTexCoord

NAME

glViewport – set the viewport

C SPECIFICATION

void **glViewport**(GLint *x*,
GLint *y*,
GLsizei *width*,
GLsizei *height*)

PARAMETERS

x, y

Specify the lower left corner of the viewport rectangle, in pixels. The default is (0,0).

width, height

Specify the width and height, respectively, of the viewport. When a GL context is *first* attached to a window, *width* and *height* are set to the dimensions of that window.

DESCRIPTION

glViewport specifies the affine transformation of *x* and *y* from normalized device coordinates to window coordinates. Let (x_{nd}, y_{nd}) be normalized device coordinates. Then the window coordinates (x_w, y_w) are computed as follows:

$$x_w = (x_{nd}+1)\left\lfloor \frac{width}{2} \right\rfloor + x$$

$$y_w = (y_{nd}+1)\left\lfloor \frac{height}{2} \right\rfloor + y$$

Viewport width and height are silently clamped to a range that depends on the implementation. This range is queried by calling **glGet** with argument **GL_MAX_VIEWPORT_DIMS**.

ERRORS

GL_INVALID_VALUE is generated if either *width* or *height* is negative.

GL_INVALID_OPERATION is generated if **glViewport** is called between a call to **glBegin** and the corresponding call to **glEnd**.

ASSOCIATED GETS

glGet with argument **GL_VIEWPORT**
glGet with argument **GL_MAX_VIEWPORT_DIMS**

SEE ALSO

glDepthRange

Chapter 6

GLU Reference Pages

This chapter contains the reference pages, in alphabetical order, for all the routines comprising the OpenGL Utility Library (GLU). The routines are listed below.

gluBeginCurve, gluEndCurve	gluLoadSamplingMatrices	gluPickMatrix
gluBeginPolygon, gluEndPolygon	gluLookAt	gluProject
gluBeginSurface, gluEndSurface	gluNewNurbsRenderer	gluPwlCurve
gluBeginTrim, gluEndTrim	gluNewQuadric	gluQuadricCallback
gluBuild1DMipmaps	gluNewTess	gluQuadricDrawStyle
gluBuild2DMipmaps	gluNextContour	gluQuadricNormals
gluCylinder	gluNurbsCallback	gluQuadricOrientation
gluDeleteNurbsRenderer	gluNurbsCurve	gluQuadricTexture
gluDeleteQuadric	gluNurbsProperty	gluScaleImage
gluDeleteTess	gluNurbsSurface	gluSphere
gluDisk	gluOrtho2D	gluTessCallback
gluErrorString	gluPartialDisk	gluTessVertex
gluGetNurbsProperty	gluPerspective	gluUnProject

NAME

gluBeginCurve, gluEndCurve – delimit a NURBS curve definition

C SPECIFICATION

void **gluBeginCurve**(GLUnurbsObj *nobj*)
void **gluEndCurve**(GLUnurbsObj *nobj*)

PARAMETERS

nobj Specifies the NURBS object (created with **gluNewNurbsRenderer**).

DESCRIPTION

Use **gluBeginCurve** to mark the beginning of a NURBS curve definition. After calling **gluBeginCurve**, make one or more calls to **gluNurbsCurve** to define the attributes of the curve. Exactly one of the calls to **gluNurbsCurve** must have a curve type of **GL_MAP1_VERTEX_3** or **GL_MAP1_VERTEX_4**. To mark the end of the NURBS curve definition, call **gluEndCurve**.

OpenGL evaluators are used to render the NURBS curve as a series of line segments. Evaluator state is preserved during rendering with **glPushAttrib(GL_EVAL_BIT)** and **glPopAttrib()**. See the **glPushAttrib** reference page for details on exactly what state these calls preserve.

EXAMPLE

The following commands render a textured NURBS curve with normals; texture coordinates and normals are also specified as NURBS curves:

```
gluBeginCurve(nobj);
    gluNurbsCurve(nobj, ..., GL_MAP1_TEXTURE_COORD_2);
    gluNurbsCurve(nobj, ..., GL_MAP1_NORMAL);
    gluNurbsCurve(nobj, ..., GL_MAP1_VERTEX_4);
gluEndCurve(nobj);
```

SEE ALSO

gluBeginSurface, gluBeginTrim, gluNewNurbsRenderer, gluNurbsCurve, glPopAttrib, glPushAttrib

NAME

gluBeginPolygon, gluEndPolygon – delimit a polygon description

C SPECIFICATION

void **gluBeginPolygon**(GLUtriangulatorObj *tobj*)
void **gluEndPolygon**(GLUtriangulatorObj *tobj*)

PARAMETERS

tobj Specifies the tessellation object (created with **gluNewTess**).

DESCRIPTION

gluBeginPolygon and **gluEndPolygon** delimit the definition of a nonconvex polygon. To define such a polygon, first call **gluBeginPolygon**. Then define the contours of the polygon by calling **gluTessVertex** for each vertex and **gluNextContour** to start each new contour. Finally, call **gluEndPolygon** to signal the end of the definition. See the **gluTessVertex** and **gluNextContour** reference pages for more details.

Once **gluEndPolygon** is called, the polygon is tessellated, and the resulting triangles are described through callbacks. See **gluTessCallback** for descriptions of the callback functions.

EXAMPLE

A quadrilateral with a triangular hole in it can be described like this:

```
gluBeginPolygon(tobj);
    gluTessVertex(tobj, v1, v1);
    gluTessVertex(tobj, v2, v2);
    gluTessVertex(tobj, v3, v3);
    gluTessVertex(tobj, v4, v4);
gluNextContour(tobj, GLU_INTERIOR);
    gluTessVertex(tobj, v5, v5);
    gluTessVertex(tobj, v6, v6);
    gluTessVertex(tobj, v7, v7);
gluEndPolygon(tobj);
```

SEE ALSO

gluNewTess, gluNextContour, gluTessCallback, gluTessVertex

NAME

gluBeginSurface, gluEndSurface – delimit a NURBS surface definition

C SPECIFICATION

void **gluBeginSurface**(GLUnurbsObj *nobj*)
void **gluEndSurface**(GLUnurbsObj *nobj*)

PARAMETERS

nobj   Specifies the NURBS object (created with **gluNewNurbsRenderer**).

DESCRIPTION

Use **gluBeginSurface** to mark the beginning of a NURBS surface definition. After calling **gluBeginSurface**, make one or more calls to **gluNurbsSurface** to define the attributes of the surface. Exactly one of these calls to **gluNurbsSurface** must have a surface type of **GL_MAP2_VERTEX_3** or **GL_MAP2_VERTEX_4**. To mark the end of the NURBS surface definition, call **gluEndSurface**.

Trimming of NURBS surfaces is supported with **gluBeginTrim, gluPwlCurve, gluNurbsCurve**, and **gluEndTrim**. Refer to the **gluBeginTrim** reference page for details.

OpenGL evaluators are used to render the NURBS surface as a set of polygons. Evaluator state is preserved during rendering with **glPushAttrib(GL_EVAL_BIT)** and **glPopAttrib()**. See the **glPushAttrib** reference page for details on exactly what state these calls preserve.

EXAMPLE

The following commands render a textured NURBS surface with normals; the texture coordinates and normals are also described as NURBS surfaces:

```
gluBeginSurface(nobj);
    gluNurbsSurface(nobj, ..., GL_MAP2_TEXTURE_COORD_2);
    gluNurbsSurface(nobj, ..., GL_MAP2_NORMAL);
    gluNurbsSurface(nobj, ..., GL_MAP2_VERTEX_4);
gluEndSurface(nobj);
```

SEE ALSO

gluBeginCurve, gluBeginTrim, gluNewNurbsRenderer, gluNurbsCurve, gluNurbsSurface, gluPwlCurve

NAME

gluBeginTrim, **gluEndTrim** – delimit a NURBS trimming loop definition

C SPECIFICATION

void **gluBeginTrim**(GLUnurbsObj *nobj)
void **gluEndTrim**(GLUnurbsObj *nobj)

PARAMETERS

nobj Specifies the NURBS object (created with **gluNewNurbsRenderer**).

DESCRIPTION

Use **gluBeginTrim** to mark the beginning of a trimming loop, and **gluEndTrim** to mark the end of a trimming loop. A trimming loop is a set of oriented curve segments (forming a closed curve) that define boundaries of a NURBS surface. You include these trimming loops in the definition of a NURBS surface, between calls to **gluBeginSurface** and **gluEndSurface**.

The definition for a NURBS surface can contain many trimming loops. For example, if you wrote a definition for a NURBS surface that resembled a rectangle with a hole punched out, the definition would contain two trimming loops. One loop would define the outer edge of the rectangle; the other would define the hole punched out of the rectangle. The definitions of each of these trimming loops would be bracketed by a **gluBeginTrim/gluEndTrim** pair.

The definition of a single closed trimming loop can consist of multiple curve segments, each described as a piecewise linear curve (see **gluPwlCurve**) or as a single NURBS curve (see **gluNurbsCurve**), or as a combination of both in any order. The only library calls that can appear in a trimming loop definition (between the calls to **gluBeginTrim** and **gluEndTrim**) are **gluPwlCurve** and **gluNurbsCurve**.

The area of the NURBS surface that is displayed is the region in the domain to the left of the trimming curve as the curve parameter increases. Thus, the retained region of the NURBS surface is inside a counterclockwise trimming loop and outside a clockwise trimming loop. For the rectangle mentioned earlier, the trimming loop for the outer edge of the rectangle runs counterclockwise, while the trimming loop for the punched-out hole runs clockwise.

If you use more than one curve to define a single trimming loop, the curve segments must form a closed loop (that is, the endpoint of each curve must be the starting point of the next curve, and the endpoint of the final curve must be the starting point of the first curve). If the endpoints of the curve are sufficiently close together but not exactly coincident, they will be coerced to match. If the endpoints are not sufficiently close, an error results (see **gluNurbsCallback**).

If a trimming loop definition contains multiple curves, the direction of the curves must be consistent (that is, the inside must be to the left of all of the curves). Nested trimming loops are legal as long as the curve orientations alternate correctly. Trimming curves cannot be self-intersecting, nor can they intersect one another (or an error results).

If no trimming information is given for a NURBS surface, the entire surface is drawn.

EXAMPLE

This code fragment defines a trimming loop that consists of one piecewise linear curve, and two NURBS curves:

```
gluBeginTrim(nobj);
    gluPwlCurve(..., GLU_MAP1_TRIM_2);
    gluNurbsCurve(..., GLU_MAP1_TRIM_2);
    gluNurbsCurve(..., GLU_MAP1_TRIM_3);
gluEndTrim(nobj);
```

SEE ALSO

gluBeginSurface, gluNewNurbsRenderer, gluNurbsCallback, gluNurbsCurve, gluPwlCurve

NAME

gluBuild1DMipmaps – create 1-D mipmaps

C SPECIFICATION

int **gluBuild1DMipmaps**(GLenum *target*,
GLint *components*,
GLint *width*,
GLenum *format*,
GLenum *type*,
void **data*)

PARAMETERS

target Specifies the target texture. Must be **GL_TEXTURE_1D**.

components

Specifies the number of color components in the texture. Must be 1, 2, 3, or 4.

width Specifies the width of the texture image.

format Specifies the format of the pixel data. Must be one of **GL_COLOR_INDEX**, **GL_RED**, **GL_GREEN**, **GL_BLUE**, **GL_ALPHA**, **GL_RGB**, **GL_RGBA**, **GL_LUMINANCE**, and **GL_LUMINANCE_ALPHA**.

type Specifies the data type for *data*. Must be one of **GL_UNSIGNED_BYTE**, **GL_BYTE**, **GL_BITMAP**, **GL_UNSIGNED_SHORT**, **GL_SHORT**, **GL_UNSIGNED_INT**, **GL_INT**, or **GL_FLOAT**.

data Specifies a pointer to the image data in memory.

DESCRIPTION

gluBuild1DMipmaps obtains the input image and generates all mipmap images (using **gluScaleImage**) so that the input image can be used as a mipmapped texture image. **glTexImage1D** is then called to load each of the images. If the width of the input image is not a power of two, then the image is scaled to the nearest power of two before the mipmaps are generated. A return value of zero indicates success. Otherwise, a GLU error code is returned (see **gluErrorString**).

Please refer to the **glTexImage1D** and **glDrawPixels** reference pages for a description of the acceptable values for the *format* and *type* parameter, respectively.

SEE ALSO

glTexImage1D, gluBuild2DMipmaps, gluErrorString, gluScaleImage

NAME

gluBuild2DMipmaps – create 2-D mipmaps

C SPECIFICATION

int **gluBuild2DMipmaps**(GLenum *target*,
GLint *components*,
GLint *width*,
GLint *height*,
GLenum *format*,
GLenum *type*,
void **data*)

PARAMETERS

target   Specifies the target texture. Must be **GL_TEXTURE_2D**.

components
Specifies the number of color components in the texture. Must be 1, 2, 3, or 4.

width, height
Specifies the width and height, respectively, of the texture image.

format   Specifies the format of the pixel data. Must be one of: **GL_COLOR_INDEX**, **GL_RED**, **GL_GREEN**, **GL_BLUE**, **GL_ALPHA**, **GL_RGB**, **GL_RGBA**, **GL_LUMINANCE**, and **GL_LUMINANCE_ALPHA**.

type   Specifies the data type for *data*. Must be one of: **GL_UNSIGNED_BYTE**, **GL_BYTE**, **GL_BITMAP**, **GL_UNSIGNED_SHORT**, **GL_SHORT**, **GL_UNSIGNED_INT**, **GL_INT**, or **GL_FLOAT**.

data   Specifies a pointer to the image data in memory.

DESCRIPTION

gluBuild2DMipmaps obtains the input image and generates all mipmap images (using **gluScaleImage**) so that the input image can be used as a mipmapped texture image. **glTexImage2D** is then called to load each of the images. If the dimensions of the input image are not powers of two, then the image is scaled so that both the width and height are powers of two before the mipmaps are generated. A return value of 0 indicates success. Otherwise, a GLU error code is returned (see **gluError-String**). Please refer to the **glTexImage1D** and **glDrawPixels** reference pages for a description of the acceptable values for the *format* and *type* parameter, respectively.

SEE ALSO

glDrawPixels, glTexImage1D, glTexImage2D, gluBuild1DMipmaps, gluError-String, gluScaleImage

NAME

      gluCylinder – draw a cylinder

C SPECIFICATION

      void **gluCylinder**(GLUquadricObj *qobj,
                         GLdouble *baseRadius,*
                         GLdouble *topRadius,*
                         GLdouble *height,*
                         GLint *slices,*
                         GLint *stacks*)

PARAMETERS

    qobj   Specifies the quadrics object (created with **gluNewQuadric**).

    baseRadius Specifies the radius of the cylinder at $z = 0$.

    topRadius Specifies the radius of the cylinder at $z = height$.

    height   Specifies the height of the cylinder.

    slices   Specifies the number of subdivisions around the z axis.

    stacks   Specifies the number of subdivisions along the z axis.

DESCRIPTION

      gluCylinder draws a cylinder oriented along the z axis. The base of the cylinder is placed at $z = 0$, and the top at $z = height$. Like a sphere, a cylinder is subdivided around the z axis into slices, and along the z axis into stacks.

      Note that if *topRadius* is set to zero, then this routine will generate a cone.

      If the orientation is set to **GLU_OUTSIDE** (with **gluQuadricOrientation**), then any generated normals point away from the z axis. Otherwise, they point toward the z axis.

      If texturing is turned on (with **gluQuadricTexture**), then texture coordinates are generated so that t ranges linearly from 0.0 at $z = 0$ to 1.0 at $z = height$, and s ranges from 0.0 at the $+y$ axis, to 0.25 at the $+x$ axis, to 0.5 at the $-y$ axis, to 0.75 at the $-x$ axis, and back to 1.0 at the $+y$ axis.

SEE ALSO

      gluDisk, gluNewQuadric, gluPartialDisk, gluQuadricTexture, gluSphere

gluDeleteNurbsRenderer

NAME

gluDeleteNurbsRenderer – destroy a NURBS object

C SPECIFICATION

void **gluDeleteNurbsRenderer**(GLUnurbsObj *nobj*)

PARAMETERS

nobj   Specifies the NURBS object to be destroyed (created with
gluNewNurbsRenderer).

DESCRIPTION

gluDeleteNurbsRenderer destroys the NURBS object and frees any memory used by
it. Once **gluDeleteNurbsRenderer** has been called, *nobj* cannot be used again.

SEE ALSO

gluNewNurbsRenderer

NAME

gluDeleteQuadric – destroy a quadrics object

C SPECIFICATION

void **gluDeleteQuadric**(GLUquadricObj *state*)

PARAMETERS

state Specifies the quadrics object to be destroyed (created with **gluNewQuadric**).

DESCRIPTION

gluDeleteQuadric destroys the quadrics object and frees any memory used by it. Once **gluDeleteQuadric** has been called, *state* cannot be used again.

SEE ALSO

gluNewQuadric

NAME

gluDeleteTess – destroy a tessellation object

C SPECIFICATION

void **gluDeleteTess**(GLUtriangulatorObj *tobj*)

PARAMETERS

tobj Specifies the tessellation object to destroy (created with **gluNewTess**).

DESCRIPTION

gluDeleteTess destroys the indicated tessellation object and frees any memory that it used.

SEE ALSO

gluBeginPolygon, gluNewTess, gluTessCallback

NAME

gluDisk – draw a disk

C SPECIFICATION

void **gluDisk**(GLUquadricObj *qobj,
GLdouble *innerRadius*,
GLdouble *outerRadius*,
GLint *slices*,
GLint *loops*)

PARAMETERS

qobj   Specifies the quadrics object (created with **gluNewQuadric**).

innerRadius
              Specifies the inner radius of the disk (may be 0).

outerRadius Specifies the outer radius of the disk.

slices   Specifies the number of subdivisions around the z axis.

loops   Specifies the number of concentric rings about the origin into which the disk is subdivided.

DESCRIPTION

gluDisk renders a disk on the $z = 0$ plane. The disk has a radius of *outerRadius*, and contains a concentric circular hole with a radius of *innerRadius*. If *innerRadius* is 0, then no hole is generated. The disk is subdivided around the z axis into slices (like pizza slices), and also about the z axis into rings (as specified by *slices* and *loops*, respectively).

With respect to orientation, the +z side of the disk is considered to be "outside" (see **gluQuadricOrientation**). This means that if the orientation is set to GLU_OUTSIDE, then any normals generated point along the +z axis. Otherwise, they point along the –z axis.

If texturing is turned on (with **gluQuadricTexture**), texture coordinates are generated linearly such that where *r=outerRadius*, the value at $(r, 0, 0)$ is $(1, 0.5)$, at $(0, r, 0)$ it is $(0.5, 1)$, at $(-r, 0, 0)$ it is $(0, 0.5)$, and at $(0, -r, 0)$ it is $(0.5, 0)$.

SEE ALSO

gluCylinder, gluNewQuadric, gluPartialDisk, gluQuadricOrientation, gluQuadricTexture, gluSphere

NAME

    gluErrorString – produce an error string from an OpenGL or GLU error code

C SPECIFICATION

    const GLubyte* **gluErrorString**(GLenum *errorCode*)

PARAMETERS

    errorCode Specifies an OpenGL or GLU error code.

DESCRIPTION

    gluErrorString produces an error string from an OpenGL or GLU error code. The string is in an ISO Latin 1 format. For example, **gluErrorString(GL_OUT_OF_MEMORY)** returns the string *out of memory*.

    The standard GLU error codes are **GLU_INVALID_ENUM, GLU_INVALID_VALUE,** and **GLU_OUT_OF_MEMORY.** Certain other GLU functions can return specialized error codes through callbacks. Refer to the **glGetError** reference page for the list of OpenGL error codes.

SEE ALSO

    glGetError, gluNurbsCallback, gluQuadricCallback, gluTessCallback

NAME

gluGetNurbsProperty – get a NURBS property

C SPECIFICATION

void **gluGetNurbsProperty**(GLUnurbsObj *nobj,
 GLenum *property*,
 GLfloat *value*)

PARAMETERS

nobj Specifies the NURBS object (created with **gluNewNurbsRenderer**).

property Specifies the property whose value is to be fetched. Valid values are **GLU_CULLING, GLU_SAMPLING_TOLERANCE, GLU_DISPLAY_MODE,** and **GLU_AUTO_LOAD_MATRIX.**

value Specifies a pointer to the location into which the value of the named property is written.

DESCRIPTION

gluGetNurbsProperty is used to retrieve properties stored in a NURBS object. These properties affect the way that NURBS curves and surfaces are rendered. Please refer to the **gluNurbsProperty** reference page for information about what the properties are and what they do.

SEE ALSO

gluNewNurbsRenderer, gluNurbsProperty

NAME

gluLoadSamplingMatrices – load NURBS sampling and culling matrices

C SPECIFICATION

void **gluLoadSamplingMatrices**(GLUnurbsObj *nobj,
         const GLfloat *modelMatrix[16]*,
         const GLfloat *projMatrix[16]*,
         const GLint *viewport[4]*)

PARAMETERS

nobj   Specifies the NURBS object (created with **gluNewNurbsRenderer**).

modelMatrix
      Specifies a modelview matrix (as from a **glGetFloatv** call).

projMatrix Specifies a projection matrix (as from a **glGetFloatv** call).

viewport Specifies a viewport (as from a **glGetIntegerv** call).

DESCRIPTION

gluLoadSamplingMatrices uses *modelMatrix*, *projMatrix*, and *viewport* to recompute the sampling and culling matrices stored in *nobj*. The sampling matrix determines how finely a NURBS curve or surface must be tessellated to satisfy the sampling tolerance (as determined by the **GLU_SAMPLING_TOLERANCE** property). The culling matrix is used in deciding if a NURBS curve or surface should be culled before rendering (when the **GLU_CULLING** property is turned on).

gluLoadSamplingMatrices is necessary only if the **GLU_AUTO_LOAD_MATRIX** property is turned off (see **gluNurbsProperty**). Although it can be convenient to leave the **GLU_AUTO_LOAD_MATRIX** property turned on, there can be a performance penalty for doing so. (A round trip to the OpenGL server is needed to fetch the current values of the modelview matrix, projection matrix, and viewport.)

SEE ALSO

gluGetNurbsProperty, **gluNewNurbsRenderer**, **gluNurbsProperty**

NAME

gluLookAt – define a viewing transformation

C SPECIFICATION

void **gluLookAt**(GLdouble *eyex,*
                    GLdouble *eyey,*
                    GLdouble *eyez,*
                    GLdouble *centerx,*
                    GLdouble *centery,*
                    GLdouble *centerz,*
                    GLdouble *upx,*
                    GLdouble *upy,*
                    GLdouble *upz*)

PARAMETERS

eyex, eyey, eyez
          Specifies the position of the eye point.

centerx, centery, centerz
          Specifies the position of the reference point.

upx, upy, upz Specifies the direction of the up vector.

DESCRIPTION

gluLookAt creates a viewing matrix derived from an eye point, a reference point indicating the center of the scene, and an up vector. The matrix maps the reference point to the negative z axis and the eye point to the origin, so that, when a typical projection matrix is used, the center of the scene maps to the center of the viewport. Similarly, the direction described by the up vector projected onto the viewing plane is mapped to the positive y axis so that it points upward in the viewport. The up vector must not be parallel to the line of sight from the eye to the reference point.

The matrix generated by **gluLookAt** postmultiplies the current matrix.

SEE ALSO

glFrustum, gluPerspective

NAME

gluNewNurbsRenderer – create a NURBS object

C SPECIFICATION

GLUnurbsObj* **gluNewNurbsRenderer**(void)

DESCRIPTION

gluNewNurbsRenderer creates and returns a pointer to a new NURBS object. This object must be referred to when calling NURBS rendering and control functions. A return value of zero means that there is not enough memory to allocate the object.

SEE ALSO

gluBeginCurve, **gluBeginSurface**, **gluBeginTrim**, **gluDeleteNurbsRenderer**, **gluNurbsCallback**, **gluNurbsProperty**

NAME

gluNewQuadric – create a quadrics object

C SPECIFICATION

GLUquadricObj* **gluNewQuadric**(void)

DESCRIPTION

gluNewQuadric creates and returns a pointer to a new quadrics object. This object must be referred to when calling quadrics rendering and control functions. A return value of zero means that there is not enough memory to allocate the object.

SEE ALSO

gluCylinder, **gluDeleteQuadric**, **gluDisk**, **gluPartialDisk**, **gluQuadricCallback**, **gluQuadricDrawStyle**, **gluQuadricNormals**, **gluQuadricOrientation**, **gluQuadricTexture**, **gluSphere**

NAME

gluNewTess – create a tessellation object

C SPECIFICATION

GLUtriangulatorObj* **gluNewTess**(void *void*)

DESCRIPTION

gluNewTess creates and returns a pointer to a new tessellation object. This object must be referred to when calling tessellation functions. A return value of zero means that there is not enough memory to allocate the object.

SEE ALSO

gluBeginPolygon, gluDeleteTess, gluTessCallback

NAME

gluNextContour – mark the beginning of another contour

C SPECIFICATION

void **gluNextContour**(GLUtriangulatorObj *tobj,
GLenum *type*)

PARAMETERS

tobj Specifies the tessellation object (created with **gluNewTess**).

type Specifies the type of the contour being defined. Valid values are
GLU_EXTERIOR, GLU_INTERIOR, GLU_UNKNOWN, GLU_CCW, and
GLU_CW.

DESCRIPTION

gluNextContour is used in describing polygons with multiple contours. After the first contour has been described through a series of **gluTessVertex** calls, a **gluNextContour** call indicates that the previous contour is complete and that the next contour is about to begin. Another series of **gluTessVertex** calls is then used to describe the new contour. This process can be repeated until all contours have been described.

type defines what type of contour follows. The legal contour types are as follows:

GLU_EXTERIOR
> An exterior contour defines an exterior boundary of the polygon.

GLU_INTERIOR
> An interior contour defines an interior boundary of the polygon (such as a hole).

GLU_UNKNOWN
> An unknown contour is analyzed by the library to determine if it is interior or exterior.

GLU_CCW, GLU_CW
> The first GLU_CCW or GLU_CW contour defined is considered to be exterior. All other contours are considered to be exterior if they are oriented in the same direction (clockwise or counterclockwise) as the first contour, and interior if they are not.

> If one contour is of type **GLU_CCW** or **GLU_CW**, then all contours must be of the same type (if they are not, then all **GLU_CCW** and **GLU_CW** contours will be changed to **GLU_UNKNOWN**).

Note that there is no real difference between the **GLU_CCW** and **GLU_CW** contour types.

gluNextContour can be called before the first contour is described to define the type of the first contour. If **gluNextContour** is not called before the first contour, then the first contour is marked **GLU_EXTERIOR**.

EXAMPLE

A quadrilateral with a triangular hole in it can be described as follows:

```
gluBeginPolygon(tobj);
    gluTessVertex(tobj, v1, v1);
    gluTessVertex(tobj, v2, v2);
    gluTessVertex(tobj, v3, v3);
    gluTessVertex(tobj, v4, v4);
gluNextContour(tobj, GLU_INTERIOR);
    gluTessVertex(tobj, v5, v5);
    gluTessVertex(tobj, v6, v6);
    gluTessVertex(tobj, v7, v7);
gluEndPolygon(tobj);
```

SEE ALSO

gluBeginPolygon, gluNewTess, gluTessCallback, gluTessVertex

NAME

    gluNurbsCallback – define a callback for a NURBS object

C SPECIFICATION

    void **gluNurbsCallback**(GLUnurbsObj *nobj,
                                GLenum *which*,
                                void *(*fn)()*)

PARAMETERS

    nobj Specifies the NURBS object (created with **gluNewNurbsRenderer**).

    which Specifies the callback being defined. The only valid value is **GLU_ERROR**.

    fn   Specifies the function that the callback calls.

DESCRIPTION

    gluNurbsCallback is used to define a callback to be used by a NURBS object. If the specified callback is already defined, then it is replaced. If *fn* is NULL, then any existing callback is erased.

    The one legal callback is **GLU_ERROR**:

    GLU_ERROR   The error function is called when an error is encountered. Its single argument is of type GLenum, and it indicates the specific error that occurred. There are 37 errors unique to NURBS named **GLU_NURBS_ERROR1** through **GLU_NURBS_ERROR37**. Character strings describing these errors can be retrieved with **gluErrorString**.

SEE ALSO

    gluErrorString, gluNewNurbsRenderer

NAME

gluNurbsCurve – define the shape of a NURBS curve

C SPECIFICATION

void **gluNurbsCurve**(GLUnurbsObj *nobj,
                        GLint nknots,
                        GLfloat *knot,
                        GLint stride,
                        GLfloat *ctlarray,
                        GLint order,
                        GLenum type)

PARAMETERS

nobj   Specifies the NURBS object (created with **gluNewNurbsRenderer**).

nknots   Specifies the number of knots in *knot*. *nknots* equals the number of control points plus the order.

knot   Specifies an array of *nknots* nondecreasing knot values.

stride   Specifies the offset (as a number of single-precision floating-point values) between successive curve control points.

ctlarray Specifies a pointer to an array of control points. The coordinates must agree with *type*, specified below.

order   Specifies the order of the NURBS curve. *order* equals degree + 1, hence a cubic curve has an order of 4.

type   Specifies the type of the curve. If this curve is defined within a **gluBeginCurve/gluEndCurve** pair, then the type can be any of the valid one-dimensional evaluator types (such as **GL_MAP1_VERTEX_3** or **GL_MAP1_COLOR_4**). Between a **gluBeginTrim/gluEndTrim** pair, the only valid types are GLU_MAP1_TRIM_2 and GLU_MAP1_TRIM_3.

DESCRIPTION

Use **gluNurbsCurve** to describe a NURBS curve.

When **gluNurbsCurve** appears between a **gluBeginCurve/gluEndCurve** pair, it is used to describe a curve to be rendered. Positional, texture, and color coordinates are associated by presenting each as a separate **gluNurbsCurve** between a **gluBeginCurve/gluEndCurve** pair. No more than one call to **gluNurbsCurve** for each of color, position, and texture data can be made within a single **gluBeginCurve/gluEndCurve** pair. Exactly one call must be made to describe the position of the curve (a *type* of **GL_MAP1_VERTEX_3** or **GL_MAP1_VERTEX_4**).

When **gluNurbsCurve** appears between a **gluBeginTrim/gluEndTrim** pair, it is used to describe a trimming curve on a NURBS surface. If *type* is **GLU_MAP1_TRIM_2**, then it describes a curve in two-dimensional (*u* and *v*) parameter space. If it is **GLU_MAP1_TRIM_3**, then it describes a curve in two-dimensional homogeneous (*u*, *v*, and *w*) parameter space. See the **gluBeginTrim** reference page for more discussion about trimming curves.

EXAMPLE

The following commands render a textured NURBS curve with normals:

```
gluBeginCurve(nobj);
    gluNurbsCurve(nobj, ..., GL_MAP1_TEXTURE_COORD_2);
    gluNurbsCurve(nobj, ..., GL_MAP1_NORMAL);
    gluNurbsCurve(nobj, ..., GL_MAP1_VERTEX_4);
gluEndCurve(nobj);
```

SEE ALSO

gluBeginCurve, gluBeginTrim, gluNewNurbsRenderer, gluPwlCurve

NAME

gluNurbsProperty – set a NURBS property

C SPECIFICATION

void **gluNurbsProperty**(GLUnurbsObj *nobj,
GLenum *property*,
GLfloat *value*)

PARAMETERS

nobj Specifies the NURBS object (created with **gluNewNurbsRenderer**).

property Specifies the property to be set. Valid values are
GLU_SAMPLING_TOLERANCE, GLU_DISPLAY_MODE, GLU_CULLING,
and **GLU_AUTO_LOAD_MATRIX.**

value Specifies the value to which to set the indicated property.

DESCRIPTION

gluNurbsProperty is used to control properties stored in a NURBS object. These
properties affect the way that a NURBS curve is rendered. The legal values for
property are as follows:

GLU_SAMPLING_TOLERANCE

value specifies the maximum length, in pixels, of line segments or edges
of polygons used to render NURBS curves or surfaces. The NURBS code is
conservative when rendering a curve or surface, so the actual length can
be somewhat shorter. The default value is 50.0 pixels.

GLU_DISPLAY_MODE

value defines how a NURBS surface should be rendered. *value* can be set
to **GLU_FILL, GLU_OUTLINE_POLYGON,** or **GLU_OUTLINE_PATCH.**
When set to **GLU_FILL**, the surface is rendered as a set of polygons.
GLU_OUTLINE_POLYGON instructs the NURBS library to draw only the
outlines of the polygons created by tessellation. **GLU_OUTLINE_PATCH**
causes just the outlines of patches and trim curves defined by the user to
be drawn. The default value is **GLU_FILL.**

GLU_CULLING

value is a Boolean value that, when set to **GL_TRUE**, indicates that a
NURBS curve should be discarded prior to tessellation if its control points
lie outside the current viewport. The default is **GL_FALSE** (because a
NURBS curve cannot fall entirely within the convex hull of its control
points).

GLU_AUTO_LOAD_MATRIX

value is a Boolean value. When set to **GL_TRUE**, the NURBS code downloads the projection matrix, the modelview matrix, and the viewport from the OpenGL server to compute sampling and culling matrices for each NURBS curve that is rendered. Sampling and culling matrices are required to determine the tesselation of a NURBS surface into line segments or polygons and to cull a NURBS surface if it lies outside of the viewport. If this mode is set to **GL_FALSE**, then the user needs to provide a projection matrix, a modelview matrix, and a viewport for the NURBS renderer to use to construct sampling and culling matrices. This can be done with the **gluLoadSamplingMatrices** function. The default for this mode is **GL_TRUE**. Changing this mode from **GL_TRUE** to **GL_FALSE** does not affect the sampling and culling matrices until **gluLoadSamplingMatrices** is called.

SEE ALSO

gluGetNurbsProperty, gluLoadSamplingMatrices, gluNewNurbsRenderer

NAME

gluNurbsSurface – define the shape of a NURBS surface

C SPECIFICATION

void **gluNurbsSurface**(GLUnurbsObj *nobj,
                                   GLint *uknot_count,*
                                   GLfloat **uknot,*
                                   GLint *vknot_count,*
                                   GLfloat **vknot,*
                                   GLint *u_stride,*
                                   GLint *v_stride,*
                                   GLfloat **ctlarray,*
                                   GLint *uorder,*
                                   GLint *vorder,*
                                   GLenum *type*)

PARAMETERS

nobj   Specifies the NURBS object (created with **gluNewNurbsRenderer**).

uknot_count
                Specifies the number of knots in the parametric *u* direction.

uknot   Specifies an array of *uknot_count* nondecreasing knot values in the parametric *u* direction.

vknot_count
                Specifies the number of knots in the parametric *v* direction.

vknot   Specifies an array of *vknot_count* nondecreasing knot values in the parametric *v* direction.

u_stride   Specifies the offset (as a number of single-precision floating-point values) between successive control points in the parametric *u* direction in *ctlarray*.

v_stride   Specifies the offset (in single-precision floating-point values) between successive control points in the parametric *v* direction in *ctlarray*.

ctlarray   Specifies an array containing control points for the NURBS surface. The offsets between successive control points in the parametric *u* and *v* directions are given by *u_stride* and *v_stride*.

uorder   Specifies the order of the NURBS surface in the parametric *u* direction. The order is one more than the degree, hence a surface that is cubic in *u* has a *u* order of 4.

vorder   Specifies the order of the NURBS surface in the parametric *v* direction. The order is one more than the degree, hence a surface that is cubic in *v* has a *v* order of 4.

type   Specifies type of the surface. *type* can be any of the valid two-dimensional evaluator types (such as **GL_MAP2_VERTEX_3** or **GL_MAP2_COLOR_4**).

DESCRIPTION

Use **gluNurbsSurface** within a NURBS surface definition to describe the shape of a NURBS surface (before any trimming). To mark the beginning of a NURBS surface definition, use the **gluBeginSurface** command. To mark the end of a NURBS surface definition, use the **gluEndSurface** command. Call **gluNurbsSurface** within a NURBS surface definition only.

Positional, texture, and color coordinates are associated with a surface by presenting each as a separate **gluNurbsSurface** between a **gluBeginSurface/gluEndSurface** pair. No more than one call to **gluNurbsSurface** for each of color, position, and texture data can be made within a single **gluBeginSurface/gluEndSurface** pair. Exactly one call must be made to describe the position of the surface (a *type* of **GL_MAP2_VERTEX_3** or **GL_MAP2_VERTEX_4**).

A NURBS surface can be trimmed by using the commands **gluNurbsCurve** and **gluPwlCurve** between calls to **gluBeginTrim** and **gluEndTrim**.

Note that a **gluNurbsSurface** with *uknot_count* knots in the *u* direction and *vknot_count* knots in the *v* direction with orders *uorder* and *vorder* must have (*uknot_count* − *uorder*) × (*vknot_count* − *vorder*) control points.

EXAMPLE

The following commands render a textured NURBS surface with normals; the texture coordinates and normals are also NURBS surfaces:

```
gluBeginSurface(nobj);
   gluNurbsSurface(nobj, ..., GL_MAP2_TEXTURE_COORD_2);
   gluNurbsSurface(nobj, ..., GL_MAP2_NORMAL);
   gluNurbsSurface(nobj, ..., GL_MAP2_VERTEX_4);
gluEndSurface(nobj);
```

SEE ALSO

gluBeginSurface, gluBeginTrim, gluNewNurbsRenderer, gluNurbsCurve, gluPwlCurve

NAME

gluOrtho2D – define a 2-D orthographic projection matrix

C SPECIFICATION

void **gluOrtho2D**(GLdouble *left*,
　　　　　　　　 GLdouble *right*,
　　　　　　　　 GLdouble *bottom*,
　　　　　　　　 GLdouble *top*)

PARAMETERS

left, right
　　　　Specify the coordinates for the left and right vertical clipping planes.

bottom, top
　　　　Specify the coordinates for the bottom and top horizontal clipping planes.

DESCRIPTION

gluOrtho2D sets up a two-dimensional orthographic viewing region. This is equivalent to calling **glOrtho** with *near*=0 and *far*=1.

SEE ALSO

glOrtho, **gluPerspective**

NAME

gluPartialDisk – draw an arc of a disk

C SPECIFICATION

void **gluPartialDisk**(GLUquadricObj *qobj,
　　　　　　　　　　GLdouble *innerRadius*,
　　　　　　　　　　GLdouble *outerRadius*,
　　　　　　　　　　GLint *slices*,
　　　　　　　　　　GLint *loops*,
　　　　　　　　　　GLdouble *startAngle*,
　　　　　　　　　　GLdouble *sweepAngle*)

PARAMETERS

qobj　　　Specifies a quadrics object (created with **gluNewQuadric**).

innerRadius
　　　　　Specifies the inner radius of the partial disk (can be zero).

outerRadius Specifies the outer radius of the partial disk.

slices　　Specfies the number of subdivisions around the z axis.

loops　　Specifies the number of concentric rings about the origin into which the partial disk is subdivided.

startAngle Specifies the starting angle, in degrees, of the disk portion.

sweepAngle Specifies the sweep angle, in degrees, of the disk portion.

DESCRIPTION

gluPartialDisk renders a partial disk on the *z*=0 plane. A partial disk is similar to a full disk, except that only the subset of the disk from *startAngle* through *startAngle* + *sweepAngle* is included (where 0 degrees is along the +*y* axis, 90 degrees along the +*x* axis, 180 along the –*y* axis, and 270 along the –*x* axis).

The partial disk has a radius of *outerRadius*, and contains a concentric circular hole with a radius of *innerRadius*. If *innerRadius* is zero, then no hole is generated. The partial disk is subdivided around the *z* axis into slices (like pizza slices), and also about the *z* axis into rings (as specified by *slices* and *loops*, respectively).

With respect to orientation, the +*z* side of the partial disk is considered to be outside (see **gluQuadricOrientation**). This means that if the orientation is set to GLU_OUTSIDE, then any normals generated point along the +*z* axis. Otherwise, they point along the –*z* axis.

If texturing is turned on (with **gluQuadricTexture**), texture coordinates are generated linearly such that where *r=outerRadius*, the value at (*r*, 0, 0) is (1, 0.5), at (0, *r*, 0) it is (0.5, 1), at (–*r*, 0, 0) it is (0, 0.5), and at (0, –*r*, 0) it is (0.5, 0).

SEE ALSO

gluCylinder, **gluDisk**, **gluNewQuadric**, **gluQuadricOrientation**, **gluQuadricTexture**, **gluSphere**

NAME

gluPerspective – set up a perspective projection matrix

C SPECIFICATION

void **gluPerspective**(GLdouble *fovy*,
                     GLdouble *aspect*,
                     GLdouble *zNear*,
                     GLdouble *zFar*)

PARAMETERS

fovy   Specifies the field of view angle, in degrees, in the *y* direction.

aspect Specifies the aspect ratio that determines the field of view in the *x* direction. The aspect ratio is the ratio of *x* (width) to *y* (height).

zNear Specifies the distance from the viewer to the near clipping plane (always positive).

zFar   Specifies the distance from the viewer to the far clipping plane (always positive).

DESCRIPTION

gluPerspective specifies a viewing frustum into the world coordinate system. In general, the aspect ratio in **gluPerspective** should match the aspect ratio of the associated viewport. For example, *aspect*=2.0 means the viewer's angle of view is twice as wide in *x* as it is in *y*. If the viewport is twice as wide as it is tall, it displays the image without distortion.

The matrix generated by **gluPerspective** is multipled by the current matrix, just as if **glMultMatrix** were called with the generated matrix. To load the perspective matrix onto the current matrix stack instead, precede the call to **gluPerspective** with a call to **glLoadIdentity**.

SEE ALSO

glFrustum, glLoadIdentity, glMultMatrix, gluOrtho2D

NAME

gluPickMatrix – define a picking region

C SPECIFICATION

void **gluPickMatrix**(GLdouble *x*,
GLdouble *y*,
GLdouble *width*,
GLdouble *height*,
GLint *viewport[4]*)

PARAMETERS

x, y

Specify the center of a picking region in window coordinates.

width, height

Specify the width and height, respectively, of the picking region in window coordinates.

viewport

Specifies the current viewport (as from a **glGetIntegerv** call).

DESCRIPTION

gluPickMatrix creates a projection matrix that can be used to restrict drawing to a small region of the viewport. This is typically useful to determine what objects are being drawn near the cursor. Use **gluPickMatrix** to restrict drawing to a small region around the cursor. Then, enter selection mode (with **glRenderMode** and rerender the scene. All primitives that would have been drawn near the cursor are identified and stored in the selection buffer.

The matrix created by **gluPickMatrix** is multiplied by the current matrix just as if **glMultMatrix** is called with the generated matrix. To effectively use the generated pick matrix for picking, first call **glLoadIdentity** to load an identity matrix onto the perspective matrix stack. Then call **gluPickMatrix**, and finally, call a command (such as **gluPerspective**) to multiply the perspective matrix by the pick matrix.

When using **gluPickMatrix** to pick NURBS, be careful to turn off the NURBS property GLU_AUTO_LOAD_MATRIX. If GLU_AUTO_LOAD_MATRIX is not turned off, then any NURBS surface rendered is subdivided differently with the pick matrix than the way it was subdivided without the pick matrix.

EXAMPLE

When rendering a scene as follows:

```
glMatrixMode(GL_PROJECTION);
glLoadIdentity();
gluPerspective(...);
glMatrixMode(GL_MODELVIEW);
/* Draw the scene */
```

a portion of the viewport can be selected as a pick region like this:

```
glMatrixMode(GL_PROJECTION);
glLoadIdentity();
gluPickMatrix(x, y, width, height, viewport);
gluPerspective(...);
glMatrixMode(GL_MODELVIEW);
/* Draw the scene */
```

SEE ALSO

glGet, glLoadIndentity, glMultMatrix, glRenderMode, gluPerspective

NAME

gluProject – map object coordinates to window coordinates

C SPECIFICATION

int **gluProject**(GLdouble *objx*,
        GLdouble *objy*,
        GLdouble *objz*,
        const GLdouble *modelMatrix[16]*,
        const GLdouble *projMatrix[16]*,
        const GLint *viewport[4]*,
        GLdouble **winx*,
        GLdouble **winy*,
        GLdouble **winz*)

PARAMETERS

objx, objy, objz
        Specify the object coordinates.

modelMatrix   Specifies the current modelview matrix (as from a **glGetDoublev** call).

projMatrix   Specifies the current projection matrix (as from a **glGetDoublev** call).

viewport   Specifies the current viewport (as from a **glGetIntegerv** call).

winx, winy, winz
        Return the computed window coordinates.

DESCRIPTION

gluProject transforms the specified object coordinates into window coordinates using *modelMatrix*, *projMatrix*, and *viewport*. The result is stored in *winx*, *winy*, and *winz*. A return value of **GL_TRUE** indicates success, and **GL_FALSE** indicates failure.

SEE ALSO

glGet, **gluUnProject**

NAME

gluPwlCurve – describe a piecewise linear NURBS trimming curve

C SPECIFICATION

void **gluPwlCurve**(GLUnurbsObj *nobj,
                    GLint *count*,
                    GLfloat *array*,
                    GLint *stride*,
                    GLenum *type*)

PARAMETERS

nobj   Specifies the NURBS object (created with **gluNewNurbsRenderer**).

count   Specifies the number of points on the curve.

array   Specifies an array containing the curve points.

stride   Specifies the offset (a number of single-precision floating-point values) between points on the curve.

type   Specifies the type of curve. Must be either **GLU_MAP1_TRIM_2** or **GLU_MAP1_TRIM_3**.

DESCRIPTION

gluPwlCurve describes a piecewise linear trimming curve for a NURBS surface. A piecewise linear curve consists of a list of coordinates of points in the parameter space for the NURBS surface to be trimmed. These points are connected with line segments to form a curve. If the curve is an approximation to a real curve, the points should be close enough that the resulting path appears curved at the resolution used in the application.

If *type* is **GLU_MAP1_TRIM_2**, then it describes a curve in two-dimensional (*u* and *v*) parameter space. If it is **GLU_MAP1_TRIM_3**, then it describes a curve in two-dimensional homogeneous (*u*, *v*, and *w*) parameter space. Please refer to the **gluBeginTrim** reference page for more information about trimming curves.

SEE ALSO

gluBeginCurve, **gluBeginTrim**, **gluNewNurbsRenderer**, **gluNurbsCurve**

NAME

gluQuadricCallback – define a callback for a quadrics object

C SPECIFICATION

void **gluQuadricCallback**(GLUquadricObj *qobj,
                            GLenum *which*,
                            void *(*fn)()*)

PARAMETERS

qobj   Specifies the quadrics object (created with **gluNewQuadric**).

which Specifies the callback being defined. The only valid value is **GLU_ERROR**.

fn   Specifies the function to be called.

DESCRIPTION

gluQuadricCallback is used to define a new callback to be used by a quadrics object. If the specified callback is already defined, then it is replaced. If *fn* is NULL, then any existing callback is erased.

The one legal callback is **GLU_ERROR**:

GLU_ERROR   The function is called when an error is encountered. Its single argument is of type GLenum, and it indicates the specific error that occurred. Character strings describing these errors can be retrieved with the **gluErrorString** call.

SEE ALSO

gluErrorString, gluNewQuadric

NAME

gluQuadricDrawStyle – specify the draw style desired for quadrics

C SPECIFICATION

void **gluQuadricDrawStyle**(GLUquadricObj *$qobj$,
                                                    GLenum $drawStyle$)

PARAMETERS

$qobj$ Specifies the quadrics object (created with **gluNewQuadric**).

$drawStyle$ Specifies the desired draw style. Valid values are **GLU_FILL**, **GLU_LINE**, **GLU_SILHOUETTE**, and **GLU_POINT**.

DESCRIPTION

gluQuadricDrawStyle specifies the draw style for quadrics rendered with $qobj$. The legal values are as follows:

GLU_FILL   Quadrics are rendered with polygon primitives. The polygons are drawn in a counterclockwise fashion with respect to their normals (as defined with **gluQuadricOrientation**).

GLU_LINE   Quadrics are rendered as a set of lines.

GLU_SILHOUETTE
                            Quadrics are rendered as a set of lines, except that edges separating coplanar faces will not be drawn.

GLU_POINT   Quadrics are rendered as a set of points.

SEE ALSO

gluNewQuadric, gluQuadricNormals, gluQuadricOrientation, gluQuadricTexture

gluQuadricNormals

NAME

NAME

gluQuadricNormals – specify what kind of normals are desired for quadrics

C SPECIFICATION

void **gluQuadricNormals**(GLUquadricObj *qobj,
                              GLenum *normals*)

PARAMETERS

qobj   Specifes the quadrics object (created with **gluNewQuadric**).

normals Specifies the desired type of normals. Valid values are **GLU_NONE**,
GLU_FLAT, and **GLU_SMOOTH**.

DESCRIPTION

gluQuadricNormals specifies what kind of normals are desired for quadrics rendered with *qobj*. The legal values are as follows:

GLU_NONE No normals are generated.

GLU_FLAT   One normal is generated for every facet of a quadric.

GLU_SMOOTH

One normal is generated for every vertex of a quadric. This is the default.

SEE ALSO

**gluNewQuadric, gluQuadricDrawStyle, gluQuadricOrientation,
gluQuadricTexture**

NAME

gluQuadricOrientation – specify inside/outside orientation for quadrics

C SPECIFICATION

void **gluQuadricOrientation**(GLUquadricObj *qobj,
                                           GLenum *orientation*)

PARAMETERS

qobj   Specifies the quadrics object (created with **gluNewQuadric**).

orientation
                   Specifies the desired orientation. Valid values are **GLU_OUTSIDE** and **GLU_INSIDE**.

DESCRIPTION

gluQuadricOrientation specifies what kind of orientation is desired for quadrics rendered with *qobj*. The *orientation* values are as follows:

GLU_OUTSIDE
                   Quadrics are drawn with normals pointing outward.

GLU_INSIDE   Normals point inward. The default is **GLU_OUTSIDE**.

Note that the interpretation of *outward* and *inward* depends on the quadric being drawn.

SEE ALSO

gluNewQuadric, gluQuadricDrawStyle, gluQuadricNormals, gluQuadricTexture

NAME

gluQuadricTexture – specify if texturing is desired for quadrics

C SPECIFICATION

void **gluQuadricTexture**(GLUquadricObj *qobj,
GLboolean *textureCoords*)

PARAMETERS

qobj   Specifies the quadrics object (created with **gluNewQuadric**).

textureCoords Specifies a flag indicating if texture coordinates should be generated.

DESCRIPTION

gluQuadricTexture specifies if texture coordinates should be generated for quadrics rendered with *qobj*. If the value of *textureCoords* is **GL_TRUE**, then texture coordinates are generated, and if *textureCoords* is **GL_FALSE**, they are not. The default is **GL_FALSE**.

The manner in which texture coordinates are generated depends upon the specific quadric rendered.

SEE ALSO

gluNewQuadric, gluQuadricDrawStyle, gluQuadricNormals, gluQuadricOrientation

NAME

gluScaleImage – scale an image to an arbitrary size

C SPECIFICATION

int **gluScaleImage**(GLenum *format*,
 GLint *widthin*,
 GLint *heightin*,
 GLenum *typein*,
 const void **datain*,
 GLint *widthout*,
 GLint *heightout*,
 GLenum *typeout*,
 void **dataout*)

PARAMETERS

format   Specifies the format of the pixel data. The following symbolic values are valid: **GL_COLOR_INDEX, GL_STENCIL_INDEX, GL_DEPTH_COMPONENT, GL_RED, GL_GREEN, GL_BLUE, GL_ALPHA, GL_RGB, GL_RGBA, GL_LUMINANCE,** and **GL_LUMINANCE_ALPHA.**

widthin, heightin
 Specify the width and height, respectively, of the source image that is scaled.

typein   Specifies the data type for *datain*. Must be one of **GL_UNSIGNED_BYTE, GL_BYTE, GL_BITMAP, GL_UNSIGNED_SHORT, GL_SHORT, GL_UNSIGNED_INT, GL_INT,** or **GL_FLOAT.**

datain   Specifies a pointer to the source image.

widthout, heightout
 Specify the width and height, respectively, of the destination image.

typeout   Specifies the data type for *dataout*. Must be one of **GL_UNSIGNED_BYTE, GL_BYTE, GL_BITMAP, GL_UNSIGNED_SHORT, GL_SHORT, GL_UNSIGNED_INT, GL_INT,** or **GL_FLOAT.**

dataout   Specifies a pointer to the destination image.

DESCRIPTION

gluScaleImage scales a pixel image using the appropriate pixel store modes to unpack data from the source image and pack data into the destination image.

When shrinking an image, **gluScaleImage** uses a box filter to sample the source image and create pixels for the destination image. When magnifying an image, the pixels from the source image are linearly interpolated to create the destination image.

A return value of zero indicates success, otherwise a GLU error code is returned indicating what the problem was (see **gluErrorString**).

Please refer to the **glReadPixels** reference page for a description of the acceptable values for the *format*, *typein*, and *typeout* parameters.

SEE ALSO

glDrawPixels, glReadPixels, gluBuild1DMipmaps, gluBuild2DMipmaps, gluErrorString

NAME

gluSphere – draw a sphere

C SPECIFICATION

void **gluSphere**(GLUquadricObj *qobj,
                 GLdouble *radius*,
                 GLint *slices*,
                 GLint *stacks*)

PARAMETERS

qobj   Specifies the quadrics object (created with **gluNewQuadric**).

radius Specifies the radius of the sphere.

slices Specifies the number of subdivisions around the z axis (similar to lines of longitude).

stacks Specifies the number of subdivisions along the z axis (similar to lines of latitude).

DESCRIPTION

gluSphere draws a sphere of the given radius centered around the origin. The sphere is subdivided around the z axis into slices and along the z axis into stacks (similar to lines of longitude and latitude).

If the orientation is set to **GLU_OUTSIDE** (with **gluQuadricOrientation**), then any normals generated point away from the center of the sphere. Otherwise, they point toward the center of the sphere.

If texturing is turned on (with **gluQuadricTexture**), then texture coordinates are generated so that t ranges from 0.0 at z=–*radius* to 1.0 at z=*radius* (t increases linearly along longitudinal lines), and s ranges from 0.0 at the +y axis, to 0.25 at the +x axis, to 0.5 at the –y axis, to 0.75 at the –x axis, and back to 1.0 at the +y axis.

SEE ALSO

gluCylinder, **gluDisk**, **gluNewQuadric**, **gluPartialDisk**, **gluQuadricOrientation**, **gluQuadricTexture**

NAME

gluTessCallback – define a callback for a tessellation object

C SPECIFICATION

void **gluTessCallback**(GLUtriangulatorObj *tobj,
                  GLenum *which*,
                  void *(*fn)()*)

PARAMETERS

tobj   Specifies the tessellation object (created with **gluNewTess**).

which Specifies the callback being defined. The following values are valid:
     GLU_BEGIN, GLU_EDGE_FLAG, GLU_VERTEX, GLU_END, and
     GLU_ERROR.

fn   Specifies the function to be called.

DESCRIPTION

gluTessCallback is used to indicate a callback to be used by a tessellation object. If
the specified callback is already defined, then it is replaced. If *fn* is NULL, then the
existing callback is erased.

These callbacks are used by the tessellation object to describe how a polygon specified by the user is broken into triangles.

The legal callbacks are as follows:

GLU_BEGIN
       The begin callback is invoked like **glBegin** to indicate the start of a (trian-
       gle) primitive. The function takes a single argument of type GLenum
       that is either **GL_TRIANGLE_FAN, GL_TRIANGLE_STRIP**, or
       GL_TRIANGLES.

GLU_EDGE_FLAG
       The edge flag callback is similar to **glEdgeFlag**. The function takes a sin-
       gle Boolean flag that indicates which edges of the created triangles were
       part of the original polygon defined by the user, and which were created
       by the tessellation process. If the flag is **GL_TRUE**, then each vertex that
       follows begins an edge that was part of the original polygon. If the flag is
       GL_FALSE, then each vertex that follows begins an edge that was gen-
       erated by the tessellator. The edge flag callback (if defined) is invoked
       before the first vertex callback is made.

Since triangle fans and triangle strips do not support edge flags, the begin callback is not called with **GL_TRIANGLE_FAN** or **GL_TRIANGLE_STRIP** if an edge flag callback is provided. Instead, the fans and strips are converted to independent triangles.

GLU_VERTEX

The vertex callback is invoked between the begin and end callbacks. It is similar to **glVertex**, and it defines the vertices of the triangles created by the tessellation process. The function takes a pointer as its only argument. This pointer is identical to the opaque pointer provided by the user when the vertex was described (see **gluTessVertex**).

GLU_END

The end callback serves the same purpose as **glEnd**. It indicates the end of a primitive and it takes no arguments.

GLU_ERROR

The error callback is called when an error is encountered. The one argument is of type GLenum, and it indicates the specific error that occurred. There are eight errors unique to polygon tessellation, named **GLU_TESS_ERROR1** through **GLU_TESS_ERROR8**. Character strings describing these errors can be retrieved with the **gluErrorString** call.

EXAMPLE

Polygons tessellated can be rendered directly like this:

```
gluTessCallback(tobj, GLU_BEGIN, glBegin);
gluTessCallback(tobj, GLU_VERTEX, glVertex3dv);
gluTessCallback(tobj, GLU_END, glEnd);
gluBeginPolygon(tobj);
   gluTessVertex(tobj, v, v);
   ...
gluEndPolygon(tobj);
```

Typically, the tessellated polygon should be stored in a display list so that it does not need to be retessellated every time it is rendered.

SEE ALSO

glBegin, **glEdgeFlag**, **glVertex**, **gluDeleteTess**, **gluErrorString**, **gluNewTess**, **gluTessVertex**

NAME

gluTessVertex – specify a vertex on a polygon

C SPECIFICATION

void **gluTessVertex**(GLUtriangulatorObj *tobj,
                       GLdouble *v[3]*,
                       void *data*)

PARAMETERS

tobj Specifies the tessellation object (created with **gluNewTess**).

v Specifies the location of the vertex.

data
Specifies an opaque pointer passed back to the user with the vertex callback (as specified by **gluTessCallback**).

DESCRIPTION

gluTessVertex describes a vertex on a polygon that the user is defining. Successive **gluTessVertex** calls describe a closed contour. For example, if the user wants to describe a quadrilateral, then **gluTessVertex** should be called four times. **gluTessVertex** can only be called between **gluBeginPolygon** and **gluEndPolygon**. *data* normally points to a structure containing the vertex location, as well as other per-vertex attributes such as color and normal. This pointer is passed back to the user through the **GLU_VERTEX** callback after tessellation (see **gluTessCallback**).

EXAMPLE

A quadrilateral with a triangular hole in it can be described as follows:

```
gluBeginPolygon(tobj);
    gluTessVertex(tobj, v1, v1);
    gluTessVertex(tobj, v2, v2);
    gluTessVertex(tobj, v3, v3);
    gluTessVertex(tobj, v4, v4);
gluNextContour(tobj, GLU_INTERIOR);
    gluTessVertex(tobj, v5, v5);
    gluTessVertex(tobj, v6, v6);
    gluTessVertex(tobj, v7, v7);
gluEndPolygon(tobj);
```

SEE ALSO
 gluBeginPolygon, **gluNewTess**, **gluNextContour**, **gluTessCallback**

NAME

gluUnProject – map window coordinates to object coordinates

C SPECIFICATION

int **gluUnProject**(GLdouble *winx*,
                    GLdouble *winy*,
                    GLdouble *winz*,
                    const GLdouble *modelMatrix[16]*,
                    const GLdouble *projMatrix[16]*,
                    const GLint *viewport[4]*,
                    GLdouble **objx*,
                    GLdouble **objy*,
                    GLdouble **objz*)

PARAMETERS

winx, winy, winz

   Specify the window coordinates to be mapped.

modelMatrix Specifies the modelview matrix (as from a **glGetDoublev** call).

projMatrix Specifies the projection matrix (as from a **glGetDoublev** call).

viewport Specifies the viewport (as from a **glGetIntegerv** call).

objx, objy, objz Returns the computed object coordinates.

DESCRIPTION

gluUnProject maps the specified window coordinates into object coordinates using *modelMatrix*, *projMatrix*, and *viewport*. The result is stored in *objx*, *objy*, and *objz*. A return value of **GL_TRUE** indicates success, and **GL_FALSE** indicates failure.

SEE ALSO

glGet, **gluProject**

Chapter 7

GLX Reference Pages

This chapter contains the reference pages, in alphabetical order, for all the routines comprising the OpenGL extension to X (GLX). The reference pages are listed below. Note that there is a **glXIntro** page, which gives an overview of OpenGL in the X Window System; you might want to start with this page.

glXChooseVisual	glXGetConfig	glXQueryExtension
glXCopyContext	glXGetCurrentContext	glXQueryVersion
glXCreateContext	glXGetCurrentDrawable	glXSwapBuffers
glXCreateGLXPixmap	glXIntro	glXUseXFont
glXDestroyContext	glXIsDirect	glXWaitGL
glXDestroyGLXPixmap	glXMakeCurrent	glXWaitX

NAME

glXChooseVisual – return a visual that matches specified attributes

C SPECIFICATION

XVisualInfo* **glXChooseVisual**(Display **dpy*,
                              int *screen*,
                              int **attribList*)

PARAMETERS

dpy   Specifies the connection to the X server.

screen   Specifies the screen number.

attribList
            Specifies a list of Boolean attributes and integer attribute/value pairs. The last attribute must be **None**.

DESCRIPTION

glXChooseVisual returns a pointer to an XVisualInfo structure describing the visual that best meets a minimum specification. The Boolean GLX attributes of the visual that is returned will match the specified values, and the integer GLX attributes will meet or exceed the specified minimum values. If no conforming visual exists, **NULL** is returned. To free the data returned by this function, use **XFree**.

All Boolean GLX attributes default to **False** except **GLX_USE_GL**, which defaults to **True**. All integer GLX attributes default to zero. Default specifications are superseded by attributes included in *attribList*. Boolean attributes included in *attribList* are understood to be **True**. Integer attributes are followed immediately by the corresponding desired or minimum value. The list must be terminated with **None**.

The interpretations of the various GLX visual attributes are as follows:

GLX_USE_GL   Ignored. Only visuals that can be rendered with GLX are considered.

GLX_BUFFER_SIZE Must be followed by a nonnegative integer that indicates the desired color index buffer size. The smallest index buffer of at least the specified size is preferred. Ignored if **GLX_RGBA** is asserted.

GLX_LEVEL   Must be followed by an integer buffer-level specification. This specification is honored exactly. Buffer level zero corresponds to the default frame buffer of the display. Buffer level one is the first overlay frame buffer, level two the second overlay frame buffer, and so on. Negative buffer levels correspond to underlay frame buffers.

GLX_RGBA If present, only RGBA visuals are considered. Otherwise, only color index visuals are considered.

GLX_DOUBLEBUFFER

If present, only double-buffered visuals are considered. Otherwise, only single-buffered visuals are considered.

GLX_STEREO If present, only stereo visuals are considered. Otherwise, only monoscopic visuals are considered.

GLX_AUX_BUFFERS Must be followed by a nonnegative integer that indicates the desired number of auxiliary buffers. Visuals with the smallest number of auxiliary buffers that meets or exceeds the specified number are preferred.

GLX_RED_SIZE Must be followed by a nonnegative minimum size specification. If this value is zero, the smallest available red buffer is preferred. Otherwise, the largest available red buffer of at least the minimum size is preferred.

GLX_GREEN_SIZE Must be followed by a nonnegative minimum size specification. If this value is zero, the smallest available green buffer is preferred. Otherwise, the largest available green buffer of at least the minimum size is preferred.

GLX_BLUE_SIZE Must be followed by a nonnegative minimum size specification. If this value is zero, the smallest available blue buffer is preferred. Otherwise, the largest available blue buffer of at least the minimum size is preferred.

GLX_ALPHA_SIZE Must be followed by a nonnegative minimum size specification. If this value is zero, the smallest available alpha buffer is preferred. Otherwise, the largest available alpha buffer of at least the minimum size is preferred.

GLX_DEPTH_SIZE Must be followed by a nonnegative minimum size specification. If this value is zero, visuals with no depth buffer are preferred. Otherwise, the largest available depth buffer of at least the minimum size is preferred.

GLX_STENCIL_SIZE Must be followed by a nonnegative integer that indicates the desired number of stencil bitplanes. The smallest stencil buffer of at least the specified size is preferred. If the desired value is zero, visuals with no stencil buffer are preferred.

GLX_ACCUM_RED_SIZE

Must be followed by a nonnegative minimum size specification. If this value is zero, visuals with no red accumulation buffer are preferred. Otherwise, the largest possible red accumulation buffer of at least the minimum size is preferred.

GLX_ACCUM_GREEN_SIZE

Must be followed by a nonnegative minimum size specification. If this value is zero, visuals with no green accumulation buffer are preferred. Otherwise, the largest possible green accumulation buffer of at least the minimum size is preferred.

GLX_ACCUM_BLUE_SIZE

Must be followed by a nonnegative minimum size specification. If this value is zero, visuals with no blue accumulation buffer are preferred. Otherwise, the largest possible blue accumulation buffer of at least the minimum size is preferred.

GLX_ACCUM_ALPHA_SIZE

Must be followed by a nonnegative minimum size specification. If this value is zero, visuals with no alpha accumulation buffer are preferred. Otherwise, the largest possible alpha accumulation buffer of at least the minimum size is preferred.

EXAMPLES

attribList = {**GLX_RGBA**, **GLX_RED_SIZE**, 4, **GLX_GREEN_SIZE**, 4, **GLX_BLUE_SIZE**, 4, **None**};

Specifies a single-buffered RGB visual in the normal frame buffer, not an overlay or underlay buffer. The returned visual supports at least four bits each of red, green, and blue, and possibly no bits of alpha. It does not support color index mode, double-buffering, or stereo display. It may or may not have one or more auxiliary color buffers, a depth buffer, a stencil buffer, or an accumulation buffer.

NOTES

XVisualInfo is defined in *Xutil.h*. It is a structure that includes *visual*, *visualID*, *screen*, and *depth* elements.

glXChooseVisual is implemented as a client-side utility using only **XGetVisualInfo** and **glXGetConfig**. Calls to these two routines can be used to implement selection algorithms other than the generic one implemented by **glXChooseVisual**.

GLX implementers are strongly discouraged, but not proscribed, from changing the selection algorithm used by **glXChooseVisual**. Therefore, selections may change from release to release of the client-side library.

ERRORS

NULL is returned if an undefined GLX attribute is encountered in *attribList*.

SEE ALSO

glXCreateContext, glXGetConfig

NAME

glXCopyContext – copy state from one rendering context to another

C SPECIFICATION

void **glXCopyContext**(Display *dpy,
                         GLXContext src,
                         GLXContext dst,
                         GLuint mask)

PARAMETERS

dpy   Specifies the connection to the X server.

src   Specifies the source context.

dst   Specifies the destination context.

mask Specifies which portions of *src* state are to be copied to *dst*.

DESCRIPTION

glXCopyContext copies selected groups of state variables from *src* to *dst*. *mask* indicates which groups of state variables are to be copied. *mask* contains the bitwise OR of the same symbolic names that are passed to the OpenGL command **glPushAttrib**. The single symbolic constant **GL_ALL_ATTRIB_BITS** can be used to copy the maximum possible portion of rendering state.

The copy can be done only if the renderers named by *src* and *dst* share an address space. Two rendering contexts share an address space if both are nondirect using the same server, or if both are direct and owned by a single process. Note that in the nondirect case it is not necessary for the calling threads to share an address space, only for their related rendering contexts to share an address space.

Not all values for OpenGL state can be copied. For example, pixel pack and unpack state, render mode state, and select and feedback state are not copied. The state that can be copied is exactly the state that is manipulated by OpenGL command **glPushAttrib**.

If *src* is not the current context for the thread issuing the request, then the state of the *src* context is undefined.

NOTES

Two rendering contexts share an address space if both are nondirect using the same server, or if both are direct and owned by a single process.

A *process* is a single execution environment, implemented in a single address space, consisting of one or more threads.

A *thread* is one of a set of subprocesses that share a single address space, but maintain separate program counters, stack spaces, and other related global data. A *thread* that is the only member of its subprocess group is equivalent to a *process*.

ERRORS

BadMatch is generated if rendering contexts *src* and *dst* do not share an address space or were not created with respect to the same screen.

BadAccess is generated if *dst* is current to any thread (including the calling thread) at the time **glXCopyContext** is called.

GLX_BAD_CONTEXT is generated if either *src* or *dst* is not a valid GLX context.

BadValue is generated if undefined *mask* bits are specified.

SEE ALSO

glPushAttrib, glXCreateContext, glXIsDirect

NAME

glXCreateContext – create a new GLX rendering context

C SPECIFICATION

GLXContext **glXCreateContext**(Display **dpy*,
XVisualInfo **vis*,
GLXContext *shareList*,
Bool *direct*)

PARAMETERS

dpy Specifies the connection to the X server.

vis Specifies the visual that defines the frame buffer resources available to the rendering context. It is a pointer to an **XVisualInfo** structure, not a visual ID or a pointer to a **Visual**.

shareList Specifies the context with which to share display lists. **NULL** indicates that no sharing is to take place.

direct Specifies whether rendering is to be done with a direct connection to the graphics system if possible (**True**) or through the X server (**False**).

DESCRIPTION

glXCreateContext creates a GLX rendering context and returns its handle. This context can be used to render into both windows and GLX pixmaps. If **glXCreateContext** fails to create a rendering context, **NULL** is returned.

If *direct* is **True**, then a direct rendering context is created if the implementation supports direct rendering and the connection is to an X server that is local. If *direct* is **False**, then a rendering context that renders through the X server is always created. Direct rendering provides a performance advantage in some implementations. However, direct rendering contexts cannot be shared outside a single process, and they cannot be used to render to GLX pixmaps.

If *shareList* is not **NULL**, then all display-list indexes and definitions are shared by context *shareList* and by the newly created context. An arbitrary number of contexts can share a single display-list space. However, all rendering contexts that share a single display-list space must themselves exist in the same address space. Two rendering contexts share an address space if both are nondirect using the same server, or if both are direct and owned by a single process. Note that in the nondirect case, it is not necessary for the calling threads to share an address space, only for their related rendering contexts to share an address space.

NOTES

XVisualInfo is defined in *Xutil.h*. It is a structure that includes *visual*, *visualID*, *screen*, and *depth* elements.

A *process* is a single execution environment, implemented in a single address space, consisting of one or more threads.

A *thread* is one of a set of subprocesses that share a single address space, but maintain separate program counters, stack spaces, and other related global data. A *thread* that is the only member of its subprocess group is equivalent to a *process*.

ERRORS

NULL is returned if execution fails on the client side.

BadMatch is generated if the context to be created would not share the address space of the context specified by *shareList*, or if the specified visual is not available.

BadValue is generated if *vis* specifies an invalid screen number.

GLX_BAD_CONTEXT is generated if *shareList* is not a GLX context and is not **NULL**.

SEE ALSO

glXDestroyContext, glXGetConfig, glXIsDirect, glXMakeCurrent

NAME

glXCreateGLXPixmap – create an off-screen GLX rendering area

C SPECIFICATION

GLXPixmap **glXCreateGLXPixmap**(Display *dpy*,
XVisualInfo **vis*,
Pixmap *pixmap*)

PARAMETERS

dpy   Specifies the connection to the X server.

vis   Specifies the visual that defines the structure of the rendering area. It is a pointer to an **XVisualInfo** structure, not a visual ID or a pointer to a **Visual**.

pixmap
Specifies the X pixmap that will be used as the front left color buffer of the off-screen rendering area.

DESCRIPTION

glXCreateGLXPixmap creates an off-screen rendering area and returns its XID. Any GLX rendering context that was created with respect to *vis* can be used to render into this off-screen area. Use **glXMakeCurrent** to associate the rendering area with a GLX rendering context.

The X pixmap identified by *pixmap* is used as the front left buffer of the resulting off-screen rendering area. All other buffers specified by *vis*, including color buffers other than the front left buffer, are created without externally visible names. GLX pixmaps with double-buffering are supported. However, **glXSwapBuffers** is ignored by these pixmaps.

Direct rendering contexts cannot be used to render into GLX pixmaps.

NOTES

XVisualInfo is defined in *Xutil.h*. It is a structure that includes *visual, visualID, screen,* and *depth* elements.

ERRORS

BadMatch is generated if the depth of *pixmap* does not match the
GLX_BUFFER_SIZE value of *vis*, if *pixmap* was not created with respect to the same
screen as *vis*, or if *vis* is not a valid XVisualInfo pointer.

BadPixmap is generated if *pixmap* is not a valid pixmap.

SEE ALSO

glXCreateContext, glXIsDirect, glXMakeCurrent

NAME

glXDestroyContext – destroy a GLX context

C SPECIFICATION

void **glXDestroyContext**(Display *dpy,
                            GLXContext ctx)

PARAMETERS

dpy Specifies the connection to the X server.

ctx Specifies the GLX context to be destroyed.

DESCRIPTION

If GLX rendering context *ctx* is not current to any client, **glXDestroyContext** destroys it immediately. Otherwise, *ctx* is destroyed when it becomes not current to any client. In either case, the resource ID referenced by *ctx* is freed immediately.

ERRORS

GLX_BAD_CONTEXT is generated if *ctx* is not a valid GLX context.

SEE ALSO

glXCreateContext, glXMakeCurrent

NAME

glXDestroyGLXPixmap – destroy a GLX pixmap

C SPECIFICATION

void **glXDestroyGLXPixmap**(Display *dpy,
GLXPixmap pix)

PARAMETERS

dpy Specifies the connection to the X server.

pix Specifies the GLX pixmap to be destroyed.

DESCRIPTION

If GLX pixmap pix is not current to any client, **glXDestroyGLXPixmap** destroys it immediately. Otherwise, pix is destroyed when it becomes not current to any client. In either case, the resource ID is freed immediately.

ERRORS

GLX_BAD_DRAWABLE is generated if pix is not a valid GLX pixmap.

SEE ALSO

glXCreateGLXPixmap, glXMakeCurrent

NAME

glXGetConfig – return information about GLX visuals

C SPECIFICATION

```
int glXGetConfig( Display *dpy,
                  XVisualInfo *vis,
                  int attrib,
                  int *value )
```

PARAMETERS

dpy   Specifies the connection to the X server.

vis   Specifies the visual to be queried. It is a pointer to an **XVisualInfo** structure, not a visual ID or a pointer to a **Visual**.

attrib Specifies the visual attribute to be returned.

value Returns the requested value.

DESCRIPTION

glXGetConfig sets *value* to the *attrib* value of windows or GLX pixmaps created with respect to *vis*. **glXGetConfig** returns an error code if it fails for any reason. Otherwise, zero is returned.

attrib is one of the following:

GLX_USE_GL   **True** if OpenGL rendering is supported by this visual, **False** otherwise.

GLX_BUFFER_SIZE   Number of bits per color buffer. For RGBA visuals, GLX_BUFFER_SIZE is the sum of GLX_RED_SIZE, GLX_GREEN_SIZE, GLX_BLUE_SIZE, and GLX_ALPHA_SIZE. For color index visuals, GLX_BUFFER_SIZE is the size of the color indexes.

GLX_LEVEL   Frame buffer level of the visual. Level zero is the default frame buffer. Positive levels correspond to frame buffers that overlay the default buffer, and negative levels correspond to frame buffers that underlay the default level.

GLX_RGBA   **True** if color buffers store red, green, blue, and alpha values, **False** if they store color indexes.

GLX_DOUBLEBUFFER
                    True if color buffers exist in front/back pairs that can be swapped, **False** otherwise.

GLX_STEREO   **True** if color buffers exist in left/right pairs, **False** otherwise.

GLX_AUX_BUFFERS   Number of auxiliary color buffers that are available. Zero indicates that no auxiliary color buffers exist.

GLX_RED_SIZE   Number of bits of red stored in each color buffer. Undefined if **GLX_RGBA** is **False**.

GLX_GREEN_SIZE   Number of bits of green stored in each color buffer. Undefined if **GLX_RGBA** is **False**.

GLX_BLUE_SIZE   Number of bits of blue stored in each color buffer. Undefined if **GLX_RGBA** is **False**.

GLX_ALPHA_SIZE   Number of bits of alpha stored in each color buffer. Undefined if **GLX_RGB** is **False**.

GLX_DEPTH_SIZE   Number of bits in the depth buffer.

GLX_STENCIL_SIZE   Number of bits in the stencil buffer.

GLX_ACCUM_RED_SIZE

     Number of bits of red stored in the accumulation buffer.

GLX_ACCUM_GREEN_SIZE

     Number of bits of green stored in the accumulation buffer.

GLX_ACCUM_BLUE_SIZE

     Number of bits of blue stored in the accumulation buffer.

GLX_ACCUM_ALPHA_SIZE

     Number of bits of alpha stored in the accumulation buffer.

The X protocol allows a single visual ID to be instantiated with different numbers of bits per pixel. Windows or GLX pixmaps that will be rendered with OpenGL, however, must be instantiated with a color buffer depth of **GLX_BUFFER_SIZE**.

Although a GLX implementation can export many visuals that support OpenGL rendering, it must support at least two. One is an RGBA visual with at least one color buffer, a stencil buffer of at least 1 bit, a depth buffer of at least 12 bits, and an accumulation buffer. Alpha bitplanes are optional in this visual. However, its color buffer size must be as great as that of the deepest **TrueColor**, **DirectColor**, **PseudoColor**, or **StaticColor** visual supported on level zero, and it must itself be made available on level zero.

The other required visual is a color index one with at least one color buffer, a stencil buffer of at least 1 bit, and a depth buffer of at least 12 bits. This visual must have as many color bitplanes as the deepest **PseudoColor** or **StaticColor** visual supported on level zero, and it must itself be made available on level zero.

Applications are best written to select the visual that most closely meets their requirements. Creating windows or GLX pixmaps with unnecessary buffers can result in reduced rendering performance as well as poor resource allocation.

NOTES

XVisualInfo is defined in *Xutil.h*. It is a structure that includes *visual*, *visualID*, *screen*, and *depth* elements.

ERRORS

GLX_NO_EXTENSION is returned if *dpy* does not support the GLX extension.

GLX_BAD_SCREEN is returned if the screen of *vis* does not correspond to a screen.

GLX_BAD_ATTRIB is returned if *attrib* is not a valid GLX attribute.

GLX_BAD_VISUAL is returned if *vis* doesn't support GLX and an attribute other than **GLX_USE_GL** is requested.

SEE ALSO

glXChooseVisual, glXCreateContext

glXGetCurrentContext

NAME

glXGetCurrentContext – return the current context

C SPECIFICATION

GLXContext **glXGetCurrentContext**(void)

DESCRIPTION

glXGetCurrentContext returns the current context, as specified by **glXMakeCurrent**. If there is no current context, **NULL** is returned.

glXGetCurrentContext returns client-side information. It does not make a round trip to the server.

SEE ALSO

glXCreateContext, glXMakeCurrent

NAME

glXGetCurrentDrawable – return the current drawable

C SPECIFICATION

GLXDrawable **glXGetCurrentDrawable**(void)

DESCRIPTION

glXGetCurrentDrawable returns the current drawable, as specified by **glXMakeCurrent**. If there is no current drawable, **None** is returned.

glXGetCurrentDrawable returns client-side information. It does not make a round trip to the server.

SEE ALSO

glXCreateGLXPixmap, **glXMakeCurrent**

NAME

glXIntro – Introduction to OpenGL in the X window system

OVERVIEW

OpenGL is a high-performance 3-D-oriented renderer. It is available in the X window system through the GLX extension. Use **glXQueryExtension** and **glXQueryVersion** to establish whether the GLX extension is supported by an X server, and if so, what version is supported.

GLX extended servers make a subset of their visuals available for OpenGL rendering. Drawables created with these visuals can also be rendered using the core X renderer and with the renderer of any other X extension that is compatible with all core X visuals.

GLX extends drawables with several buffers other than the standard color buffer. These buffers include back and auxiliary color buffers, a depth buffer, a stencil buffer, and a color accumulation buffer. Some or all are included in each X visual that supports OpenGL.

To render using OpenGL into an X drawable, you must first choose a visual that defines the required OpenGL buffers. **glXChooseVisual** can be used to simplify selecting a compatible visual. If more control of the selection process is required, use **XGetVisualInfo** and **glXGetConfig** to select among all the available visuals.

Use the selected visual to create both a GLX context and an X drawable. GLX contexts are created with **glXCreateContext**, and drawables are created with either **XCreateWindow** or **glXCreateGLXPixmap**. Finally, bind the context and the drawable together using **glXMakeCurrent**. This context/drawable pair becomes the current context and current drawable, and it is used by all OpenGL commands until **glXMakeCurrent** is called with different arguments.

Both core X and OpenGL commands can be used to operate on the current drawable. The X and OpenGL command streams are not synchronized, however, except at explicitly created boundaries generated by calling **glXWaitGL**, **glXWaitX**, **XSync**, and **glFlush**.

EXAMPLES

Below is the minimum code required to create an RGBA-format, OpenGL-compatible X window and clear it to yellow. The code is correct, but it does not include any error checking. Return values *dpy*, *vi*, *cx*, *cmap*, and *win* should all be tested.

```
#include <GL/glx.h>
#include <GL/gl.h>

static int attributeList[] = { GLX_RGBA, None };

static Bool WaitForNotify(Display *d, XEvent *e, char *arg) {
    return (e->type == MapNotify) && (e->xmap.window == (Window)arg);
}

int main(int argc, char **argv) {
    Display *dpy;
    XVisualInfo *vi;
    Colormap cmap;
    XSetWindowAttributes swa;
    Window win;
    GLXContext cx;
    XEvent event;

    /* get a connection */
    dpy = XOpenDisplay(0);

    /* get an appropriate visual */
    vi = glXChooseVisual(dpy, DefaultScreen(dpy), attributeList);

    /* create a GLX context */
    cx = glXCreateContext(dpy, vi, 0, GL_FALSE);

    /* create a color map */
    cmap = XCreateColormap(dpy, RootWindow(dpy, vi->screen),
                           vi->visual, AllocNone);

    /* create a window */
    swa.colormap = cmap;
    swa.border_pixel = 0;
    swa.event_mask = StructureNotifyMask;
    win = XCreateWindow(dpy, RootWindow(dpy, vi->screen), 0, 0, 100, 100,
                        0, vi->depth, InputOutput, vi->visual,
                        CWBorderPixel|CWColormap|CWEventMask, &swa);
    XMapWindow(dpy, win);
    XIfEvent(dpy, &event, WaitForNotify, (char*)win);
```

```
        /* connect the context to the window */
        glXMakeCurrent(dpy, win, cx);

        /* clear the buffer */
        glClearColor(1,1,0,1);
        glClear(GL_COLOR_BUFFER_BIT);
        glFlush();

        /* wait a while */
        sleep(10);
    }
```

NOTES

A color map must be created and passed to **XCreateWindow**. See the example code above.

A GLX context must be created and attached to an X drawable before OpenGL commands can be executed. OpenGL commands issued while no context/drawable pair is current are ignored.

Exposure events indicate that *all* buffers associated with the specified window may be damaged and should be repainted. Although certain buffers of some visuals on some systems may never require repainting (the z-buffer, for example), it is incorrect to code assuming that these buffers will not be damaged.

GLX commands manipulate XVisualInfo structures rather than pointers to visuals or visual IDs. XVisualInfo structures contain *visual*, *visualID*, *screen*, and *depth* elements, as well as other X-specific information.

SEE ALSO

glFinish, glFlush, glXChooseVisual, glXCopyContext, glXCreateContext, glXCreateGLXPixmap, glXDestroyContext, glXGetConfig, glXIsDirect, glXMakeCurrent, glXQueryExtension, glXQueryVersion, glXSwapBuffers, glXUseXFont, glXWaitGL, glXWaitX, XCreateColormap, XCreateWindow, XSync

NAME

glXIsDirect – indicate whether direct rendering is enabled

C SPECIFICATION

Bool **glXIsDirect**(Display *dpy,
                        GLXContext ctx)

PARAMETERS

dpy Specifies the connection to the X server.

ctx Specifies the GLX context that is being queried.

DESCRIPTION

glXIsDirect returns **True** if ctx is a direct rendering context, **False** otherwise. Direct rendering contexts pass rendering commands directly from the calling process's address space to the rendering system, bypassing the X server. Nondirect rendering contexts pass all rendering commands to the X server.

ERRORS

GLX_BAD_CONTEXT is generated if ctx is not a valid GLX context.

SEE ALSO

glXCreateContext

NAME

glXMakeCurrent – attach a GLX context to a window or a GLX pixmap

C SPECIFICATION

Bool **glXMakeCurrent**(Display **dpy,*
                       GLXDrawable *draw,*
                       GLXContext *ctx*)

PARAMETERS

dpy   Specifies the connection to the X server.

draw Specifies a GLX drawable. Must be either an X window ID or a GLX pixmap ID.

ctx   Specifies a GLX rendering context that is to be attached to *draw*.

DESCRIPTION

glXMakeCurrent does two things: It makes *ctx* the current GLX rendering context of the calling thread, replacing the previously current context if there was one, and it attaches *ctx* to a GLX drawable, either a window or a GLX pixmap. As a result of these two actions, subsequent OpenGL rendering calls use rendering context *ctx* to modify GLX drawable *draw*. Because **glXMakeCurrent** always replaces the current rendering context with *ctx*, there can be only one current context per thread.

The first time *ctx* is made current to any thread, its viewport is set to the full size of *draw*. Subsequent calls by any thread to **glXMakeCurrent** with *ctx* have no effect on its viewport.

To release the current context without assigning a new one, call **glXMakeCurrent** with *draw* and *ctx* set to **None** and **NULL** respectively.

glXMakeCurrent returns **True** if it is successful, **False** otherwise. If **False** is returned, the previously current rendering context and drawable (if any) remain unchanged.

NOTES

A *process* is a single-execution environment, implemented in a single address space, consisting of one or more threads.

A *thread* is one of a set of subprocesses that share a single address space, but maintain separate program counters, stack spaces, and other related global data. A *thread* that is the only member of its subprocess group is equivalent to a *process*.

ERRORS

BadMatch is generated if *draw* was not created with the same X screen and visual as *ctx*.

BadAccess is generated if *ctx* was current to another thread at the time **glXMakeCurrent** was called.

GLX_BAD_DRAWABLE is generated if *draw* is not a valid GLX drawable.

GLX_BAD_CONTEXT is generated if *ctx* is not a valid GLX context.

GLX_BAD_CONTEXT_STATE is generated if the rendering context current to the calling thread has OpenGL renderer state **GL_FEEDBACK** or **GL_SELECT**.

SEE ALSO

glXCreateContext, glXCreateGLXPixmap

NAME

glXQueryExtension – indicate whether the GLX extension is supported

C SPECIFICATION

Bool **glXQueryExtension**(Display **dpy,*
                                        int **errorBase,*
                                        int **eventBase*)

PARAMETERS

dpy   Specifies the connection to the X server.

errorBase Returns the base error code of the GLX extension.

eventBase Returns the base event code of the GLX extension.

DESCRIPTION

glXQueryExtension returns **True** if the X server of connection *dpy* supports the GLX extension, **False** otherwise. If **True** is returned, then *errorBase* and *eventBase* return the error base and event base of the GLX extension. Otherwise, *errorBase* and *eventBase* are unchanged.

errorBase and *eventBase* do not return values if they are specified as **NULL**.

NOTES

eventBase is included for future extensions. GLX does not currently define any events.

SEE ALSO

glXQueryVersion

NAME

glXQueryVersion – return the version numbers of the GLX extension

C SPECIFICATION

Bool **glXQueryVersion**(Display *dpy,
int *major,
int *minor)

PARAMETERS

dpy   Specifies the connection to the X server.

major Returns the major version number of the GLX extension.

minor Returns the minor version number of the GLX extension.

DESCRIPTION

glXQueryVersion returns the major and minor version numbers of the GLX extension implemented by the server associated with connection *dpy*. Implementations with the same major version number are upward compatible, meaning that the implementation with the higher minor number is a superset of the version with the lower minor number.

major and *minor* do not return values if they are specified as **NULL**.

ERRORS

glXQueryVersion returns **False** if it fails, **True** otherwise. *major* and *minor* are not updated when **False** is returned.

SEE ALSO

glXQueryExtension

NAME

glXSwapBuffers – exchange front and back buffers

C SPECIFICATION

void **glXSwapBuffers**(Display *dpy,
                          Window *window*)

PARAMETERS

dpy   Specifies the connection to the X server.

window
           Specifies the window whose buffers are to be swapped.

DESCRIPTION

glXSwapBuffers exchanges the front and back buffers of *window*. The exchange typically takes place during the vertical retrace of the monitor, rather than immediately after **glXSwapBuffers** is called. All GLX rendering contexts share the same notion of which are front buffers and which are back buffers.

An implicit **glFlush** is done by **glXSwapBuffers** before it returns. Subsequent OpenGL commands can be issued immediately after calling **glXSwapBuffers**, but are not executed until the buffer exchange is completed.

If *window* was not created with respect to a double-buffered visual, **glXSwapBuffers** has no effect, and no error is generated.

NOTES

Synchronization of multiple GLX contexts rendering to the same double-buffered window is the responsibility of the clients. The X Synchronization Extension can be used to facilitate such cooperation.

SEE ALSO

glFlush

NAME

glXUseXFont – create bitmap display lists from an X font

C SPECIFICATION

void **glXUseXFont**(Font *font,*
int *first,*
int *count,*
int *listBase*)

PARAMETERS

font   Specifies the font from which character glyphs are to be taken.

first   Specifies the index of the first glyph to be taken.

count   Specifies the number of glyphs to be taken.

listBase Specifies the index of the first display list to be generated.

DESCRIPTION

glXUseXFont generates *count* display lists, named *listBase* through *listBase+count*–1, each containing a single **glBitmap** command. The parameters of the **glBitmap** command of display list *listBase+i* are derived from glyph *first+i*. Bitmap parameters *xorig, yorig, width,* and *height* are computed from font metrics as *descent–1, –lbearing, rbearing–lbearing,* and *ascent+descent*, respectively. *xmove* is taken from the glyph's *width* metric, and *ymove* is set to zero. Finally, the glyph's image is converted to the appropriate format for **glBitmap**.

Using **glXUseXFont** may be more efficient than accessing the X font and generating the display lists explicitly, both because the display lists are created on the server without requiring a round trip of the glyph data, and because the server may choose to delay the creation of each bitmap until it is accessed.

Empty display lists are created for all glyphs that are requested and are not defined in *font*. **glXUseXFont** is ignored if there is no current GLX context.

ERRORS

BadFont is generated if *font* is not a valid font.

GLX_BAD_CONTEXT_STATE is generated if the current GLX context is in display-list construction mode.

glXUseXFont

SEE ALSO

glBitmap, glXMakeCurrent

NAME

    glXWaitGL – complete GL execution prior to subsequent X calls

C SPECIFICATION

    void **glXWaitGL**(void)

DESCRIPTION

    OpenGL rendering calls made prior to **glXWaitGL** are guaranteed to be executed before X rendering calls made after **glXWaitGL**. Although this same result can be achieved using **glFinish**, **glXWaitGL** does not require a round trip to the server, and it is therefore more efficient in cases where client and server are on separate machines.

    glXWaitGL is ignored if there is no current GLX context.

NOTES

    glXWaitGL may or may not flush the X stream.

SEE ALSO

    glFinish, glFlush, glXWaitX, XSync

NAME

glXWaitX – complete X execution prior to subsequent OpenGL calls

C SPECIFICATION

void **glXWaitX**(void)

DESCRIPTION

X rendering calls made prior to **glXWaitX** are guaranteed to be executed before OpenGL rendering calls made after **glXWaitX**. Although this same result can be achieved using **XSync**, **glXWaitX** does not require a round trip to the server, and it is therefore more efficient in cases where client and server are on separate machines.

glXWaitX is ignored if there is no current GLX context.

NOTES

glXWaitX may or may not flush the OpenGL stream.

SEE ALSO

glFinish, glFlush, glXWaitGL, XSync